# THE NEW FRONTIERS OF JIHAD

RADICAL
ISLAM
IN EUROPE

**Alison Pargeter** is a Senior Research Associate at the Centre of International Studies at the University of Cambridge, where she is also a visiting scholar at Pembroke College. She has conducted numerous research projects on issues related to political Islam, violence and radicalization in Europe, North Africa and the Middle East.

# THE NEW FRONTIERS OF JIHAD

## RADICAL ISLAM IN EUROPE

### ALISON PARGETER

I.B. TAURIS

LONDON · NEW YORK

Published in 2008 by I.B.Tauris & Co. Ltd
6 Salem Road, London W2 4BU
175 Fifth Avenue, New York, NY 10010
www.ibtauris.com

ISBN: 978 1 84511 391 9

A full CIP record for this book is available from the British Library
A full CIP record for this book is available from the Library of Congress

Library of Congress catalog card: available

Typeset in Goudy Old Style by A. & D. Worthington, Newmarket, Suffolk
Printed and bound in Great Britain by TJ International Ltd, Padstow, Cornwall

# CONTENTS

*To*
*Ahmed*

# INTRODUCTION

The arrests of scores of terrorist suspects across Europe following 9/11, as well as the attacks in London and Madrid, were a stark reminder that the continent was host to militant Islamists of varying hues. In some cases these radicals had been resident in the continent for decades and had been quietly working away to further the cause of jihad, largely against their own regimes in the Islamic world. From veterans of the war in Afghanistan, to members of Middle Eastern insurgent groups, to second-generation immigrants and European converts, these radicals have all contributed to the image of Europe as a breeding ground for religiously inspired political violence. Yet very little is known about exactly who these Islamists are, why they are here and how and why they became involved in the world of militant Islam.

Much of the commentary that has appeared in the post-9/11 era has tended to lump all of these Islamists into one basket, as if they all share the same aims and objectives and as if they are part of one globalized movement whose primary target is the West. In fact analysts and the media often talk about 'globalized Islam', 'international terrorism', and the 'global war on terror' as if we are dealing with one monolithic movement that has been born out of the modern era. Similarly it is widely assumed that these Islamists are somehow linked to or share the same ideology as Al-Qa'ida and Osama Bin Ladin. Yet in many cases these links and perceived aspirations are often more tenuous than is suggested and the particularities of the various groups and movements are regularly overlooked. Yet it is these very particularities and differences that have given the Islamist movement its flavour and colour and that help to explain the varying motivations of those who have taken up the cause of jihad. Moreover, despite the assertion by commentators and by many Islamists themselves that they represent a unified body working towards the same goal of establishing an Islamic state, the Islamist movement in Europe is as plagued by division, petty in-fighting and battles of egos as any ideological movement anywhere else in the world.

Moreover the assertions that those committing or supporting these acts of terrorism have been driven to hatred for the West by issues such as the Iraq war or Afghanistan also require further inspection. Indeed such assumptions fail to take into account the fact that anti-Western discourse is neither new nor the domain of the jihadists alone. Not only has it been used by Islamists since the early awakenings of the political Islamist movement that was conceived in the 1920s largely in response to the fall of the Ottoman Empire and to Western colonialism, it has long been used by a whole host of constituencies in the Middle East as a rallying cry. From the secularists to the nationalists to the left-wing movements, they have all sought to use anti-Westernism as a legitimizing factor. In fact a discourse that rejects the West and what the West stands for is intrinsically tied up with societies in the Islamic world and is symptomatic of the acute crisis that the region has been experiencing for decades. It is this very crisis that has been expressed by the Islamist movement since the early 1980s not only in the Islamic world, but also among Muslim communities in Europe and that at the most extreme end of the spectrum has become a cry of pain and despair. Indeed, radical Islam in Europe, as in the Islamic world, appears increasingly to have become an ideology of desperation, driven by frustration, helplessness and a sense of impotence.

Furthermore the post-9/11 world has left policymakers scratching their heads about the best way to tackle radicalism head on. As more and more alleged plots have been uncovered on the continent, there have been increasingly desperate attempts to understand how and why young Muslims in Europe have become so wrapped up in this militant ideology and how to devise strategies to prevent it from happening. Yet many of these attempts have placed this radicalism within a vacuum, as if what is occurring in Europe is somehow separated from the wider Islamic world. Europe of course is important in itself, but the radicalism that has developed in various European countries cannot simply be explained away by issues such as marginalization, integration or access to social justice. The issue is far wider and far more complex. Indeed if we want to understand the roots of this radicalism, it has to be placed in the context of broader developments in the Islamic world.

Based upon research I have been conducting over the past few years among Muslim communities in Europe, and the many conversations I have had with Islamists, from both the moderate and more radical end of the spectrum, this book seeks to offer an understanding of the particularities of the various Islamist camps operating in Europe and to show how, while they may be in Europe, much of the politics played out by these various groups and individuals is a direct result of what is occurring in the Islamic world. In fact Muslim communities in Europe have largely reflected events in the

Islamic world or have been shaped by powers outside the continent.

Given the definitional minefield that accompanies any work on such issues, I should make clear that this book is primarily about those parts of the Muslim community that have taken up Islamic activism or who are involved in what is generally termed 'political Islam'. This covers those who take up militancy or who espouse the use of violence as a vehicle through which to achieve their objectives, which I broadly refer to as militants or jihadists. It also covers those who I refer to as moderates, by which I mean specifically those who have taken up Islamic activism or who follow the ideology of groups such as the Muslim Brotherhood that do not generally espouse violence. Indeed these groups often refer to themselves as the moderate camp. Therefore I am not referring to Muslim communities more widely, or even those who are practising Muslims when I use the term 'moderate', as it has a specific political meaning. Indeed it should be remembered that there are large numbers of non-practising Muslims in Europe and even many practising Muslims who do not go to the mosque except to celebrate Islamic holidays, let alone subscribe to the same ideology as those involved in the Islamist scene. Therefore, although this book goes some way to explore the relationship between the Islamists and the wider Muslim communities in which they are situated, it should not be forgotten that in the European context both militants and moderates alike are minorities within a minority.

The first chapters of the book deal with how Muslim communities in Europe became Islamicized as a direct result of the religious revivalism that swept the Middle East after the Iranian Revolution of 1979. Chapter 1 focuses on the first wave of Islamists who came to Europe mainly in the 1980s seeking refuge from persecution in their countries of origin. It was this group of highly motivated idealists, from those at the more moderate end such as the Muslim Brotherhood to the hardcore jihadists such as the Syrian Abu Musab Al-Suri, who were to plant the seeds of militant Islamism in the continent and to act as guides for the younger generation. Many of them were veterans of the war in Afghanistan and their primary objective was to topple their own governments and replace them with Islamic ones. As such it was the failure of the states in the Middle East that resulted in Europe having to absorb these militants. Chapter 2 explains how during the 1980s and 1990s Europe became a melting pot of Islamist ideologies, partly as a result of the Saudi money that was sloshing around the continent combined with the brains of those in the various Islamist organizations, especially the Muslim Brotherhood, that sought to expand their influence in the continent. This chapter also covers the Rushdie crisis, as, perhaps more than any other event, it demonstrates how Muslim communities in the UK became hostage to the ambitions and power struggles of Middle East states. Chapter 3 focuses on how Europe became host to jihadist recruitment networks and looks in particular at the Bosnia case, which, while it was particularly important for a number of Egyptian Islamists such as Anwar Shaban who was based in Italy, failed to really capture the hearts and minds of the Islamic world, largely because it was in Europe and culturally a million miles away from Afghanistan and the Middle East.

The next set of chapters deal with how Middle Eastern politics were played out more directly in Europe. Starting with the various nationalistic insurgent groups who were forced to set up bases in Europe after they were pushed out of their own countries, Chapter 4 looks at what Europe meant for these various groups and how they used the facilities and advantages of being in Europe to continue their struggle against their own regimes thousands of miles away. It touches on groups such as the Libyan Islamic Fighting Group (LIFG), the Egyptian Al-Jama'a Al-Islamiya and the Algerian Groupe Islamique Armée (GIA) and their support networks. Chapter 5 takes a closer look at some of the personalities involved in the militant Islamist scene in Europe and at how this scene was characterized by internal conflict and petty rivalry, as well as how feuds between some of the groups or within the groups were mediated in Europe. Chapter 6 focuses more specifically on the Algerian armed groups that had perhaps the greatest influence on the European radical stage during the 1990s when the Algerian struggle was the great hope of the jihadist movement. This chapter explores the complex relationship between the Algerian Islamist groups and Algeria's former colonizer, France, and focuses on the string of bomb attacks against the French mainland in the mid-1990s. It looks at how Algerian radicals used France, as well as second-generation Algerian immigrants residing there, to try to effect change in Algeria.

The latter chapters focus mainly on what is often referred to as the new breed of radical Islamists and offer an explanation as to what is driving these individuals. These chapters try to explain how the nature of the militants operating in Europe changed from the early proponents of jihad who sought to bring down their own regimes to the nihilistic type of mindless violence perpetrated by the newer generation. Chapter 7 looks first at the impact that Osama Bin Ladin and 9/11 had on the floundering jihadist movement in Europe and beyond. It tackles the issue of globalized Islam and looks at whether Europe itself played a role in the radicalization of those jihadists who carried out acts of terrorism. Chapter 8 looks at the Madrid bombings that were perpetrated mainly by Moroccans and argues that they may have been as much to do with the Moroccan–Spanish relationship as with the wider international context. Moreover it looks at the similarities between those who perpetrated the Madrid attacks and those who blew themselves up in Casablanca the year before and argues that both attacks were born out of the same desperation and cultural mindset.

Chapter 9 covers the London bombings and looks at the issue of second-generation Pakistani communities in the UK and argues that some of the assumptions made about this group of young men require greater examination. As such the chapter explores issues of alienation and anger among second-generation south Asian communities in the UK and assesses to what extent this can really be considered as a radicalizing factor. The chapter also addresses the issue of foreign policy as a motivating factor in radicalization among young jihadists in Europe. Chapter 10 explores the subject of European converts to Islam who have been a consistent, albeit small, feature of the European jihadist scene since the first years that Islamic revivalism hit the continent. The chapter looks at the attraction that Islam holds for some of those who have converted to radical interpretations of Islam and argues that despite assertions that converts are 'Westernizing' Islam, in fact they are often seeking something that is outside the European experience and view pure Islam as something that originates in the Islamic world. It looks at what drove some of these converts such as London bomber Germaine Lindsay and shoe-bomber Richard Reid to turn against their own societies in such an acute and violent way. Lastly Chapter 11 deals with the Danish cartoon crisis which encapsulated the fact that, despite all these years of being in Europe, those Islamists seeking to make use of the crisis still had to take the issue to the Middle East for any meaningful action to occur. It also symbolized the dilemma in which those in the moderate camp in Europe have found themselves in the post-9/11 world, as they are caught between trying to work with European authorities in order to be accepted and at the same time having to play to their own constituencies who in many cases still feel that they remain outside of mainstream European society.

# CHAPTER 1

# THE FIRST WAVE OF RADICALS

In the early 1980s a young Syrian, Mustafa Set Mariam Naser, also known as Abu Musab Al-Suri, arrived in Europe having fled his home country just a few years earlier in fear of his life. The fair-skinned, red-headed Al-Suri had been brought up in a deeply religious and conservative middle-class family in the ancient and beautiful city of Aleppo, a city famed for its Islamist activism. After finishing school he went on to train at university as a mechanical engineer, but soon found a higher calling in life and abandoned his studies to become part of Syria's underground Islamist opposition. He joined a group called the Fighting Vanguard (Al-Tali'ah Al-Muqatila) that was led by Sheikh Marwan Hadid, which was a militant offshoot of the Syrian Muslim Brotherhood (Ikhwan Muslimeen) – a Sunni fundamentalist movement that had originated in Egypt in the 1920s and which had spread across the Middle East and whose adherents sought the establishment of an Islamic state. The Fighting Vanguard opposed the ruling Ba'athist government of Syrian President Hafez Al-Assad and sought to overthrow it by force in order to establish *sharia* (Islamic) law. Al-Suri and the Fighting Vanguard's objection to the Al-Assad regime was that it was aggressively nationalist and secular. This alienated the traditional and religious classes, of which Al-Suri was a part, which feared that the Ba'athist regime with its modernist ideas was threatening not only their position and status but the very social fabric of the country.

Joining such an opposition movement was an extremely dangerous move for Al-Suri. Like many other regimes in the Middle East at that time the secular Ba'athist government in Syria stopped at nothing to repress its Islamist opponents, who were viewed as reactionary forces opposed to modernity and progress. After the regime launched a particularly ferocious assault in 1981 following an uprising in the town of Hamma that had pitted some members of the Brotherhood against the security forces, many Islamists fled the country, including Al-Suri, who escaped to the relative safety of neighbouring Jordan where the monarchy displayed a rather more tolerant attitude towards the Islamist movement. Still keen to pursue his Islamist ideals,

Al-Suri joined the Syrian branch of the Muslim Brotherhood in Jordan that was made up from other exiles who had fled the brutalities of the Al-Assad regime. He began working for their military wing, training new recruits in military camps there. He also spent some time engaged in similar activities in Iraq where he was appointed a member of the Syrian Brotherhood's supreme military leadership. It was not that the secular Ba'athist regime of Saddam Hussein in Iraq was any more open to the presence of Islamists than the Syrians, but rather that the Iraqi regime saw the opportunity to support Syrian opposition movements as a means of irritating and weakening its Ba'athist rivals in Damascus and thus was willing to host and give protection to the Syrian Brotherhood.

However, this willingness of the Brotherhood to make alliances with secular regimes such as that of Saddam Hussein never sat very comfortably with the impassioned purist Al-Suri who sought a more strident movement that would see the triumph of Islamist rule in the region. The young Syrian became increasingly disillusioned with the Muslim Brotherhood and escaped to Europe. His first port of call was France where he had hoped to resume his engineering studies which had been interrupted when he left Syria. While he was there, although he managed in 1984 to achieve a black belt in judo, he was not able to complete his education.[1] Indeed it was not long before he was sidetracked once again, as his love of jihad and his homeland pushed him to abandon his studies and to try to work from his adopted home in Europe to further the cause of bringing down the Syrian regime.

Whilst in France Al-Suri joined forces with a leading Syrian Islamist, the legendary Sheikh Adnan Al-Ackla, who was still inside Syria, and the two men set about trying to restructure the Syrian jihadist movement that had been shattered after the Hamma incident in 1981. However, in 1985 Al-Ackla was himself arrested with other remnants of the Fighting Vanguard, leaving Al-Suri to form his own fledgling Syrian jihadist group from the far away lands of Europe. It was also in 1985 that Al-Suri moved to Spain where he settled in the Andalusian city of Granada with its rich and glorious Islamic history. Al-Suri started his own import–export business, married a Spanish convert to Islam and obtained dual Syrian–Spanish citizenship. Despite being so far from his home country, the young Syrian did not lose sight of his main ambition, which was to fight the jihad in his beloved Syria. While in Spain he continued trying to gather money and to develop his own Syrian Islamist organization.

However, like many Islamists at the time, Al-Suri was lured by events in Afghanistan, where the Arab mujahideen were fighting alongside their Afghan brothers to oust the Soviets from the country. If he could not get back into Syria to fight, Afghanistan was an appealing alternative, not least because it had become a magnet for the new jihadist wave that was sweeping the Islamic world, attracting thousands of fighters. In 1987 Al-Suri travelled to Pakistan and on into Afghanistan in order to fight against the 'godless communists' that were backing the Syrian regime as well as the other secular governments in the region. During his time there Al-Suri was to meet some of the top jihadists of the day including Sheikh Sayid Imam Al-Sharif, better known as Dr Fadl, who was a leading member of the Egyptian Al-Jihad group and who was for a time close to Al-Qa'ida ideologue Ayman Al-Zawahiri. Al-Suri also met Osama Bin Ladin, and while he shared some of the Saudi billionaire's ideas, he felt that he was rather conceited. In an e-mail sent several years later, which was recovered after the fall of Kabul in 2001, Al-Suri complained about Bin Ladin's love of appearing on the media, noting, 'I think our brother has caught the disease of screens, flashes, fans, and applause.'[2] Yet these men, along with others he met in Afghanistan, were to shape Al-Suri's future thinking about the nature of jihad and the jihadist movement.

After the defeat of the Soviets in 1991, Al-Suri went back to Spain. However, keen to be at the heart of the action, it was not long before he moved to London, which by then had become the centre of the European radical scene. He had been invited to the UK to work with a group of Algerians and other radicals who were focusing their attentions on producing propaganda about the Islamist struggle that was unfolding in Algeria. Al-Suri was ideally suited to this role. He considered himself as somewhat of an intellectual and theoretician and made great efforts in writing jihadist literature. In fact he was keen to develop his theories of jihad that could be applied to those fighting anywhere in the world and produced tomes with titles such as 'The Sunna in Damascus', 'Muslims in Central Asia and the New Islamic Struggle', and 'The Next Islamic Battle'. Al-Suri seemed to view himself as the chronicler of the entire jihad movement and lamented in a language that betrayed his engineer's mind:

> Where are the studies? Where are the instructions, the creativity to put in place the variables and the non-variables of the next movement? Where is the methodological basis for the international dawa for jihad that we started calling for? Where is its theoretical basis that we have to build upon and continue?[3]

In 1996 he established a Bureau for the Study of Islamic Conflicts, through which he succeeded in setting up an interview for Osama Bin Ladin with the American CNN channel. It was as if Al-Suri with his middle-class background was bent on intellectualizing what was essentially a series of armed insurgencies against the ruling regimes of the Islamic world. However, his writings certainly had a big impact, resulting in people referring to him as one of the geniuses of the mujahideen.

Despite Al-Suri's ambitions to take up a course in media and political science in London, he is alleged to have come under increasing pressure from the British intelligence services during the 1990s and decided to leave. In 1997 he returned to Afghanistan, which by that time was in the grip of Mullah Omar and the Taliban, where he established his own camp and continued to produce works on the jihad. By 2004 Al-Suri had become one of the most wanted militants in the world and had been accused of being part of Al-Qa'ida. His name had been connected to the bombings in Madrid in 2004 and London in 2005, although in exactly what context is still unclear. Al-Suri also had a US$5 million reward placed on his head, something he allegedly described as 'silly'. In October 2005 his luck finally ran out and he was arrested in Pakistan and handed over to the US authorities.

## Young idealists

Particularities aside, Al-Suri's experience is by no means unique. Indeed his story is similar to that of many young Islamist activists who were forced to seek safety in Europe in the 1980s and early 1990s. The rather precarious path trodden by Al-Suri was typical of the first wave of Islamist radicals who, largely by default, found themselves in Europe but whose hearts and ambitions remained firmly in their homelands. This situation was directly related to the circumstances in the Arab world where the failings of the post-colonial independence experiment were becoming increasingly apparent. The progressive secular nationalist regimes, like the Syrian, the Libyan and the Egyptian, that had promised so much had ultimately failed to meet even the most basic socio-economic needs for much of their populations. At the same time the elites of these countries had become mired in corruption and focused their attentions, as well as their investments, in Europe and the West more widely, serving to further alienate themselves from their populations. In addition the increasing reliance by all the regimes in the region on repressive authoritarian measures as a means of prohibiting any genuine political opposition to emerge had prompted many people to seek alternatives.

It was in the 1980s that political Islam arrived on the scene and came to offer new hope in this respect. The success of the populist Islamic Shi'ite revolution in Iran in 1979, combined with efforts by Saudi Arabia and other Gulf states to promote Sunni Islam, including backing the mujahideen in Afghanistan, gave people new aspirations that Islam could bring about the change that they craved and somehow bring about more equitable societies. Political Islam came to be viewed as a morally fastidious and viable alternative to the status quo, and opposition movements of an Islamist hue began to spring up across the region. However, these countries had become so stagnant that they were unable even to absorb their own political opponents and took to employing the tools of repression with even greater ferocity to deal with their Islamists, forcing many to seek safety elsewhere. Europe, with its tradition of accepting others and its asylum policies, was the obvious place for those fleeing persecution, and they came to follow in the footsteps of the thousands of immigrants who had moved to Europe in search of work in the 1960s and 1970s, bringing a new flavour and new dimension to the Muslim migrant communities in the continent.

Given the nature of the regimes in the Middle East, many of those who came to Europe seeking refuge at this time came from the nationalist states of Egypt and Syria, whose Islamist movements were perhaps the most developed. They included figures such as the Egyptian Anwar Shaban, who had been a member of the militant Egyptian Al-Jama'a Al-Islamiya group that was heavily persecuted in Egypt. Shaban escaped to Afghanistan and then sought asylum in Italy at the beginning of the 1990s. Once in Italy his fiery oratory style attracted a group of followers and it was not long before he set up a mosque in Milan, which allegedly became a key jihadist recruitment centre.[4] Another Egyptian who trod a similar path was Talaat Fouad Qassem. Like Abu Musab Al-Suri, Qassem was also an engineering student and joined the Al-Jama'a Al-Islamiya group and soon became the leader of the movement in his university faculty and then of the whole Al-Minya University at a time when the Al-Jama'a Al-Islamiya had been able to take over most of the country's universities, imposing their rigid ideology on both students and staff. After being arrested for his activities and a brief spell in prison, Qassem escaped from Egypt and went to Afghanistan to join the jihad, where he remained until 1992 when the jihadists were forced to find a new refuge. According to one report, after he fled Qassem 'stopped by several countries looking for a base for his message until he settled in Denmark, where he obtained political asylum'.[5]

On the Syrian front, apart from Al-Suri, other figures included Imad Eddin Barakat Yarkas, also known as Abu Dahdah, who came to Europe and who was the leader of a wide-ranging Islamist network in Spain. In September 2005 he was sentenced to 27 years in prison, 12 on charges of leading a terrorist group and a further 15 for conspiracy in the 9/11 attacks. Similarly, the well-known preacher Omar Bakri Mohamed, who regularly hit the headlines in the UK with his anti-Western diatribes, also came from Syria at this time. Surprisingly, given his somewhat oafish appearance, Bakri Mohamed was born into a wealthy Aleppo family and studied law at Damascus University. He joined the Syrian Muslim Brotherhood but was forced to leave the country in fear of his life. After a short spell in Beirut and Saudi Arabia, Bakri Mohamed was granted asylum in Britain in the mid-1980s. Along with fellow Syrian Islamist Farid Kassim, he established Hizb ut Tahrir in the UK and went on to gain a reputation for being one of the most hardened and radical espousers of violent jihad until he was excluded from Britain in 2005. In fact the uncompromising stance of the Syrian regime towards its opposition, especially in the clamp-down of the 1980s, meant that many Syrians ended up in Europe at this time. Many of them were linked to the Syrian Muslim Brotherhood, so much so that a number of them were able to set up an important base in Germany, in the beautiful and historic town of Aachen (Aix-la-Chapelle) that became a key Syrian Brotherhood hub. They joined established Syrian figures there, including Issam Al-Attar, the former General Guide of the Syrian Brotherhood who moved away from the movement in the 1970s ostensibly because of infighting within the group. One commentator has gone so far as to suggest that 'Aachen was one of the main exile refuges of the Syrian branch [of the Muslim Brotherhood], to the extent that some observes have attributed to it, probably in exaggerated terms, the role of coordinator of the Islamic uprising in Syria during the three or four years up to 1982.'[6] It is true that this is somewhat of an exaggeration, but the vigour of the Syrians who had arrived at this time meant that Aachen came to represent an important centre for Islamist radicals in Europe.

Like Al-Suri, many of these Islamists were young idealists who were products of the internal social and political upheavals of their own societies and who had become involved in political Islam as a means of challenging their own governments. It was these men who were to lay down the roots of militant Islam in Europe. After being forced out of their own countries they had little choice but to settle in Europe, although some passed through Saudi Arabia or Afghanistan on their way. Indeed Saudi Arabia represented a special haven for them, as it was considered the centre of the Islamic world and a place of 'pure Islam'. These Islamists, who were full of the fervour of their new-found ideology, were extremely attracted to the Wahabist version of Islam practised in Saudi Arabia, which offered a refreshing antidote to the traditional Islam generally practised by the regimes of the region. Even those regimes that proclaimed themselves as secular continued to rely on traditional forms of Islam as a means of bolstering their own legitimacy. Therefore for those Islamists who sought to bring down their regimes, the purity and simplicity of Wahabism held a special appeal, so much so that Saudi Arabia was for the Islamists what Moscow represented for the communists during the Soviet era. Yet it was in Europe that these fugitives felt most free to engage in political activism and to openly condemn their own governments without fear of persecution or of being sent back to their own countries. Indeed, being in Europe was not going to prevent them from trying to fulfil their dream of creating a 'true' Islamic state in the Islamic world.

## Jihad and new Islamic thinking

What constituted the 'true' Islamic state, however, was a highly contentious issue and one that was debated fiercely among the various schools of thought that were prevalent at the time. Indeed the 1970s and 1980s had seen a mushrooming of different strands and ideologies that were essentially a response to the political environment of the day. What all of these different ideologies shared, however, was the belief that the answer to society's problems lay in Islam, or more specifically in purifying Islam and going back to the roots of the religion and to the golden age of the Prophet and the *salaf* (ancestors i.e. companions of the Prophet) and to the core texts of the Qu'ran and the *hadith* (sayings of the Prophet).

This was an idea that gained great currency in the late nineteenth century in Egypt and was expounded by a number of scholars such as Jamal Al-Din Al-Afghani, Muhammad Abdu and later Rashid Ridha who were proponents of what is known as *salafiyah* or *salafism*, i.e. returning to the time of the ancestors. The movement developed largely in response to the challenges that Western colonial occupation and modernity had brought and that had forced Arabs to confront their own backwardness in relation to the West's technological and scientific advances. These scholars argued that it was by stripping away the *biddah* (innovations) and superstitions that had come to dilute and corrupt Islam and by getting back to its Islamic roots that Arab society could move on and meet the challenge of Westernization head on. By the early twentieth century this *salafist* revivalist trend had spread to other countries, including Algeria and Morocco, where it became part of the discourse of the national struggle against the foreign colonialist powers. These reformist ideas were of course also in line with the rigid Wahabism of Saudi Arabia – itself a revivalist movement that had sought salvation in purity.

The idea of returning to the time of the *salaf* was also to characterize the entire political Islamist movement of the twentieth century. It was the basis upon which Hassan Al-Banna, who had been greatly influenced by Rashid Ridha, formed his Muslim Brotherhood movement in 1928, which is generally considered to be the first articulation of political Islam, as it sought the establishment of an Islamic state that would act as an alternative to the political systems of the day. Like the revivalist movement of the nineteenth century, the Brotherhood was also created as a response to colonialism and

Westernization that Al-Banna believed was corrupting Egyptian society. He once asserted, 'Western civilization has invaded us by force and with aggression on the level of science and money, of politics and luxury, of pleasures and negligence, and of various aspects of a life that are comfortable, exciting and seductive.'[7] Indeed the Muslim Brotherhood and its various offshoots tried to portray themselves as 'the guardians of the native popular culture against the distortions of foreign and secularist ideologies'.[8]

Although the Brotherhood does not shy away from the concept of fighting jihad when Muslims are under attack – something they regard as *Fard al-Ain* (individual religious duty) – the movement is generally considered to represent the moderate school of political Islam. Rather than advocating coups or revolutions, they have favoured a slow bottom-up approach that seeks to educate the population to prepare it for the eventual establishment of an Islamic state. However, it was through one of the Brotherhood's key thinkers, Sayid Qutb, that more militant offshoots were to develop. Qutb was heavily influenced by the Indian-born scholar Abu Al-Ala Mawdudi, who used the term *jahiliyyah* (pre-Islamic ignorance) to describe contemporary Muslim society and who believed that such ignorance had to be countered through the total sovereignty and rule of God (*al-hakimiyya*). In his writings from prison during the 1960s Qutb built upon these ideas as he came increasingly to express his bitterness with Egypt's secular revolution and asserted that jihad should be applied against the rulers. Qutb's disgust with the society in which he found himself was evident. In his most famous book, *Milestones*, he bemoans, 'There are people – exponents of Islam – who are defeated before this filth in which *Jahiliyyah* is steeped, even to the extent that they search for resemblances to Islam among this rubbish heap of the West, and also among the evil and dirty materialism of the East.'[9] Qutb was a controversial figure whose ideas sowed division within the Muslim Brotherhood. Some, including the then Supreme Guide, Dr Hassan Al-Hodeibi, found his ideas unacceptable. Yet his translating of his political aspirations into a complete rejection of existing social order and society encapsulated the utter desperation of the time. Indeed the 'politics of despair' had now acquired a 'religious' theory.[10] This was to prove a potent mix.

Qutb was to inspire a new breed of Islamists who sought to take up arms against their own regimes, and he unleashed the tide of jihadist movements that sprung up not only in Egypt but also across the region. Many of these jihadists sought justification for such ideas from within Islamic history. One of the most important Islamic sources that they looked to was the medieval Syrian scholar Ibn Taymiya. In his *fatwas* Ibn Taymiya had outlined situations in which Muslim rulers should be considered as *kufar* (apostate) and therefore could be fought against.[11] Consequently jihad against such heretics or apostates was not only allowed but obligatory. This appealed to those militants who were frustrated by the Muslim Brotherhood's slow and laboured approach, not to mention its willingness to ally itself with regimes when it suited its agenda. Indeed for some the Brotherhood had become part of the everyday reality rather than the alternative.

Egyptian militant Mohamed Abdelsalam Faraj, who was one of the main proponents of jihadist thinking in his day, was one of those for whom the Brotherhood's policy of working through charitable and religious societies was deeply flawed. He disdainfully declared, 'Is the Islamic state going to be established by such works and pieties? The immediate answer is without doubt: No ... The Islamic state can only be established through struggle, jihad, against oneself, against the devil, against the infidels and against the hypocrites. And this struggle to build the Islamic state should start immediately ... must be launched in one big strike.'[12] This desire to strike against the rulers of the day was shared by other militants such as Sayid Imam Abdelaziz Al-Sharif, known as Dr Fadl, who was the emir of the Al-Jihad group until he fell out with Ayman Al-Zawahiri in 1993. Dr Fadl was famed for his book *Al Umdah fi Idad al Uddah li Jihad* (The Foundations of Preparation for Jihad), which laid down a kind of constitution for jihadist combat and came to shape much of the jihadist discourse and thinking.

Yet even among these jihadists there were different shades of interpretation and different nuances. While those who followed the ideas of the likes of Mohamed Abdelsalam Faraj were prepared to declare the rulers as *kufar* and therefore as a legitimate target, others went further and pronounced the whole of society as apostate. These others belong to the strand that is often labelled as *takfiri*. *Takfir* means to pronounce others as being *kufar*, the punishment for which in strict Islamic terms is death. Plainly all the groups that were declaring their own regimes as apostate and were willing to take up arms against them were employing the concept of *takfir*, as was Sayid Qutb. However, the term has been applied mainly to those who were considered to be the most extreme in their thinking.

This includes the group that became known as Al-Takfir wal Hijra, which emerged in Egypt in the 1970s and was led by the highly charismatic Shukri Mustafa. Mustafa pronounced the whole of Egyptian society as *kufar* and his group did their utmost to separate themselves from it. Mustafa and his band of militants pooled their resources and lived communally in a simple way without electricity or the trappings of modern life in order to replicate the life of the Prophet. They shunned all those who were not a part of them, in some cases leaving behind their wives who would not agree to join their communes, and meted out severe punishments to deserters. In spite of the association of the term *takfir* with extreme violence, Mustafa and his group did not in fact take up arms against the society they had condemned. Instead they sought to bring Muslims to their group through proselytizing, with the eventual aim of confronting society through jihad when they had prepared themselves sufficiently. This was in marked contrast to the Al-Jihad-type thinking that favoured immediate action and the infiltration of political and military institutions. However, in 1977 the group assassinated the Minister for Religious Affairs after they had captured him in an attempt to force the regime into releasing some of their members from prison, resulting in Mustafa's execution.

Therefore the concept of pronouncing *takfir* on society was more of a theological exercise for Shukri Mustafa and other groups who followed a similar path. In fact the only group that indulged in widespread massacres of their own population was the Algerian Groupe Islamique Armée (GIA), which rejected the label *takfiri*. This rejection is not surprising, as *takfiri* was the term used by regimes to label their jihadist opponents as a means of discrediting them and taking away their popular legitimacy. Shukri Mustafa's group rejected the name Al-Takfir wal Hijra, referring to themselves as Al-Jama'at Al-Muslimeen (The Muslim Group) instead. The term was and continues to be so disliked that accusing groups or individuals of being *takfiri* became one way in which militants tried to discredit each other.

It is clear therefore that there were many groups on the scene who all had their own particular ideas and interpretations of what it meant to fight jihad for the Islamic state. As famous Syrian Islamic scholar Abu Buseer Al-Tartousi remarked, the jihadist scene was characterized by fruitless debates and long arguments over whether regimes were *kufar* and therefore legitimate targets and whether they represented 'a major kufr or a minor kufr'.[13] Indeed the problem for many of these jihadist groups that had sprung up within the Qutbist tradition was that they had limited popular appeal and consisted of small groups of individuals who were on the margins of society. Perhaps the only exception in the Egyptian case was Al-Jama'a Al-Islamiya, which was able to attract a wider popular appeal as its focus encompassed religious and social aspects as well as jihad. Yet for many militants their dreams were much greater than their capabilities. As Abu Buseer Al-Tartousi recalled, a member of one jihadist group told him about his group's strategy which comprised confronting 'the kufar, the mortadeen (those who leave Islam) and all heretics everywhere on every piece of land on earth'.[14] When Abu Buseer asked how many people there were in the group, the jihadist replied that they numbered from a few dozen to a few hundred at most! Yet these groups were full of conviction that they could somehow bring down their regimes and allow the glory of the Islamic state to flourish. Somewhat ironically it was to Afghanistan, which was not part of the Arab world, that they turned in order to make that dream a reality.

## The Afghanistan factor

The idea of going to defend one's fellow Muslims from the communist Soviet superpower had a broad appeal among many Muslim populations. Individuals from across the Arab world rallied to the cause and responded to the various *fatwas* (religious rulings) being issued both by official religious establishments, such as Al-Azhar in Cairo, and important Islamic scholars such as the Saudi Sheikh Abdulaziz Bin Baez and the Syrian Ikhwan leader Sa'id Hawwa, instructing Muslims to go to liberate their brothers in Afghanistan.[15] This clearly gave the Afghan struggle a strong religious legitimacy and an internationalist flavour that enabled it to touch a chord with Muslims wherever they might be. Ironically the cause of Palestine, which had been dear to the hearts of Muslims for years, was not to be the scene of the first great contemporary jihadist success. It is surely one of the great ironies of the Afghanistan struggle that Abdullah Azzam, who is considered to be the father of the Afghan Arabs, was Palestinian and yet chose to fight against the Soviets rather than Israel. It seems that Azzam disliked the secular orientation of some of the Palestinian groups that were fighting against Israel and sought instead to focus on creating an Islamic state. In fact Palestine was the great cause of the secular regimes such Libya, Iraq and Syria, while the monarchies and the Islamists threw their energies behind Afghanistan, as it offered the opportunity for a specifically Islamist victory. Moreover these alliances were all part of the wider Cold War scenario that was at its zenith at the time.

However, many of the regimes in the Middle East and North Africa, including the secular ones, were prepared to turn a blind eye to the fact that so many of their nationals were streaming into Afghanistan to join the jihad. The Egyptian government even took the opportunity to release radicals from prison on the condition that they continued their jihad in Afghanistan rather than at home.[16] Some Algerians have also suggested that the Algerian regime encouraged their nationals to join up, declaring, 'The government also helped send young Algerians to Afghanistan. Saudi Arabia paid for the tickets; they'd go to Mecca and then to Afghanistan.'[17] It was as if these states had not even contemplated the longer-term consequences of sending scores of highly ideologically motivated and restless young men off to the battlefield. Yet it was relatively easy for the recruits to get to Afghanistan, as all they needed to do was to get to Saudi Arabia, from where they were offered cut-price tickets to fly straight to Pakistan.

Some of the volunteers were already committed jihadists in their own countries. The Libyan Abu Munder Al-Saidi, for example, who went on to become the spiritual leader of the main militant Libyan group, the Libyan

Islamic Fighting Group (LIFG), was already a member of a militant cell in Libya that aspired to remove the Qadhafi regime by force before he joined the Afghan struggle in the late 1980s.[18] Others, however, were not involved in Islamic activism, but were simply attracted by the idea of struggling to defend their fellow Muslims against an external infidel aggressor and had little conception of the complexities of the battle they were joining. In fact the jihad offered the volunteers a simplistic and emotive message based on a strict black and white interpretation of Islam that seemed to be full of solutions.[19] For some the opportunity provided a real-life adventure and the chance to see a bit of the world. Others were attracted to the idea of military action. As the Saudi scholar Dr Mussa Al-Qarni, who is considered to be one of the ideologues of the Afghanistan jihad, noted:

> Many of the Arab youths who joined the Jihad had not received any Islamic education. Many of them had been living a life of deviance, and some were only directed to the straight path immediately before they went to wage Jihad. I personally know young men who were deviant or even extremely so who joined Jihad and were killed, and we ask God that they be martyrs. Some of these men were attracted to the path of Jihad. ... When these men came along they were unaware of the prayer or ablution rules. They only came to fight.[20]

Some of the volunteers, on the other hand, went to Afghanistan to perform humanitarian and charitable work, and groups such as the Muslim Brotherhood were heavily involved in these activities. The Brotherhood was in its element in Afghanistan, as it finally had an open space in which to flourish and to put its principles of providing charitable work as a means of preparing society for the establishment of an Islamic state into practice without the usual restrictions of the state. Moreover the moral pressure to get involved in these activities was such that, as one member of the Libyan Ikhwan (Brotherhood) has described, 'How could we say no?'[21] In addition the Ikhwan offered support to the struggle by collecting money and sending consultants to the mujahideen. It also sent teachers and doctors from all over the world to work in Afghanistan and set up educational establishments in Peshawar in Pakistan such as the Al-Dawa wa Jihad University, where the spiritual leader of the Afghan jihad, Sheikh Abdullah Azzam, used to lecture. The Ikhwan also took it upon itself to play the role of facilitator. In 1980 key Egyptian Brother Kamal Sananiri brought together the leaders of the various Afghani organizations to a meeting in Mecca where they signed a declaration to the effect that they would give up their individual organizations and merge them into the Islamic Union for Afghani Mujahideen.[22] The Ikhwan also worked as an intermediary between the mujahideen and the Pakistani and Saudi authorities. However, the Brotherhood's role in

Afghanistan was not restricted solely to humanitarian and political work, as a handful of members of the movement also took up arms against the Soviet forces. According to some sources the Ikhwan had two military training camps inside Afghanistan.[23]

While for some of the volunteers Afghanistan turned out to be little more than a brief summer adventure, for others it proved to be a fiercely radicalizing experience. The coming together of Islamists from across the Muslim world brought a sense of shared purpose. Indeed, despite the very real and deep national divisions and differences that persisted among the fighters, not to mention the antagonistic relationship between the Arab and Afghan mujahideen, it also brought to the volunteers a sense of being part of the *ummah* (one Muslim nation). In addition, the Afghanistan experience also exposed some volunteers to the more militant ideas that were doing the rounds in the camps. For those from countries such as Morocco or Libya, for example, that followed what is generally considered to be the moderate Maliki school of Islam, mixing with Islamists who espoused more rigid interpretations of the faith was a radicalizing experience, as was coming into contact with organized jihadist groups who were advocating taking the struggle back to their own countries.[24]

Perhaps the most powerful effect of the war, however, was to make the Arab Afghans believe that they were truly invincible. After they had triumphed over a world superpower, they felt they could take on the world. In fact, despite the internationalized character of the Afghanistan experience, after the war the majority of mujahideen fractured back into nationalistic groups with specific nationalistic aims of bringing down their own governments. These fighters founded or joined many of the Islamist opposition groups in their country of origin, such as the Libyan Islamic Fighting Group (LIFG), the Egyptian Al-Jihad, the Algerian Front Islamique du Salut (FIS), as well as its more radical offshoot, the Groupe Islamique Armée (GIA), apparently forgetting that what had assisted them in Afghanistan had not only been the fact that they had pooled their resources into one battle and were fighting alongside Afghan units, but also that they had been bolstered by support from the West and from the US in particular who were equally keen to bring down the Soviet superpower. It seems these jihadists had not fully comprehended the extent to which their own struggle was just part of a much bigger battle being fought out on the world stage.

It was not long before these idealistic young men came to the sorry and sobering realization that they were in fact no match for the security services of their own countries, which, as they woke up to the dangers of the returning veterans, clamped down even harder on their own Islamist movements. The Libyan regime, for example, made it extremely difficult for the veterans to even return to the country, and the LIFG leadership was forced to either remain in Afghanistan or to seek refuge in Europe, mostly in the UK. Likewise the Egyptian regime began taking harsh measures against the fighters, trying them before military courts *in absentia* and issuing death sentences for the elite of the Arab Afghans.[25] The Algerian regime also began trying to crush its Islamist opponents following the outbreak of the civil war in 1992 after the army had cancelled the elections that the Islamist party, the FIS, looked set to win.

To make matters worse Pakistan, where many of the fighters who could not return home were residing, decided it was time for the mujahideen to leave. According to figures published by the Pakistani government at the time, there were 2,800 Arabs left in Pakistan in 1992.[26] Of this number, 594 were Egyptian, 291 Algerian, 52 Moroccan and 63 Tunisian. The Pakistani security services therefore started pushing them out of the country and forced them to close the mujahideen offices there. One of the reasons behind Pakistan's decision to oust the mujahideen was that they were not keen to upset the secular Arab regimes that were complaining loudly about those Arab militants who had returned from the front lines and who were now beginning to create havoc at home. Indeed the secular nationalist governments of the region were taking steps to ensure that the returnees could not wage jihad against their own regimes. As one Saudi spokesman for the Arab Afghans in Jeddah complained, 'The Algerians cannot go to Algeria, the Syrians cannot go to Syria or the Iraqis to Iraq.'[27] As a result many veterans of the Afghanistan jihad found themselves embittered and unwanted both by their home countries and by the lands they had fought so hard to liberate. In fact for some of the volunteers who had gone to Afghanistan as young idealists aspiring to become the heroes of the Islamic world, it seemed as though their adventure had suddenly gone horribly wrong. As one Algerian fighter described, they began feeling like 'fugitive criminals on the run'.[28] Another complained bitterly, 'I hoped after years of jihad that I would be appreciated by any Arab country, but the Afghan Arabs are chased wherever they go. Algeria? I cannot even come close to its borders. I feel after years of Afghani jihad that I was tricked.'[29]

This realization by the regimes of the Middle East and North Africa that they had become the target of the mujahideen resulted in a wave of Islamists, including Afghan veterans, being forced to flee to Europe, mainly to the UK, France and Germany. Indeed, as a result of these various clamp-downs, a number of veterans who had been radicalized by their experience of jihad found themselves in Europe, as there was nowhere else for them to go. However, the refugees who could not go back were primarily the citizens of the secular nationalist regimes, as the protection given to Islamist groups and to Afghan veterans by countries such as Saudi Arabia, Yemen and Kuwait, and to a certain extent Morocco and Jordan, meant that the fighters from those countries could return home. As a result Saudis and Yemenis were not a major feature of the European radical scene in the 1980s and early 1990s. It was rather the Egyptians and the poorer Maghrebi veterans who ended up scattered across the various countries of Europe, those who, commensurate with the status, wealth and perceived sophistication of their own countries, had often been regarded by jihadists from other parts of the Middle East as being on the lowest rung of the militant Islamist ladder.

However, it was this group who had been spewed out by their own countries who were to establish the base of Islamic radicalism inside Europe and who were to have a major influence on the nature of Islamist communities there. While these individuals escaped to Europe as a refuge, they also came to the continent with their own cultural baggage. In fact it was surely ironic that after they had struggled against the secular nature of their own governments and fought against the godless Soviets in Afghanistan, they suddenly found themselves in the heart of perhaps the most secular continent on the planet. These militants, along with many of the more moderate Islamists who had sought refuge in Europe, generally associated Europe with the evils of the Crusades, colonialism and moral degeneration. Furthermore, despite the fact that these Islamists accused their own regimes of being supported by the Soviet Union, they also blamed the West for backing these same secularist elites that they held responsible for destroying their own societies and cultures. A jihadist manifesto of 1986 called the Arab leaders, 'a fifth column that gnaws the bones of Muslim society at the behest of foreign powers. They lost their will and sold their honour and dignity. ... They paved the way for colonialism and exploitation.'[30]

However, while they might have had such misgivings about their new environment, for most of these individuals Europe was simply a place of refuge from where they hoped to continue their struggle to wrestle the lands of the Middle East from the hands of the secular nationalists and to restore Islamic rule in the region, even if the idea of what actually constituted Islamic rule meant different things to different people. They were not interested in Europe as such, but they viewed it as a useful and convenient place where they could set up Islamic centres and organizations and keep the flame of struggle burning in the lands of their birth.

CHAPTER 2

# EUROPE AS ISLAMIC
# MELTING POT

The Iranian revolution of 1979 was an earth-shattering event whose repercussions were to be felt not only in the Middle East but also among Muslim communities the world over, including in Europe. An editorial from the UK-based publication *Crescent International* summed up the feelings surrounding the event by declaring, 'The Islamic Revolution in Iran is a powerful assertion of the Islamic political culture. It has brought the era of Muslims' decline to an end.'[1] The revolution in which the Ayatollah Khomeini overthrew the Shah did indeed herald the end of an era. It marked a closing chapter on the idealism of the Arab nationalist movement that had sprung up in the 1950s and 1960s and confirmed the failures of the secular nationalist regimes that had themselves triumphed over the crumbling colonialist-backed monarchies just a few decades earlier. It was surely ironic that it took a Persian Shi'ite revolution to bring an end to the Arab nationalist ideal that had promised to liberate Muslims from oppression and imperialism.

Whilst Khomeini's revolution signalled the end of one set of ideas, it also ushered in a new era and importantly a new ideology. Despite the fact that the overwhelming majority of Muslims in the Middle East and Europe are Sunni, it was Khomeini's Shi'ite revolution that served to unleash a new tide of Islamist activism that was to change the face of the Middle East and beyond. The importance and appeal of the Iranian revolution was that a populist movement had successfully ousted a Western-backed regime that was perceived to be rotten to the core and that was widely hated across the region, not least because of the Shah's willingness to deal with Israel. That it had overthrown such a seemingly powerful regime through an Islamist movement served to bring hope to many Muslims that answers could be found in their own cultural roots and that the Islamic state could be re-created in the contemporary world. Events in Iran marked the beginning of a new Islamic

16

consciousness that was to reverberate around the Arab world and was also reflected among Muslim communities in Europe.

The revolution came as a surprise not only to the regimes of the Middle East but also to the Islamists themselves – both those from the Brotherhood and those of a more radical bent. The Brotherhood and many of those who had formed the various radical movements that had sprung up at this time came largely from the middle classes and remained primarily elitist organizations focused around university campuses. The Brotherhood in particular had worked to appeal to the intelligentsia and had never advocated mass revolution as a means of achieving its objectives or even been interested in the idea of overturning regimes through popular revolt. Even Ayman Al-Zawahiri's Al-Jihad group in Egypt had the specific objective of targeting military personnel within the regime to get them to join the Islamist movement as a means of staging an internal coup, rather along the lines by which the secular Nasser regime had come to power in the 1950s. The Iranian revolution therefore opened the eyes of these Sunni Islamists to the possibilities that political Islam could be popular and that they needed to up their game in order to awaken Islamist sensibilities at the grass-roots level.

That is not to suggest that there was no Islamist activism in Europe prior to the Iranian revolution. Certainly the inklings of a political Islamic consciousness were already present. As the immigrant communities that had arrived in Europe in the 1950s and 1960s became more settled and began bringing their families to join them in their adopted homes, they began building mosques and Islamic community centres as a means of replicating the social fabric of their home countries. However, these were based largely upon national lines and were set up mostly to serve specific communities. The Moroccan community in Belgium established mosques there in the early 1970s, as did the Turkish community in Germany. Groups from the Indian sub-continent such as the Jama'at-e-Islami also began to establish bases in Europe. At the same time, Saudi Arabia and other rich states of the Middle East provided funds for the construction of mosques. The Saudi royal family contributed £2 million for the building of the large Central Mosque in London and also provided financial assistance to projects such as the setting up of the Munich Islamic Centre in 1960 and the Islamic Cultural Centre in Brussels in 1969. Likewise the Brotherhood was also active in the 1960s and 1970s, particularly among students who, free from the constraints of the region, were able to express their Islamist aspirations. For some this was an exhilarating experience that exposed them to the new ideas doing the rounds in Muslim communities at the time.[2] Yet it was the Iranian experience that ignited a new wave of Islamist revivalism in Europe, as it did in the Middle East, and became a symbol of hope and of resistance against imperialist-backed oppression.

This revivalism was actively encouraged by the new regime in Tehran, which sought to export its revolution. It began to disseminate propaganda throughout the world and offered Muslims the opportunity to study at its religious institutes. Many Muslims from Europe travelled to Iran to see the new theocracy in action and returned full of vigour to spread the Islamic message. The Iranian revolution was also important in another aspect because it gave rise to a new awareness among Muslims that they were part of the global *ummah*. Despite the fact that this was an old and highly abstract concept, the establishment of an Islamic state in the Middle East made people believe that the *ummah* was a reality. As the founder of the UK's Muslim Parliament, Kalim Siddiqui, noted shortly after the revolution, 'Islamic activities before the Revolution in Iran used to be more of a waste of energy over minor issues. The Revolution provided a target of attack. The [Islamic movement] now directly and uncompromisingly attacks *kufr* and its agents within and outside the *Ummah*.'[3]

However, it was not long before the initial euphoria that surrounded the triumph of the Islamic revolution in Iran began to ebb away. Despite the celebrations and elation about the unity of the *ummah*, it seemed that the conservative Islamic monarchies as well as the Islamists who aspired to the establishment of the *Khilafah* (Islamic state) could not move beyond their own prejudices. This was because many Sunnis could not come to terms with the Shi'ite aspect of the new Iranian state. The Muslim Brotherhood, for example, initially declared its support for the revolution and criticized the fact that the Egyptian regime had given refuge to the deposed Shah of Iran. However, as one former member of the organization has described, 'The international Muslim Brotherhood ... wanted to engage with the Islamic revolution and establish contacts but at the same time they were constrained by the popular mistrust of Iranians and Shias in the Arab world. In other words they did not want to alienate their core constituencies.'[4] Among some groups this ambivalence turned to downright mistrust and hostility. Anti-Shi'ite publications began to be spread in Egypt discrediting the Islamic credentials of the Shi'ites and questioning the intentions of the Iranian revolution.[5] Yet this mistrust went beyond the traditional antagonisms between the Sunni and Shi'ite sects of Islam; it also tapped into long-standing anxieties about the Persian Empire.

The Arab world had long viewed Iran as a rival power and had considered its Iraqi neighbour as the eastern gate of the Arab nation protecting it against the expansionist intentions of the Persians. This was especially the case for the other states of the Gulf and Saudi Arabia especially. Moreover Saudi Arabia, along with Sunni Pakistan, feared the new Shi'ite theocracy in

Tehran, not least because both states had their own Shi'ite minorities which they feared would become emboldened by the Iranian revolution.[6] By 1979 the Shi'ites in Saudi Arabia were getting restless and at the end of that year riots had broken out and at least 20 people had been killed and hundreds arrested as the regime moved to suppress them.

Therefore, despite the utopian vision of the *ummah*, it was not long before the revolution set off a regional power struggle to win the hearts and minds of Muslims. By extension the revived Islamic consciousness among Muslim communities in Europe became hostage to the ambitions of the states of the Middle East and Asia. As one commentator noted, 'The Muslims of Britain have become easy prey for the international Islamic forces fighting each other for the spoils.'[7] These international Islamic forces included not only Saudi Arabia, but also the other Gulf states such as Kuwait and Qatar. However, the competition also extended to the nationalist regimes that had long rivalled the conservative monarchies and who, despite their secular orientation, were prepared to use their oil wealth to fund Islamic groups and organizations to try to extend their own reach. Despite his complete intolerance to political Islam at home, Libya's Colonel Qadhafi, who routinely describes Islamists as *zindiq* (heretics), provided support to a range of Islamic groups in Europe. At the same time that he was suppressing the Libyan branch of the Muslim Brotherhood inside Libya he was allegedly giving financial assistance to the international Muslim Brotherhood centre in London.[8] In fact Qadhafi used the Libyan Islamic Call Society, an organization set up ostensibly to spread Libyan propaganda and influence across the globe, to fund various Islamic activities such as the publication of the *Al-Qalam* Islamic journal in Lisbon.[9] The Islamic Call Society also organized conferences in Europe, such as the one held in Utrecht in April 1986 to mark the opening of a mosque and Islamic library.[10] This conference was attended by various Islamic representatives in Europe including Sheikh Zaki Badawi, the Egyptian head of the Muslim College in London. Similarly, the secular Ba'athist regime in Iraq provided £2 million for the construction of the Saddam Hussein mosque in Birmingham in 1988. Despite their strong aversion to these secular-oriented regimes and what they were doing to their own Islamists, the various Islamic groups and organizations in Europe seem to have been more than ready accept their assistance and support.

As a result of this new activism and the sudden inflow of cash from the various regimes in the Middle East, the number of mosques and Islamic cultural centres opening in Europe mushroomed. In Britain, for example, the 51 mosques that were registered in 1979 had increased to 329 by 1985.[11] During the same period the number of places of worship in France increased from 136 to 766.[12] Many of these mosques or Islamic cultural centres were located in garages, private houses or disused buildings and in some cases were left to be run by Islamic organizations that were not tied to the formal state of any Middle Eastern country. They worked to lobby European governments to get them to respect the religious rights of their Muslim communities, such as *halal* slaughtering and Muslim burial.

## The Saudi–Ikhwan axis planted in Europe

Of all the regimes in the Middle East, it was Saudi Arabia that proved to be by far the most successful at spreading its influence beyond its borders and promoting its own ultra-orthodox Wahabist version of Islam. Since coming into existence as a modern state in 1932 the Kingdom of Saudi Arabia has viewed itself as the protector of Islam, mainly because it is home to the two holy cities of Mecca and Medina. In addition, the fact that the kingdom was founded on an alliance between the Saudi chieftain Mohammed Bin Saud and the preacher Mohammed Ibn Abdul Wahab has meant that Islam has always been an important source of legitimacy for the royal family and has underpinned the Saudi state. Wahabism, as espoused by Ibn Abdul Wahab, was a purist reformist movement, which feared that innovation and superstition were corrupting the faith and which sought a return to the original Islamic texts. In fact when Ibn Abdul Wahab began preaching among the Bedouins of the Najd in the eighteenth century, his ideas were quickly dismissed by the traditional centres of Islamic learning such as Al-Azhar, who considered his teachings to be simplistic and erroneous to the point of heresy.[13] Certainly Wahabism sought to strip Islam back to basics. For example, Wahabists destroyed the shrine to the Prophet's daughter, Fatima Zahra, when they conquered Mecca and Medina in 1803, as they viewed worshipping shrines and saints as immoral and deviant.[14] Yet this missionary zeal was not confined to the Arabian peninsula. In 1801, for example, Wahabists attacked the Shi'ite city of Kerbala in Iraq and sacked the shrine of Imam Hussein. Therefore, since its inception, the Saudi state has considered itself to have an almost divine mission to spread its revivalist Islam beyond its borders.

It was the kingdom's vast oil wealth, however, that enabled it to export its Islam to the wider world in a big way and it spent millions of dollars on propaganda, channelling funds into Islamic centres, organizations and schools across the world, including Europe. In 1977 the Saudis opened a Paris office of the Muslim World League which had been established in Mecca in 1962 as a means of spreading Wahabism. It also backed initiatives such as the Association des Etudiants Islamiques de France (AEIF) which was founded in France in 1963 by the Indian scholar Muhammad Hamidullah and which was close to one faction of the Syrian branch of the Muslim Brotherhood and counted Sudanese Islamist Hassan Al-Turabi among its members.[15] While these efforts were driven partly by missionary zeal, they were also strongly motivated by politics, namely the politics of the Cold War and of survival. One of the reasons why Saudi Arabia sought to increase its influence was to counter the Arab nationalist regimes of the Middle East that had toppled monarchies just like theirs across the region and were winning the backing of the Soviet Union. Moreover the Saudi regime was becoming increasingly alarmed by its own internal opposition which was spouting a more militant version of Islam. The armed takeover of the most sacred Meccan mosque by a group of Saudi militants in 1979 particularly unnerved the regime and made it intent on trying to preserve its political legitimacy by emphasizing its Wahabist credentials.

Therefore, while Saudi Arabia's attempts to extend its reach pre-dated 1979, it was the Iranian revolution that brought a new challenge, and all the stops were pulled out to counter the new Persian danger. The Saudis continued to finance large and expensive mosques all over the world. According to one Iranian sympathizer based in London, shortly after the revolution the Saudis donated US$60,000 for a mosque to be built in New Zealand on the condition that it would have nothing to do with those who supported the Islamic revolution in Iran.[16] The kingdom also financed the large and imposing mosques in Rome and Madrid among others. In fact King Fahd, who ruled from 1982 until 2005, personally financed the building of 210 Islamic centres and supported more than 1,500 mosques and 202 colleges and almost 2,000 schools for educating Muslim children in non-Islamic countries, including Europe.[17]

Saudi Arabia also increased the work of its charitable organizations, including those with offices in Europe such as the Muslim World League and the World Assembly of Muslim Youth (WAMY). These organizations concentrated significant efforts on *dawa* (call to Islam) activities and by 1992 the Muslim World League alone had over 1,000 *dawa* workers across the world. This *dawa* activity was aimed not only at existing Muslims but also at new converts. In 1989, for example, the WAMY head office in Saudi Arabia asked its branches in Europe to collect the names and addresses of all the converts to Islam that they came into contact with.[18] New converts were invited in many cases to study in Saudi Arabia free of charge and encouraged to spend time in the kingdom. According to the head of the Dawa Department at that time, Hamid Al-Radadi, 'Our main aim in the *dawa* work is to preach to the Muslims first with the specific objectives of directing them to the right concept of Islam and correcting any misconceptions they may hold.'[19] Clearly the 'right' concept of Islam was that of Saudi Wahabist Islam.

In addition the Saudis actively sought to bring existing Islamic structures and organizations under their control. For example, the Saudi-run
UK and Eire branch of the Council of Mosques sought to control the
training of imams 'to enable them to propagate Islam in its right perspective'.[20] Furthermore, as one UK imam noted, 'The new mortar [to build
the mosques] did not come without a price. There were often conditions
laid down as to *Eid* timings and even content of sermons.'[21] This increasing
Saudi influence and interference were greatly resented by those within the
Muslim community who took a more pro-Iranian line. Kalim Siddiqui, for
example, complained in 1982, 'in recent years the Saudis have financed large
"Islamic councils" in Asia, Europe, Africa and North America to project
themselves as "Islamic". ... These councils try to buy out the local leadership of Muslim communities by donations and all-inclusive trips to various
"Islamic conferences" all over the world.'[22] However, through this *dawa* work
and the endless supplies of money that was there to support it, Saudi Arabia
succeeded in creating a new generation of young Islamists who were keen to
impose their rigid ideology on Muslim communities around the world.

One of the main beneficiaries of this Saudi 'largesse' was the Muslim
Brotherhood. Despite the fact that in the post-9/11 era the Brotherhood has
sought to distance itself from the Saudis, the ideas, aspirations and needs of
the two camps neatly coincided in the latter half of the twentieth century
making the relationship a mutually beneficial one. The Muslim Brotherhood
is a controversial organization that has inspired much debate over the years.
It describes itself as pacific and has tended to refrain from the use of violence
or from advocating revolution against the state, preferring the approach of
working from the bottom up, educating and instilling Islamic values into the
population. However, the involvement of some branches of the Brotherhood
in violence, such as the Syrian Ikhwan who took up arms against the Al-
Assad regime, or its support for suicide bombing in Palestine and its sometimes ambiguous relations with more militant elements, have led some to
doubt the group's true intentions. Yet the Brotherhood is a large and fluid
organization that has been able to contain a range of viewpoints and has
been characterized by its flexibility and its overriding ability to adapt to the
prevailing environment. Moreover the Brotherhood is considered to be not
only the first articulation of political Islam but also the source and mother
of all Islamist groups.

The Brotherhood's appeal and ability to spread beyond the borders of
Egypt arose partly out of its simple and conservative message that made a
play to tradition and struck a chord with populations in countries as diverse
as Syria, Libya and Morocco. The movement was also successful because it
had been able to encapsulate the sense of loss, albeit largely abstract, felt by

many Arabs after the end of the Ottoman caliphate and to tap into fears about the encroaching modernity that appeared to be imported from the West. Added to this was its policy of engaging in charitable and welfare work, enabling it to fill the vacuum that the state in many countries of the region had left woefully empty and thus bolstering its popularity. It was therefore not surprising that the movement came into confrontation with the secular nationalist regimes of the day, and the Brotherhood came to be regarded with deep suspicion. It was not long therefore before the Ikhwan were being considered as opponents of the ruling regimes and these regimes moved to suppress them.

As a result of these clamp-downs, and especially that by the Egyptian regime in the 1950s, the Ikhwan needed a refuge, and it was Saudi Arabia that came to the rescue. Whilst it was partly a means for the Saudi establishment to shore itself up further against the nationalist regimes, it was also an opportunity for the Saudis to use the Brotherhood to fill the gaps in their own society and institutions. The Saudis were suffering from a lack of qualified personnel and offered the Ikhwan, who were generally members of the educated intelligentsia, posts within the administration and government. The relationship was therefore a coming together of the brains and intellect of the Ikhwan and the money and power of the Saudi state.

As a result the Ikhwan succeeded in penetrating the Saudi establishment to the highest level. The Ikhwan's former Supreme Guide, Mamoun Al-Hodeibi, for example, worked as a personal consultant to Prince Nayef Abdul Aziz, and King Fahd's personal physician was also a Muslim Brother. Sayid Qutb's brother Mohammed worked as an academic in the Saudi kingdom and wrote a number of texts on *tawhid* (monotheism or the oneness of God) for the school curriculum there.[23] As the current Supreme Guide of the Brotherhood, Mohamed Mehdi Akef, who worked as a consultant for WAMY in Riyadh in the 1970s, commented, 'The Muslim Brotherhood is like a beauty spot on the face of Saudi Arabia because of what it provided the country.'[24]

The Saudis also gave the Ikhwan key posts in many of their charitable organizations, including those in Europe. According to the influential Islamic scholar Sheikh Yusuf Al-Qaradawi, it was a group of Ikhwan led by the Egyptian Said Ramadan, who eventually settled in Germany, that convinced the Saudi authorities to set up perhaps their most important organization, the Muslim World League, in the first place.[25] By staffing some of the offices of the World League, the Ikhwan were able to spread their influence across Europe. In fact, the tolerance displayed to the Brotherhood in Europe, combined with generous financial support from the Gulf, prompted it to set up an international arm. In 1981 Muslim Brother Mustafa Al-Mashour fled his home country of Egypt and sought refuge in Kuwait. With the backing of funders from the Gulf he set up an international branch of the Brotherhood in Germany in July 1982. Its aim was to bring together all the Ikhwani threads from around the world and it allied itself with other Islamic organizations that shared a similar ideology including the Jama'at-e-Islami of Pakistan, the Islamic Party of Malaysia and the Refah Party of Turkey. The freedom with which Al-Mashour could manoeuvre in Europe impressed some of the Brotherhood leaders who had come from inside the Islamic world. As one noted, 'Leaders of the *Ikhwan* organizations were surprised by the Western openness to Islam and the facilities that were given to fugitive Islamic leaders.'[26] However, others were less optimistic. A number of Egyptian Brothers, for example, came to resent the freedom that those in Europe were given, as they felt the access of those in Europe to the international media allowed them to bolster their own credentials, eclipsing the local struggle in Egypt.[27]

It was through this network, supported by Saudi finances, that the Brotherhood was able to spread across Europe. In 1983, for example, a group of Moroccan and Tunisian Brothers set up the Union des Organisations Islamiques en France (UOIF), which sought to spread Islam from the Ikhwani perspective. In 1989, under the sponsorship of the Dean of the Bin Saud University in Riyadh, Abdullah Al-Turki, the Saudis set up the Islamische Konzil Deutschland (Islamic Council of Germany). Turki appointed the Egyptian Ibrahim Al-Zayat, who is close to the Ikhwan, to run this new organization.[28] In 1997 the Egyptian Ikhwan Dr Kamal Helbawy set up the Muslim Association of Britain, which was established to 'promote and propagate the principles of positive Muslim interaction with all elements of society to reflect, project and convey the message of Islam in its pure and unblemished form'.[29] Although many of these centres did not link themselves publicly with the Brotherhood, as the Ikhwan has traditionally shied away from proclaiming its affiliation to the movement, not least because of fear of the security services of its country of origin that were operating inside Europe, they were generally run by those who had adopted an Ikhwanist ideology and outlook. Therefore by the 1980s, political Islam was on the rise in Europe and organizations such as those run by the Brotherhood, as well as the Saudi establishment, sought, with great excitement, to promote the *ummah* and the new era of Islamic consciousness.

## The Rushdie crisis

However, it was not long before the fragility of the concept of the *ummah* was to make itself felt once again, this time right in the heart of Europe. After novelist Salman Rushdie published his novel *The Satanic Verses* in 1988, there was a great outpouring of anger by Muslims both in the West and the Islamic world who deemed parts of the novel blasphemous. Yet while the crisis served to heighten a sense of Islamic consciousness not felt since the Iranian revolution, it also brought to the fore the deep divisions that existed within the Muslim community both in the UK and beyond. Indeed the crisis over Rushdie's novel revealed the extent to which Muslims in Europe were tied directly to the politics of the Muslim world, as Saudi Arabia and Iran fought to dominate Islamic communities beyond their own borders. As such this crisis can be placed in the context of the old rivalries of the immediate post-Iranian revolution period.

Although the novel had provoked negative responses in India, various groups in the UK and their external backers tried to take the lead in the campaign against Rushdie primarily as a means of enhancing their own credentials as leaders of the Muslim communities there. The first to take up the cause in the UK was the Leicester Islamic Foundation. This organization, which had been set up in the early 1970s, was closely linked to the Pakistani group Jama'at-e-Islami, which was not dissimilar to the Muslim Brotherhood. The Foundation now sits in the middle of lush green fields in Markfield, a few miles outside the city of Leicester. After the Foundation had been alerted to the content of the book by Jama'at-e-Islami's offices in India, its leaders, along with its group of networked organizations, launched a campaign against the novel. The Foundation was closely linked to Saudi Arabia, which was keen to lead the way on the crisis, and worked with the Saudi Islamic Cultural Centre in London to set up a UK Action Committee on Islamic Affairs to mobilize action. Muslim Brotherhood strongholds in the UK, such as the Muslim Welfare House in Finsbury Park in North London, which is adjacent to the underground station and tucked behind what was Abu Hamza Al-Masri's famous mosque, also joined in.

The Action Committee, which described *The Satanic Verses* as 'The most offensive, filthy and abusive book ever written by any hostile enemy of Islam',[30] encouraged local Muslim organizations to demand the book be banned and compensation be paid to 'an agreed Islamic charity in Britain'.[31] This was surely an indication of how poorly the Committee had understood the society in which it was living. The Committee also demanded the British government extend the blasphemy law to include Islam. However, it was unable to bring any real pressure to bear and, frustrated by the lack of success, the head of the Leicester Islamic Foundation decided to take the matter to the heart of the Islamic world where he knew he would be greeted with a sympathetic ear. He travelled to Saudi Arabia where he consulted with the leadership of the Organization of the Islamic Conference (OIC) – an inter-governmental organization whose headquarters are based in the Saudi Arabian city of Jeddah. OIC member states called at once for *The Satanic Verses* to be banned.

At the same time local community leaders from the Indian sub-continent were trying to do their bit to defend the honour of the Muslims. This parallel effort was led by the Bradford Council of Mosques, which, while it did not have the sophistication or clout to lead a politicized campaign, succeeded in tapping into grass-roots feeling that saw the novel as an attack on the Muslim community as a whole. They organized a large demonstration in Bradford at which *The Satanic Verses* was burnt – an image that was broadcast on television screens across Europe and shocked the European public, who saw the book burning as an attempted form of censorship in its own backyard and the antithesis of what European society stood for. However, the demonstration was not solely about religious matters. It also offered a way for young disaffected Muslim immigrants to express their general dissatisfaction with life and their frustrations about being a minority community in Britain. According to one commentator who recalled the events, 'A large number of anti-Rushdie demonstrators were young. Many were not religious, only a handful could recite the Qu'ran, and most flouted traditional Muslim taboos on sex and drink. They felt resentful about the treatment of Muslims, disenchanted by left-wing politics and were looking for new ways of expressing their disaffection.'[32] Islam became for these young people a rallying cry associated with identity and politics and a means to express their frustration at feeling somewhat alienated in Western society. It was these grass-roots demonstrations that catapulted the affair into the media spotlight, leaving the Saudi-backed Action Committee feeling as though the rug had been pulled from under its feet.

By this point, however, the Khomeini regime in Tehran had seen in the crisis an opportunity to raise its standing as leader of the *ummah* and to challenge Saudi Arabia's hegemony over the Muslim faith. It was also a chance to deflect attention away from a number of uncomfortable domestic difficulties the Iranian regime was facing, such as the ceasefire Tehran had signed with Iraq, which marked its failure to defeat the Saddam Hussein regime after a long and bloody war. The fact that Saudi Arabia had provided financial assistance to secular Ba'athist Iraq in this war had greatly irked the Iranian regime and made it all the more imperative to challenge the Saudis. The Rushdie affair provided such an opportunity.

In a bold attempt to take control of the crisis, on 14 February 1989 Khomeini shocked the world by issuing a *fatwa* against Rushdie, condemning him to death. Fred Halliday has rightly argued, 'Khomeini's call for the death of Salman Rushdie ... was a means of meeting his two main policy goals – mobilization at home, confrontation internationally.'[33] Yet the *fatwa* was also an attempt by Khomeini to extend his influence into the very heart of Muslim communities in Europe and to wrestle the leadership role from the Saudis. He was demonstrating that, 'for him, the universal mission of Islam did not stop at national frontiers, but included populations which had emigrated to Europe and which were seen as Islamic enclaves, the bridge-heads of the Muslim nation'.[34] The next manoeuvre by the Saudi clerics was to argue that Rushdie should not be killed automatically but rather should stand trial in an Islamic court. At the same time both the Saudis and the Iranians sought to mobilize support through the OIC. Despite Iran's hard lobbying to get the OIC to endorse Khomeini's *fatwa*, at its meeting of foreign ministers in March 1989 it instead called on members to prohibit Rushdie's entry into all Muslim countries, implicitly marking a Saudi Arabian victory.

Therefore what had started largely as a local protest involving a novel by a British author and Muslim communities in Britain had by now become a major issue in the international relations of the Middle East. This Saudi-Iranian competition also kept the affair burning in Europe, encouraging outbursts of protest and violence against the novel. These protests were not limited to the UK but reverberated around Muslim communities in various European states. In Italy, the Padua bookshop of the Mondadori publishing company, which had produced a translation of *The Satanic Verses*, was set on fire. At the same time, a group calling themselves the 'Guardians of the Revolution' threatened to blow up the monument to Italian writer Dante Alighieri in Ravenna because of the insults to the Prophet in *The Divine Comedy*. Muslims in Holland and Belgium meanwhile also travelled to London to take part in demonstrations against the novel. In Paris a demonstration was organized by the Saudi-backed group La Voix d'Islam, with supporters chanting for Rushdie's death, although a significant proportion of the protestors had come directly from Bradford. This prompted the French daily *Le Monde* to write, 'Rushdie's book is a godsend to those who, in the name of the defence of an offended Islam, dream of taking control in the West of communities who are often disoriented, badly integrated, both in social and religious terms.'[35] However, a poll conducted by the French *Nouvel Observateur* suggested that only 9 per cent of Muslims in France agreed with Khomeni's *fatwa*, 47 per cent wanted the book banned, whilst 25 per cent accepted Rushdie's right to publish the novel and 19 per cent had no opinion.[36] Yet this new Islamic consciousness and radicalism was clearly growing in France. In February 1989 French singer Véronique Sanson performed a song titled 'Allah' at the Paris Olympia Hall and after just one performance of the song received a death threat.[37] The Rusdhie crisis also dovetailed with the issue of the Islamic veil that had erupted after a French school had prohibited three girls from wearing the *hijab* on school premises.[38] The veil issue was seen by some elements of the French Islamic community as another direct assault on Muslims, and the affair took on a political dimension.

However, it was in March 1989 that the conflict between the two regional superpowers in the Middle East was to take lives in Europe when two leading figures within the Belgium Muslim community, Imam Abdullah Al-Ahdal and his Tunisian assistant Salem el-Behir, were shot dead after the imam, who was a representative of the Muslim World League, had made an apparently lenient statement on Belgian television saying he did not believe the novel should be banned in Belgium because it was a democratic country.[39] It is believed that the two victims were killed by an Iranian-backed group, possibly with links to Hizbollah.

The crisis and responses within the Islamic world to Khomeini's *fatwa* also provoked debate within Muslim communities in Europe. There was hugely divergent opinion over whether Rushdie deserved death. Figures such as the Saudi Dr Mughram Ali Al-Ghamdi, who was the chairman of the UK Action Committee, opted for a less confrontational approach and tried to focus attention on what the British government should do to ban the book rather than on inciting violence. Al-Ghamdi, who referred to *The Satanic Verses* as the 'filthiest-ever sacrilege against Islam',[40] explained, 'This book has caused real, genuine and universal hurt. We are doing all we can within the legal framework of the country to get it banned and the author punished for blaspheming Islam. ... But Britain is not a Muslim country. Islamic laws do not apply here and even in Islamic countries it is not for individuals to take the law into their own hands.'[41] Yet this approach was considered to be too soft, especially among some sections of British Asian youth who had been especially touched by the affair. At the time of the crisis Tariq Modood noted:

> What perhaps cannot be denied and is worth noting is that by his intervention the Ayatollah rose in Asian estimation. Not because the majority wished Rushdie killed, let alone wanted to kill him. It was because he was considered to have stood up for Islamic dignity and sensibilities against the West and in contrast to Arab silence. Initially, Asian Muslims had looked to Saudi Arabia as the spiritual leader of Sunni Islam to speak out. They were baffled by the silence and dismayed when they recalled the trouble that that government had gone to to prevent the showing of *Death of a Princess*[42] on British television: were the Guardians of the Holy places more concerned with the honour of the royal family than of Muhammad?[43]

Modood also explained how the grass-roots of the British Asian community felt let down by the London-based secular Asians who backed the calls for free speech and supported Rushdie's right to say what he wanted.

As the crisis ratcheted up, Saudi Arabia began to fear a possible rupture in its relations with Western governments if it did not step in to calm the situation and so was forced to retract from its original position. The Saudi-owned London-based Arabic newspaper *Al-Sharq Al-Awsat* published articles urging Muslims to focus on showing Islam's good-natured attributes to the West rather than getting involved in violence. Zaki Badawi, the Egyptian scholar and head of the London Muslim College who had close links to the Saudi establishment and who had initially labelled the book 'an outrageous attack' and who had written to every UK mosque to express his condemnation of the novel, claimed he would offer Rushdie sanctuary in his home if the author was chased to his door.[44] This brought him much criticism from more hardline elements which felt that nothing short of death would be sufficient. Indeed Sir Iqbal Sacranie of the UK Action Committee, who went on to run the Muslim Council of Britain, famously exclaimed, 'Death, perhaps, is a bit too easy for him ... his mind must be tormented for the rest of his life unless he asks for forgiveness to Almighty Allah.'[45]

## Advocating separation

Beyond the immediate ramifications of the Rushdie affair, the crisis also served to consolidate a sense within some parts of the Muslim communities in Europe that they were under attack and that their values were incompatible with those of the host country in which they found themselves. Immigrants living in Europe may have been far removed from the competition being played out by the major powers in the Middle East, but they were acutely sensitive to appeals framed in terms of defence and honour of their traditions.[46] This goes some way to explain the particularly emotional response to *The Satanic Verses* in Britain.

This need to defend one's cultural values and the fear of being 'tainted' by being in the West was picked up and advocated by figures such as Shabbir Akhtar, who was a member of the Bradford Council of Mosques and who in 1989 exclaimed, 'Those Muslims who find it intolerable to live in the UK contaminated with the Rushdie virus need to seriously consider the Islamic alternatives of emigration to the House of Islam or a declaration of holy war (jihad) on the House of Rejection.'[47] Surely Akhtar's comments do not differ substantially from those made by the legendary fighter in Afghanistan, Abdullah Azzam, who was one of the main proponents of jihad and who in the 1980s noted, 'You shouldn't live in a place where you cannot worship Allah such as in the European and Western countries, the countries of the apostates. You should emigrate away from corrupt societies – don't live in them.'[48] Azzam's comments were motivated primarily by the desire to encourage volunteers to join the jihad, but they also served to strengthen the idea that the West was a negative influence on Muslims and Islam. By extension such ideas also promoted the belief that the West continued to be the root of all the ills in the Muslim world and that it was bent on destroying Islamic culture and values. The Gulf-backed Islamic organizations claimed that what was at stake was the authenticity of Islamic ideas, as defined by them, versus the perfidies of a Western world intent on emasculating their authenticity.[49] As such these regimes and Islamist organizations promoting their ideology were able to tap into natural feelings of alienation and misplacement among migrant communities and channel this into a new Islamic awareness.

That is not to suggest that these kinds of feelings were not there before Salman Rushdie published his novel, but rather that it brought them to the fore and made it part of an acceptable political discourse. It also corresponded to the trend in the Islamic world to use Islam as a vehicle through which to express discontent and dissatisfaction. The Saudis and other Islamists had long tried to emphasize to Muslims living in the West that they were different from the societies they had settled in and that their primary loyalty lay with the *ummah*. One of the main reasons behind Saudi proselytizing was to try to bring nominal Muslims back to the straight path from which they had wandered.[50] The Saudis especially tried to encourage segregation and lobbied for separate Islamic education in line with their own societal values. They also encouraged local Muslim leaders to become more proactive in lobbying on such Islamic issues. In 1988, for example, the Council of Mosques approached local imams across the UK and told them they should be warning Muslims of the 'dangers of remaining unconcerned or passive over school policies, especially on sex education'.[51] This was not a deliberate attempt to create strife or conflict in the West, but was rather a reflection of the mindset of Saudi Arabia itself as well as of the political Islamist movement more widely that had been born out of a reaction to Western modernization and secularism. Indeed, despite aligning itself politically with the West, the Saudi Arabian establishment has long promoted a discourse that is deeply antagonistic to Western cultural values. It was and indeed continues to be part and parcel of life for Saudi scholars and preachers to rail against the evils of Western degradation and as a result much of the Saudi propaganda doing the rounds in Europe was overtly hostile to the West and carried a significant emphasis on how Muslim minorities could survive the dangers of being forced to live in a non-Muslim environment. The *Muslim World League Journal* of March 1995, for example, noted, 'The hostility and antagonism of the Christians and Jews against Islam is nothing but really a socio-cultural attack on the Muslim community.'[52]

Yet the Rushdie crisis gave a greater political dimension to this issue, and the attempts by states in the Middle East to expand their influence encouraged some Muslims living in the West to consider themselves as an extension of the Islamic world rather than simply as isolated migrant communities within European states. Kalim Siddiqui argued after the Rushdie affair that in order to survive as Muslims in Britain the community should develop its own institutions without dependence on the British state or government and should 'plug into the global grid of the power of Islam'.[53] Indeed for some in the Islamist movement their objectives came increasingly to focus on isolating Muslim communities and trying to ensure that they could operate under their own separate rules and institutions which would preserve them from the moral dangers and ambiguities associated with living in Europe.

Therefore while most Muslims in the continent, in spite of being touched by the Rushdie affair, remained detached from the politics of the Islamist movement, there was an increased Islamic awareness and radicalism among Muslim communities in Europe that developed in the 1980s and 1990s. This, however, was as much a result of the influence of the major Islamic states in the Middle East and the developments that were occurring in the region itself as it was of the presence of a number of radicals who were fleeing persecution from their own governments. However, it was the mixing of these two elements, combined with the large amounts of money being poured into Islamic organizations in the continent from various sources, that made Europe a melting pot of Islamic ideas, ideologies and activism.

# CHAPTER 3

# RECRUITMENT FOR JIHAD

O mar Bakri Mohamed, the firebrand radical and head of the British group Al-Muhajiroun, told a television reporter in 1997, 'If I lived in Saudi Arabia, I could never get away with what I do here, ha ha.'[1] Although Bakri was referring to Britain, where he had been granted political asylum from his home country of Syria, his comment sums up what Europe represented for many of those of a radical persuasion who found themselves living in the continent for one reason or another. Europe, with its tradition of tolerance and a lack of real interest in what was going on within its various Islamic communities, represented a free space where militants and moderates alike could continue their struggle against their own governments or against the 'infidels' in various locations around the world.

The first holy struggle that presented an opportunity for the aspiring radicals in Europe was of course the Afghan jihad, and during the 1980s a number of Islamists based in Europe were prepared to do their bit in the fight against the Soviets. In view of the fact that the Afghanistan war was part of the Cold War experience, Western governments appeared to have no problem with the idea of Muslims going to fight there. After all, they were fighting the same communist enemy, and the Afghan jihad had been supported by the Central Intelligence Agency (CIA) as well as by Western ally Saudi Arabia. As a result Islamists were able to move between Afghanistan and Europe with relative ease. As one analyst has observed, 'I have not been able to detect a coherent or systematic effort to discourage European Muslims from travelling to Afghanistan during the war.'[2] Indeed the Afghan resistance had various offices around Europe, including an information office in Paris.[3] Even the father of the Afghan jihad, Sheikh Abdullah Azzam, took time out from the front line to travel around North America and Europe promoting the Afghani jihad. He asked his audiences to support the struggle financially, requesting they send cheques to the various bank accounts he had opened in Western countries. In 1988 Azzam participated in a conference on jihad at the Al-Farouq mosque in Brooklyn, which was home to a branch of the Al-Kifah charity founded by Osama Bin Ladin. The charity was opened to provide financial support for widows and orphans of jihadists but in fact is alleged to have recruited around 200 jihadists to fight in Afghanistan.[4]

At the same time the various Saudi charitable organizations operating in Europe sought support for the Afghan jihad from among the Muslim migrant communities there. Moroccan Islamist Mohamed Al-Guerbouzi, for example, who came to the UK as a teenager in 1974, described how he had been alerted to the Afghan jihad by sheikhs and scholars who came to Europe in the 1980s to spread the news about what was going on in Afghanistan and Palestine.[5] Guerbouzi recounts how he felt saddened by what he had heard and sought to do something to assist his fellow Muslims. He was given the chance when the International Islamic Relief Organization, which belongs to the Saudi government, asked for help for the Afghan refugees in Pakistan. Guerbouzi began assisting by collecting clothes and medicine to be sent out to the refugee camps. However, it was not long before staff in the organization asked him to go with them to Pakistan to work there. He went to Peshawar in 1991 using his Moroccan passport, as at that time there was no problem for Arab nationals wanting to move in and out of Afghanistan. Abu Musab Al-Suri had also been convinced to go to Afghanistan from his European refuge. Despite these efforts by numerous organizations to recruit in Europe, however, the vast majority of the Afghan volunteers at this time came from the Arab world. Yet it was the end of the war in Afghanistan and the subsequent displacement of the fighters that was to result in the development of major jihadist recruitment networks across the European continent.

## Jihad in Bosnia

With Afghanistan over, some of the veterans tried to find another Islamic battlefield where they could continue the jihad. Some headed to Chechnya, some to Tajikistan and others to Kashmir. None of these locations were as glamorous as Afghanistan, and only Chechnya really struck a chord with the Arabs. This was largely because of the presence of Chechen communities in a number of Arab countries, including Jordan and Syria, and a general awareness among Islamists that the Soviet Union was communist and therefore infidel. However, these hot spots provided a place to go and a cause to fight for. Other veterans found refuge in those Middle Eastern countries that were willing to host them. The Sudanese regime, for example, was happy to welcome the veterans and in 1992 opened its doors to them on a large scale, resulting in Khartoum becoming a major base for figures such as Osama Bin Ladin, as well as for Algerian and Libyan jihadists. One of the motivations for the Sudanese regime to allow them in was that it sought to strengthen its

Islamist credentials in the face of its ongoing struggle with Christian separatists in the south. Yemen also provided refuge for some veterans who were prepared to work with the regime as a means of suppressing the socialist currents in the country. Likewise countries such as Saudi Arabia had no problem with allowing the veterans to reside in the kingdom, partly as a continuing means of bolstering themselves against the secular nationalist regimes but also because they supported their objectives.

Some, however, sought and were granted asylum in Europe, giving rise to an influx of war-hardened radicals into the continent. Some settled down into life in the West and left their jihadist past behind them in the battlefields of Afghanistan. Others were still hungry for action and they were soon given the opportunity to continue their struggle through the jihadist front that opened up in Bosnia in 1992. In March of that year, as the former Yugoslavia was breaking up, Bosnia-Herzegovina, in which the majority of Muslims in the country lived, declared its independence, prompting heavy retaliation by Serbian militias and an ensuing ethnic cleansing campaign by the Slobodan Milošević regime against the Muslim population. Bosnia would not seem the most obvious place in which to wage a holy war given that the Balkans rang few bells in the minds of the majority of Arabs and that the ultimate aim was still to create an Islamic state in the Middle East, but the outbreak of the crisis proved a kind of godsend for some of the veterans who had nowhere else to go.

One of the most important Afghan veterans who made his way to Bosnia was the charismatic Saudi preacher and fighter Abu Abdel Aziz, sometimes referred to as Barbaros. Abu Abdel Aziz recounted how he first went to Bosnia, explaining:

> When Jihad in Afghanistan was over, with the conquest of Kabul, I went with four of those who participated in Afghanistan to Bosnia to check out the landscape. We wanted to see things with a closer eye. I wanted to find out the truth to what is reported by the Western media. And surely, as was reported, there was persecution of Bosnian Muslims. Many were slaughtered, others were killed, while others were forced to exile. The chastity of their women was infringed upon for the simple reason that they were Muslims. The Christians took advantage of the fact that the Muslims were defenceless with no arms. They recalled their age-old hatred.[6]

Abu Abdel Aziz became the emir of the Arab Afghan fighters in Bosnia and led one of the two mujahideen factions that were operating in the war under the command of the Bosnian army. The other group was led by Al-Zubair Al-Haili, who was also a Saudi and who had also been in Afghanistan. Al-Haili's group consisted mainly of fighters from Saudi Arabia and the Gulf region, while Abu Abdel Aziz's faction, called Kattibat Al-Mujahideen, consisted mainly of North African fighters. One veteran reportedly told another willing new recruit, 'If you want laughter join Zubair's group and if you want good organization join the *Kattibat*.'[7]

Like Abdullah Azzam in the Afghanistan war, Abu Abdel Aziz sought religious sanction for the new project. He went to the heart of the Islamic establishment, Saudi Arabia, and met with prominent scholars including Sheikh Nasir Ad-Din Al-Albani, Sheikh Abdulaziz Bin Baez and Sheikh Muhammad Bin Otheimin, who all gave their backing to the war.[8] While he was in the kingdom, Abu Abdel Aziz also travelled around giving lectures and encouraging people to join his new jihad. Throughout the war he also continued to seek support from various other places. In November 1994, for example, he attended a conference organized by the militant Pakistani group Lashkar-e-Toiba (LET), where he was introduced as an Indian Muslim living in Saudi Arabia who was playing a heroic role in helping the Muslims of Bosnia in their fight against the Christian Serbs.[9]

However, the real brains behind Abu Abdel Aziz's faction lay in the Egyptian Afghan veterans who were the real theoreticians and political strategists of the Bosnian jihad. After being forced out of Afghanistan, these Egyptians, who were mainly members of the militant Egyptian group Al-Jama'a Al-Islamiya, sought and were granted political asylum in Europe. These included figures such as Talaat Fouad Qassem, who, along with seven of his group, settled in Copenhagen. Qassem was unable to return to Egypt as he had been sentenced *in absentia* to death by an Egyptian court in 1992 and as a result was granted asylum in Denmark. Vienna was another key base for the group, as were Italy and the Netherlands. From Western Europe these Egyptians, along with their cohorts inside Bosnia, such as Egyptian Afghan veterans Wahiuddin Misri, who was killed in 1993 aged just 21, and Moataz Billah, succeeded in setting up a network to support the jihad there.

One of the most influential figures among these Egyptians was Sheikh Anwar Shaban, who was granted asylum in Italy, as his political activities against the Egyptian state meant that he could not return home. A few years before the Bosnian war broke out Shaban, with the help of a few other Islamists, set up a mosque in Viale Jenner in Milan. The mosque is a large garage-like structure in a bland and busy street in a rather unglamorous part of Italy's main northern city. Shaban, who was 'well-versed in several languages and one who had memorized the entire *hadith* collection of Sahih Muslim',[10] set about preaching Islam and producing Islamic literature and soon became popular among the local Muslim community. After the Bosnian war broke out Shaban seems to have taken it upon himself to make his Islamic Centre a recruitment hub for the jihad that was taking place in

Italy's backyard. Shaban is alleged to have developed a large network to send willing young recruits to do their bit for the holy struggle.

It is easy to see how Shaban could have impressed the young, mostly North African, immigrants who made up much of his congregation. Italy's North African community is much less developed than that of France and Belgium, as immigration to the country is a relatively new phenomenon. In fact immigrants from Tunisia and Algeria in Italy often consider North Africans who reside in Italy to be on the lowest rung of the immigrant ladder.[11] It is common wisdom among these migrant communities in Italy that while they might mostly arrive in the poor southern port of Naples, where surviving as an illegal immigrant is extremely tough, those who are able move on to the northern cities such as Milan or Turin, and those of a better calibre and who have the real brains and money move out of Italy altogether and settle in France or the UK. Apart from the Egyptians, who have a longer presence in the country, many North Africans residing in Italy are there on an illegal basis, are poorly educated and are struggling to survive in a country that has a reputation for being one of the less immigrant-friendly nations in Europe. For these young men, far away from home, without the language of the host society and generally without the company of women, the mosque can offer comfort and a feeling of brotherly warmth. As can the attention of a friendly imam.

Part of Shaban's particular appeal lay in his oratorical skills. Egyptians are well known for being excellent speakers and preachers, and the fact that Shaban could speak a number of languages would have meant that he cut an impressive figure to those around him. North Africa in particular has a major problem with literacy, and while many speak their own dialect of Arabic few have a good command of standard Arabic – the language of the Qu'ran. Any preacher who can speak Arabic would automatically be considered as someone to look up to and respect. This fact, combined with the videos and stories directly from the front lines, as well as returning fighters who passed through the mosque, was bound to make a deep impression on some of these unworldly young men who had little to hope for or to aspire to. Indeed, looking at the young North African men hunched against the Milan winter in their heavy jackets looking uncomfortably out of place while they wait for Friday prayers to begin, it is clear to see how characters such as Anwar Shaban might offer a spark of hope and respite.

One such recruit was a young Tunisian, Karray Kamel Bin Ali, known as Abu Hamza. Karray Kamel was working in the Fiat factory in Turin but abandoned his job to join the Bosnian jihad in 1992. He recounted how he was moved to go to Bosnia:

One day, whilst we were at midday prayers, the Imam asked us to return in the afternoon for the afternoon prayers to listen to a Sheikh who had returned from Bosnia. This old man related what was happening to Muslims in Bosnia and he started crying. I started to cry with him. I have never suffered so much in my life as I did on that day. We watched a video showing girls who had been raped, old people assassinated, mosques and houses in Bosnia burned. ... I could not continue to remain still. Three days later I went directly to Travnik.[12]

Karray Kamel trained for just three months before being sent to the front line.[13] He survived the war and, like many others, stayed on in Bosnia, marrying a Bosnian woman called Arnaut Halima. However, he was later sentenced to nine years in prison after being convicted of killing an Egyptian, Hisham Diaba, in 1997 in Zenica.

Likewise the Moroccan L'Houssaine Kherchtou was another poor immigrant who was working illegally in a bakery in Milan but who allegedly signed up for jihad after attending Shaban's mosque. He was sent to the Al-Farouq camp in Afghanistan near Khost through the Egyptian's network, where he allegedly ended up working with Bin Ladin.[14] Kherchtou was to turn up several years later in Kenya, where in 1998 he agreed to work with US intelligence services after Bin Ladin had allegedly refused to give him money to complete a flying course and to fund medical treatment for his wife who was very ill.[15]

However, Shaban was also able to attract a number of more educated recruits such as one young Syrian from a conservative family who had been sent to Italy to study medicine. He reportedly attended Shaban's mosque and after listening to the imam's descriptions of the tragedy in Bosnia was persuaded to go and fight there.[16] In addition, it was through Shaban that Italy also became a conduit for jihadists in the Arab world who wanted to get into Bosnia. In fact Shaban's network became almost legendary, and stories about his exploits reached far into the Arab world. Mahmoud Al-Saidi, known as Ibn Walid Al-Masri, for example, reportedly heard about the plight of Bosnian Muslims while at home in Egypt. Al-Masri was a peasant from the impoverished Al-Said region of Egypt and whose only capital asset was just one cow. When he inquired about how to join the jihad there he was told to go through Anwar Shaban.[17] Al-Masri therefore sold his cow in order to raise the funds to get himself to Italy, from where Shaban is alleged to have facilitated his passage to Bosnia.

Shaban, however, was not content to remain in Italy and wanted a piece of the action. He saw himself as an important player and began shuttling between Bosnia and his Milan base. While he was in Bosnia he took part in some of the fighting but focused his efforts mainly on his forte, which was preaching. He made use of his oratorical skills to give inspiring speeches of encouragement to the mujahideen just before they went into battle. Shaban even took his wife and children with him to Bosnia and it is reported that his 12-year-old son Aadam participated in some of the military operations. His younger sons, who were aged nine and ten, were not let off fulfilling their jihad duties either and reportedly undertook training in the military camps. Shaban, however, was to meet his death in Bosnia at the hands of Croat soldiers at a checkpoint near Zepce.

Recruits to Bosnia were drawn not only from the immigrant communities of Italy but also from other European countries. A number of North African immigrants from France, for example, also joined the Bosnian war. Some went for very short periods of time to get a taste of what the jihad was all about. These include figures such as Hamel Marzoug, who spent just two months in Bosnia in the winter of 1992, where he was in a brigade with a dozen European Arabs tasked with attacking Serbian positions around Muslim villages.[18] According to some souces, Marzoug, who was sentenced to death in Morocco in 1995 after having been accused of launching an attack on a McDonalds in Casablanca, had, along with a few others, gone through a sort of military preparation in Germany through a network that appears to have been headed by the Tunisian Abdelrazak Arroum, who was also allegedly securing the passage of arms into the Balkans.[19]

Others came from Germany, such as Abu Musa Al-Turki, a German of Turkish origin who travelled to Bosnia where, as well as fighting, he also acted as as a cameraman, recording the triumphs of the mujahideen before he was killed in July 1995. Another Turkish Muslim called Abu Muslim at-Turki, from Britain, was also martyred in Bosnia in 1993.[20] Like many other *shaheed* (martyrs), Abu Muslim at-Turki's last days were immortalized in a highly romanticized biographical sketch, the purpose of which was to encourage other young men to take up the cause of jihad. It reads:

> A Turkish brother who lived all his life in Britain, but, who lived a life of a Kafir. He was married to an English woman, and he did not used to pray and did not used to practice anything of Islam. And then Allah guided him to the Straight Path, and when he heard of Bosnia, he said to himself that: 'I must go to Bosnia and I must repent and I must fight against the Kuffar as maybe Allah will forgive me for what I have done in the past.'[21]

Keen to take part in the jihad, Abu Muslim, so the story goes, began to cry every time he was not picked to take part in a military operation. On one such occasion it was reported:

> Abu-Muslim cried and cried like a baby and said to the Emir: 'Fear Allah.'
> The brothers there said to him: 'Do not shout and cry so loud, as maybe the Serbs, they will hear you.'

Abu-Muslim replied: 'By Allah, if you do not put me in this operation, I will cry so loudly that the whole country will hear me.'

He said to the Emir: 'Put me in this operation, even at the back as the last one.'

The Emir said to him 'Are you sure? I will put you at the back.'

He (Abu-Muslim) said: 'Put me anywhere in this operation ... right at the back ... but include me in this operation.'

And so he went and he took part in this operation; and even though he was at the end, the course of the fighting changed, so that the back became the front, and he was killed ... by a bullet in his heart. The body was returned by the Croats after three months. It was smelling of musk, and no change had come on his body. And all the brothers there said that his body had become more beautiful and white since the last time they saw him.[22]

This flowery language is typical of how many of the biographies of martyrs were written and which belie the harsh realities of the war. In fact they all laud the bravery of the victims, giving them almost divine attributes. These accounts were circulated as key recruitment tools. Another such excerpt about a Libyan who was martyred in Bosnia reads:

Three of us were in a small trench. Dr Abu Baker Al-Libbi was testing his Qu'ranic recitation skills because he learned how to keep the book of Allah by heart whilst he was serving on the front and when he was in the trenches for six months. ... The lion Abu Baker stood up and said 'I will go to Abi Muath the Emir and ask his permission.' We asked him, 'permission to do what?' He said 'Permission that I go myself and silence this evil trench' ... and he went truly to AbiMuath Al-Kuwaiti. He asked him to be given permission and he was given it ... and he was so happy. ... Minutes after he left he was killed.[23]

The religious devotion of these mujahideen was such that even after Abu Baker had died and been buried, when they realized that they had interred him facing the wrong direction, i.e. not towards the Qiblah (the direction of the Ka'aba, the sacred stone of Islam in Mecca), they dug his body up again under the orders of their sheikh and reburied him facing the right direction. The story continues:

After a month, we dug up the grave, and ... as we dug him up, we saw that his body was still intact, not even rotten or smelling or anything, and blood was still coming from his wound which he had in his neck. This is amazing because, I've seen Serbs, dead Serbs, which after one hour, have started to smell, you cannot even approach these bodies, and after a day they've become black as charcoal. ... After a week there's a stench. Now I'm telling you this for bodies that are on top of the ground, this brother was buried under the ground for one month and he was completely intact.[24]

## Old rivalries flourish

As with the Rushdie affair in the 1980s, the Bosnia conflict also became hostage to the ambitions of the old Middle Eastern rivals, Iran and Saudi Arabia, as they sought to extend their influence further into Europe. The Saudi information machine used the war as another opportunity to churn out propaganda about the Bosnian crisis. The *Muslim World League Journal*, for example, commented in 1995, 'Bosnian Muslims are suffering from the horrendous crimes committed against them by the Serbian armies. ... The city of Sarajevo is under indiscriminate bombardment and sniper fire from Serbs who shoot at hospitals, cemeteries and passers-by.' The article also makes it clear that the West was to blame for the situation, noting, 'The West, which is talking about humanity, human rights and their abuses and prevention and cruelty to animals, is failing to save the lives of the defence-less Bosnian civilians in their backyard.'[25] In fact some were beginning to frame the Bosnian crisis in terms of a clash between Islam and the West. One commentator in the Saudi Arabian newspaper *Al-Riad* described the Bosnian fighting as a 'prelude to the war between Islam and the West'.[26] Graphic accounts of the rape and mistreatment of Bosnian women began to be circulated not only around the Middle East but also among Muslim communities in Europe. There were even complaints that some of the Saudi money that was going into Bosnia was being squandered on propaganda efforts rather than going to the needy. For example, relief money was alleg-edly spent on producing thick full-colour glossy magazines such as *Sarajevo*, which was printed entirely in Arabic.[27]

Saudi Arabia and other Gulf states were also willing to give large dona-tions to assist Bosnian Muslim refugees. King Fahd reportedly gave US$8 million of his personal fortune to support the Bosnians, while Sheikh Jaber Ahmed Al-Sabah, the emir of Kuwait, donated US$3 million.[28] However, these sums were just the icing on the cake. By 1993, according to the *Muslim World League Journal*, Saudi Arabia had supplied US$65 million of aid to Bosnia, the United Arab Emirates US$5 million, and Pakistan had pledged US$30 million.[29] The Saudis established special aid organizations for Bosnia such as the Saudi High Committee for Aid to Bosnia-Herzegovina, which was set up by Prince Salman Ben Abdulaziz. Funds were channelled through this and other charities and organizations that were operating in Bosnia. Scores of Islamic charitable organizations opened offices in Bosnia, many of them run from the Gulf. The networks built up by these agencies, however, also proved useful in supplying weapons to the fighters. As one journalist who was in Bosnia during the war noted, 'Sometimes hidden under boxes of flour and cooking oil that trundled into Travnik and Zenica lay freshly greased Kalashnikovs and boxes of ammunition.'[30]

Also in Bosnia, the Saudi–Ikhwan axis came into play again and, as in the Afghan jihad, the Muslim Brotherhood played an important role. The Brotherhood had taken an interest right from the beginning of the conflict. In September 1992 the imam of the main Zagreb mosque, Mustafa Ceric, organized a conference on the protection of human rights in Bosnia. Attending this event were key figures from the Arab world who were associated with the Brotherhood, including the Egyptian scholars Sheikh Yusuf Al-Qaradawi and Sheikh Muhammad Al-Ghazali. The Brotherhood in Egypt also launched initiatives in support of the Bosnian refugees and a number of its members went to work in refugee camps in Croatia. The Egyptian Ikhwan also tried to use the Bosnian conflict as a means of putting pressure on the Egyptian regime to support the Bosnian jihad.

Not to be outdone by the Saudis and their allies, Iran was also willing to spend money in Bosnia in order to spread its influence in what it viewed as a bridgehead into Europe. In May 1994 Tehran tried to display its commitment to the Bosnians by opening a new embassy in Sarajevo. It also openly flouted the arms embargo that had been imposed by the United Nations in 1991. In May 1994, for example, an Iranian air force transport plane, loaded with explosives and material for weapons production, landed in Zagreb, its cargo bound for the Bosnian army.[31]

This rivalry between the two big Middle Eastern states fostered resentment among Muslims in Bosnia, some of whom felt they were simply pawns in a much bigger game. One Islamic Aid worker there complained, 'The Iranians will not work in an area where there are no [rival] Saudis.'[32] There was also a significant degree of resentment at the attempts by the various external actors to impose their own Islamic values on the Bosnians and the tying of aid to certain conditions. As one Muslim expressed, 'Don't think the Iranians are in Sarajevo to express solidarity with their fellow Muslims. That would be naive in the extreme. Once they are in the field they have power to use aid as a weapon: "We will give you aid, but you must follow our line." '[33] Likewise the Saudis were keen to make Bosnian Muslims, who had a reputation for being secular and part of cosmopolitan Europe, follow their own strict interpretation of Islam. Women, for example, were expected to wear the *hijab* and men were encouraged to attend the mosque regularly. This effort to impose Islamic values on the local population was simultaneously carried out on the ground by the Arab mujahideen. In 1993 the Egyptian Imad Al-Misri published a pamphlet titled 'The Opinions that We Need to Correct' which laid out the errors in Bosnian Islam, such as the attachment to nationalism and to democracy.[34] These efforts to 'Islamicize' the population often took violent forms, and reports emerged of enforced and crudely carried out circumcisions and other forms of brutality.[35]

Muslim communities in Europe also became part of this assistance network and collected money for Bosnia. At one end of the spectrum were organizations such as the Islamic Relief charity that was founded by Dr Hany El Banna in Birmingham in 1984, which raised large sums through *zakat* and other means. At the other end of the scale were small local fundraising efforts such as the football tournament held in Wolverhampton in the UK in February 1993 which raised £355 for Bosnian refugees. At the same time, some of the charities that had offices in Bosnia sought to raise funds from Muslims in Europe. The United Arab Emirates charity Human Appeals International, for example, which had opened offices in Zagreb and Tuzla, collected funds for Bosnia in Denmark, which was home to Al-Jama'a Al-Islamiya member Talaat Fouad Qassem.[36] However, European Muslim communities did not only focus on charitable works; there were also calls for military jihad. The Awaz Forum held a meeting in the UK in May 1993 at which they 'lamented the lack of armed effort from the Muslim world to fight on behalf of their suffering brothers'.[37] The Muslim Parliament in Britain went so far as to put forward a proposal that money should be raised from British Muslims to buy arms for those fighting in Bosnia. This proposal was not accepted by the British authorities, although the Muslim Parliament continued in its bid to create a volunteer force to help the Bosnians.

Europe also became a place for weapons deals to be brokered and for arms to be transited into the Balkans. One important player in one of these networks was the Third World Relief Agency, which was set up in 1987 and was run by a Sudanese Islamist, El-Fatih Hassanein. This charitable front enabled Hassanein, who worked on a Sudanese diplomatic passport, to channel huge sums of money into Croatia and Slovenia and finally to Bosnia through Austrian banks. Investigators claimed that the charity had links to the blind Sheikh Omar Abdel Rahman, who was convicted in the US in relation to the 1993 bombing of the World Trade Center and who is the spiritual guide of Al-Jama'a Al-Islamiya.[38] Rahman allegedly made telephone calls to the charity that had agreed to sell his videos and recorded sermons in mosques around Europe. The charity allegedly brokered major arms deals to ensure that the fighters in Bosnia were supplied with weaponry. In fact in 1993, 30 Bosnians and Turks were indicted in Bavaria on weapons and racketeering charges for negotiating illegal arms deals in Germany.[39] However, the German authorities, along with the Austrians, seemed to have quietly allowed the activities of the charity to continue and refrained from closing it down during the war. Austrian officials claimed they did not act because it was not illegal to negotiate a weapons deal on Austrian soil so long as the transaction took place elsewhere. However, one Austrian official acknowledged to the media that 'public pressure to support Bosnia's Muslims allowed them to turn a blind eye to the agency's activities'.[40] Some have also suggested that part of Austria's keenness to support the Bosnian Muslims might have been driven by its close ties to Iran, which was its third largest business partner at the time.[41] Indeed across much of Europe there seems to have been a feeling that the activities of these jihadists were relatively harmless. The British tried to give the impression that they were not supporting the mujahideen by refusing in 1993 to issue visas to representatives of the Islamic movement in Bosnia who wanted to hold a meeting on the crisis in London. However, there appears to have been little concerted effort by the British or other European states to prevent volunteers from travelling to join the jihad.

Yet despite all these efforts as well as the growing Islamic consciousness among European Muslim communities that had been fuelled by events such as the Salman Rushdie affair and the proximity of Bosnia to Western Europe, even this crisis in the neighbouring Balkans did not succeed in attracting large numbers of Muslims. In fact, the Bosnian jihad was never to have the same impact or appeal as the Afghanistan one. This was due to a combination of factors. Firstly, the Arab states, and Saudi Arabia in particular, were not keen to upset their Western government allies who were deeply engaged in the region, and as a result trod a much more careful line than they had done in Afghanistan. Moreover, although Saudi Arabia was still willing to channel cash into the war, it was more reticent when it came to actually encouraging jihad. Even the religious scholars who had given their blessing to the war were aware of the limitations. Sheikh Nasir Ad-Din Al-Albani, for instance, cautioned Abu Abdel Aziz that the Arab mujahideen should not attack in Bosnia, but rather 'dig in and be at the most advanced defence lines to defend those persecuted'.[42] It seems that, although they had to support the concept of jihad, which after all was a religious duty, the Saudi official religious establishment did not back the struggle in the same way they had done in Afghanistan.

On a more practical level Saudi Arabia was not in a position to facilitate the passage of large numbers of recruits into Bosnia in the way it had done in the Afghanistan jihad, where it had laid on transport to fly volunteers directly into Pakistan. In addition, whereas many regimes in the Middle East had been willing to turn a blind eye to the recruits who went to Afghanistan, their experience of the radicalized returnees and the corresponding growth of Islamist militant movements in the region meant that they were not willing to show the same degree of laxity in relation to Bosnia. Some regimes even stepped in to try to halt some of the Bosnian efforts. The Egyptian authorities, for example, accused the Human Relief Agency, which was operating in Bosnia, of acting as a front, through its international network, for the activities of the Egyptian group Al-Jihad and tried to clamp down on the organization.[43]

Moreover, for many Muslims the Bosnian war was not as clear-cut as the Afghani case, in which a foreign invader had entered the country. Bosnia presented a much more complex picture, related to internal fragmentation and crisis. Added to which was the fact that the Serbs had traditionally been considered the friends of the Palestinians, and Milošević had maintained good relations with some of the secular regimes in the Middle East, including Iraq and Libya. Moreover the Serbs and Milošević in particular had a reputation for being anti-Western. Yet perhaps more important than all of these factors was the fact that, for many Arabs, European Bosnia seemed culturally and religiously a million miles away. Those who went were shocked by the secular nature of the Bosnian Muslims, whose Europeanized tradition was far removed from the communities of the Arab world where Islamicism had been enjoying a revival for the past decade. The Bosnians' reputation soon spread around the Arab world. One young Saudi, Abu Jandal, recounted how he had wanted to fight in Bosnia but was advised by other Saudi jihadists to go to spread *salafism* in Eritrea instead. They told him, 'Go anywhere apart from Bosnia, because in Bosnia you will find moral degeneration and many temptations. The blonde European girls might sway you.'[44]

This 'moral degeneration' of the Bosnians was not lost on the emir of the Afghan Arabs, Abu Abdel Aziz, who himself complained in 1994 that there were not enough religious scholars to give *dawa* to the local population. Abu Abdel Aziz also protested that there were only a small number of volunteers who had come to join the jihad and he criticized the calibre and lack of religious knowledge of the small number who had made it. In an interview in 1994 he complained:

> Believe me dear brother, until now, two years since we established our base there, there isn't a single scholar in our midst for us to seek his religious judgement. For the small number of youth that make it here, we ask them do *Da'wa*, and they reply, 'We came here seeking martyrdom. We did not come to sit in mosques and public squares to teach people and educate them. All we wish for is a bullet that hits our chests through which we reach *shahada* [martyrdom].'[45]

Abu Abdel Aziz also protested that money raised in the name of the mujahideen was not reaching them. All in all, Abu Abdel Aziz's comments reflect the paltry state of the Bosnian jihad. They also reflect that fact that the Islamic missionary zeal of the Arab mujahideen did not have the same appeal among the local community as it had in Afghanistan. The Bosnians considered themselves part of Europe and were not ready to give up their more secularized lifestyle to return to the way of the *sharia*. It seems that this very black and white interpretation of Islam that the mujahideen hoped to spread was only workable in less developed societies such as Afghanistan, and that being Muslim and part of the *ummah* was not sufficient to overcome the very real cultural differences that persisted.

Another factor that may have weakened the jihad in Bosnia was that many of the key players in the jihadist front, such as Osama Bin Ladin, appear not to have been particularly interested. Despite the assertions contained in a document released by the district court of Illinois in the US case against the former head of the Islamic Benevolence Foundation, Enaam Arnaout, that Al-Qa'ida was intent on establishing a base of operations in Europe through Bosnia against its 'true enemy, the United States',[46] it seems that Bin Ladin was much more lukewarm about the whole project. Like many other Afghan veterans seeking a new home, Bin Ladin had opted to go to Sudan in 1992 after Khartoum had offered to host the mujahideen. From his new base Bin Ladin sent an Al-Qa'ida representative to Bosnia to meet with local leaders there and to report back on the situation. This emissary reportedly met with Abu Abdel Aziz and other leaders, although the discussions appear to have focused primarily around possible business opportunities in Croatia.[47] In the end it appears that Bin Ladin did not take the Bosnian jihad to his heart. According to a spokesman for the Arab fighters in Bosnia, Imad Al-Hussein, also known as Abu Hamza Al-Suri, Bin Ladin did not want the Arabs to go to Bosnia because it was surrounded by *kufar* states and its geographical situation was extremely difficult.[48] Indeed, in a rare interview he gave to British journalist Robert Fisk in 1993 from his Sudanese base, Bin Ladin explained that although he felt for the Bosnian crisis, 'the situation there does not provide the same opportunities as Afghanistan. A small number of mujahideen have gone to fight in Bosnia-Herzegovina but the Croats won't allow the mujahideen in through Croatia as the Pakistanis did with Afghanistan.'[49]

Other sources, including Osama Bin Ladin's one-time bodyguard, have suggested that the real reason why Bin Ladin did not want to develop the jihad in Bosnia was because the Egyptian Al-Jama'a Al-Islamiya had got there before him.[50] As a result of the Egyptians having muscled in on the scene, Bin Ladin chose instead to focus his efforts on Somalia, where he was convinced that the US was trying to create a base for itself. It seems therefore that, just as in Afghanistan, the old petty nationalistic rivalries were very much present. In fact Anwar Shaban looks to have tried to do his utmost to create his own jihadist empire and to eclipse those being fought in other parts of the world. In a fax he sent to a potential donor in Qatar he tried to impress upon the recipient the importance of Bosnia, writing, 'the Islamic projects in Europe must have absolute priority, considering how making these place stable bases for Muslims can be useful for Muslims all over the world'.[51]

It appears therefore that there was no overarching jihadist strategy at this time and that despite the continued emphasis on the global *ummah*, the various factions were still pulling in different directions and had different agendas that they wanted to fulfil. Bosnia seems to have been mainly a convenient place of refuge where those North Africans and Syrians who were unable to return to their countries of origin could continue to engage in a holy struggle. However, despite all the propaganda, the Bosnian jihad did not really amount to anything very much. In fact it marked the beginning of the decline of the scattered jihadist movement, which throughout the 1990s failed to achieve anything like the success it had scored against the communist Soviets in Afghanistan.

However, as far as Western Europe was concerned, the Bosnian crisis did have an impact, albeit limited, beyond those immediately engaged in the various networks: it served to heighten feelings among Muslim communities that while the West had been prepared to go thousands of miles to strike against Saddam Hussein in 1990, it was slow to assist Muslims who were being massacred on its doorstep. Some Muslims who were living in Europe complained that the Bosnian war had made them feel vulnerable because it had proved that Western governments had shown no compassion even for white Muslims who were part of the same continent. Prominent convert Yusuf Islam, formerly the singer Cat Stevens, wrote of the Bosnian crisis in 1997, 'Something had changed with the event of the Bosnian war, our perception of reality had taken a mighty leap forward. These European Muslims were being killed simply because they were Muslim. In fact many of them had already adopted Western cultural values: there were mixed marriages, some of them even shared a cigarette and a glass of beer with their neighbours, but that didn't help them – because they still had Muslim names.'[52] Although these sentiments may have been heightened because Yusuf Islam was a convert to the faith, the Bosnian conflict became adopted as part of the discourse of Islamists in Europe and came to represent another example of the Western world's perceived disregard for Islam and Muslims.

# CHAPTER 4

# ISLAMIST OPPOSITION GROUPS AND EUROPEAN SUPPORT NETWORKS

B y the mid-1990s the trickle of radical Islamists seeking out a place of refuge in Europe had developed into a steady stream. This stream was made up not only of those who were fleeing Afghanistan but also from those who had joined national insurgent movements in their own countries and for whom the dream of toppling their own regimes and establishing an Islamic state had turned into a horrific nightmare. Indeed, as the regimes of the Middle East and North Africa woke up to what it meant to be faced with hardened war veterans who had gained a kind of public legitimacy following their triumph in Afghanistan and who had extended their networks into the local arena, they responded by clamping down with the greatest ferocity. Furthermore the shock of what had happened in Algeria after the army cancelled the elections that the Islamists were set to win in 1992, when the state found itself facing a widespread armed Islamist rebellion, rang alarm bells across the region, and other regimes were determined not to allow the same thing to happen to them. These regimes did not shy away from using the most brutal methods to eliminate the various Islamist groups that had sprung up to challenge them, prompting many of those who had managed to escape death or arrest taking their chances by fleeing abroad. As radical Egyptian cleric Abu Hamza Al-Masri, with characteristic drama, remarked, 'Physical exile far from my homeland is much easier for me and for many like me than the exile of our souls, the slaughter of our faith and our values, and the amputation of our tongues as the price of returning to our homeland.'[1] Once in Europe these militants sought to stay connected to the struggle at home and it was not long before Europe became a hive of activity, giving the various nationalist opposition groups a foothold in the continent.

It was not only the Islamists who fled the region at this time. Others who were displaced by the war in Algeria, for example, also joined the throngs that were making their way to Europe. In addition the flows of immigrants trying to escape the desperate social and economic conditions across North Africa also increased during this period, bolstering the existing Muslim communities that had settled in the continent in previous decades. These communities appear to have been considered by the newly arrived, highly politicized Islamists as a pool of potential supporters among whom they could try to operate and spread the word. Certainly the various nationalist groups did their best to garner support from these communities in order to keep the dream of creating Islamic states in their homelands alive.

One of these groups was the Libyan Islamic Fighting Group (LIFG). Rather uniquely this group was formed outside Libya, having first been established in the camps of Afghanistan around 1990. Although small, the LIFG developed a reputation for producing excellent and well-disciplined fighters. It had also allegedly elicited admiration in Afghanistan, as it was one of the first groups to introduce theological teachings in its training camps, bringing in preachers from the Gulf to supplement the military diet with a theological one.[2] Yet the LIFG remained fiercely nationalistic and its main aim was to return to Libya to overthrow the security-obsessed Qadhafi regime. Although returning proved to be more difficult than the group had anticipated, some of its members managed to smuggle themselves back into the country, where they were able to garner support from among some parts of the population. Given the gargantuan nature of their task, the LIFG decided on a long-term approach, lying low and gathering weapons and men until it was ready to mount a challenge to the regime. However, this plan was disrupted in 1995 when, in spite of its alleged military prowess, the group was discovered as a result of a bungled operation to rescue one of its members from hospital where he was being held under armed guard. Qadhafi launched an all-out offensive against the group, forcing many to flee in fear for their lives. The majority went to the UK, where they joined their brothers who had not been able to get back into Libya after Afghanistan. Many gravitated to the lively northern city of Manchester where there was already a growing Libyan community and from where they continued to dream of bringing the Qadhafi regime to its knees.

Like the LIFG, the Egyptian Al-Jama'a Al-Islamiya also came under renewed pressure in the 1990s. The group was larger and more important than the LIFG, having secured a major support base inside Egypt during the 1970s and 1980s when President Sadat gave them space in which to operate as a means of countering his leftist and secular opponents. The group had sprung out of the university campuses where it focused most of its efforts on

Islamicizing the population. It ran initiatives such as the 'Week of Muslim Girls', in which it gave out free or very cheap Islamic clothing to female students, lauding victories when some girls who had come to the university without the *hijab* returned home acceptably attired. The group had become so strong by the late 1970s that its members were able to impose their own ideology not only on the student population but also on the university lecturers and administrators. They enforced segregation of the sexes and also ensured that lectures and meetings were halted when it was time to pray, removing those lecturers who would not comply. However, the group came under increasing pressure after President Mubarak came to power and this was increased after the returning Afghan veterans breathed new life and militancy into the group in the early 1990s, prompting a number of attacks on politicians, secular intellectuals and members of the country's Christian community, not to mention foreign tourists. By this time the group had become so entrenched in some areas of Cairo that in 1992 Sheikh Gaber, the movement's military leader, boasted that the impoverished slums of the Embaba district of Cairo, which served as home to many disenfranchised migrants from the rural Al-Said area, had become an Islamic republic where *sharia* law ruled.[3] Although this was an overstatement, the district had certainly become a bastion of Islamist militancy. The state responded by sending 14,000 soldiers into Embaba, where they remained for six weeks rooting out thousands of suspects. From this point the state upped the ante and launched major efforts to eliminate the threat, resulting in hundreds of deaths. This renewed pressure meant that members of the group fled abroad and those who were outside Egypt could not countenance going home. By the 1990s there were thought to be around 150 members of Al-Jama'a Al-Islamiya in Europe, 40 of whom had managed to obtain residency. They were scattered across Denmark, Romania, Greece, Britain, Germany and Spain.[4]

Some members of the smaller Egyptian Al-Jihad group led by Dr Fadl and then by Ayman Al-Zawahiri also settled in Europe. Al-Jihad was never able to garner as much support as the larger Al-Jama'a Al-Islamiya, although this was partly because the group decided to focus its strategy on winning over military personnel with the aim of staging a coup rather than appealing to the grass-roots. Various members of the group ended up in London and Al-Zawahiri himself spent some time in Europe, reportedly being offered asylum in Denmark in 1991. He is also alleged to have spent some time in Switzerland.[5]

While all these nationalist movements altered the complexion of the Islamist communities in Europe, the group that was to have perhaps the greatest impact on the European radical scene during the 1990s was the

Algerian Groupe Islamique Armée (GIA).[6] The GIA was formed inside Algeria after the cancellation of the 1992 elections. It brought together a disparate group of militants including Afghan veterans, frustrated members of the more moderate Front Islamique du Salut (FIS) and those who had been involved in the numerous armed groups that had sprung up in the 1980s. It was officially formed at a meeting in the Baraki suburb of Algiers, at which Abdelhaq Layada was appointed as the new group's emir. The GIA had a particular popular legitimacy because it was seen to be avenging itself on the regime for denying the country the Islamist government it had voted for. As the country slid into a cruel and vicious civil war, the GIA came to gain a reputation for being one of the most ferocious militant Islamist opposition forces, not least because of its willingness to indulge in the kill-ing of civilians. As the security forces responded with equal brutality, many members of the GIA fled to Europe. Many settled in Europe, mostly in France, but also spread out to other countries including Belgium, Italy and the UK.

Meanwhile militants from Tunisia, Morocco, Syria and Iraq had been unable to develop any real nationalist insurgency movements inside their own countries. There were some attempts, such as the tiny Islamic Front in Tunisia, which in 1995 claimed responsibility for the murder of four police-men and warned all foreigners to leave the country.[7] However, the repressive nature of the Ben Ali regime, which had been perhaps more aggressively secular in its approach than any other regime in the region, forced the Front outside of the country and it was never able to gain any real presence there or indeed elsewhere. The remnants of this group, along with other individ-uals from Tunisia, Morocco, Syria and Iraq, however, became part of the European radical scene, orbiting around the other militant groups that had gained a foothold in Europe. Like the other groups they also tried to rally for their own cause among migrant populations, but owing to their limited size and organizational capacity were never able to develop any real weight.

In many cases the regimes of the region did not distinguish between the militant and the more moderate strands of their Islamist opposition movements, which meant that it was not just those at the militant end who espoused fighting jihad against their own governments who were pushed out. The moderates also fled for their lives. This included groups such as the FIS, which, owing to their large numbers, were to develop a strong network in exile in Europe, even setting up their own ruling council abroad; the Tunisian An-Nahda party, which was run by Sheikh Rachid Al-Ghannouchi who settled in the north London suburb of Sudbury Hill; and the smaller Libyan Muslim Brotherhood, which was based in Manchester and London. Like their more radical counterparts, these groups also tried to develop a

European base from where they could continue with their Islamist activities and promote the cause against their own regimes.

Despite their general distrust of and concerns about Western culture and values, Europe initially did not mean very much for the majority of these Islamists who simply needed somewhere they could feel safe. As one former member of Al-Jama'a Al-Islamiya, Osama Rushdi, described when he was forced to flee Albania in 1993 after a number of Egyptians who had settled in Tirana at the time of the Bosnian crisis were handed back to Cairo, he rushed to Tirana airport and got on the next flight which happened to be transiting via the Netherlands, where he settled. He recalled that as a country the Netherlands meant nothing to him because at that time he had no idea of differences between the various European states and was merely seeking safety.[8] In a similar vein, the exiled member of the FIS, Djaffar Al-Houari, who had been expelled from France to Burkina Faso after he had been arrested for his Islamist activities, fled Burkina Faso in 1995 for fear of being handed over to Sudan. He noted, 'At the airport, we took the first plane to Europe. Its destination was London ... but it's true that I would have preferred to go to a continental country, preferably Denmark.'[9] Even radical Jordanian preacher Abu Qatada Al-Filistini, who became famous for his vitriolic pronouncements against the evils of the Western world and who had settled in London, declared, 'I have no problem with Britain. ... Britain doesn't represent anything for me now. My case is with the regime in my country. My case is with these regimes, with these *taghout* [ungodly hegemonies].'[10] This view was reiterated by Sheikh Rifai Ahmed Taha, an important member of the Al-Jama'a Al-Islamiya, who, although not in Europe himself, explained, 'We do not aim to commit any activity in Europe or any other country. Our goals are open and clear, to bring down the Egyptian regime, and to support the internal conflict through advertising our plight externally through our members who live in the West.'[11] In fact these Islamists were more concerned with how to avoid the security services of their own countries that were active across the continent. Taha himself complained about the Egyptian security forces in Europe, noting, 'The Egyptian secret service continues to send its agents to commit certain crimes and start tongues wagging in some Islamic centres [in Europe]. We have learnt that the Egyptian secret service are recruiting members from other nationalities to ambush our members so that these attacks appear as normal crimes without political aims.'[12]

However, in time these Islamists came to realize that Europe could in fact serve as a useful centre from which they could assist the struggle back home. The various groups used their adopted homes as a base from which they could disseminate propaganda, try to muster support among migrant communities and pressurize the regimes of the region. They also set up support networks to raise funds, provide false documentation and in some cases to smuggle arms back to the insurgents. All this activity was to change the face of migrant Muslim communities in Europe and, more importantly, the way in which such communities were perceived. Indeed it was the presence of so many radical elements and activists that gave Europe the reputation of being a hotbed of Islamic extremism. London in particular came to be dubbed 'Londonistan' – a term first coined by the French security services who had become increasingly frustrated at the UK's unwillingness to hand over suspects wanted on terrorist charges in France. Abu Musab Al-Suri went even further and described London as the 'new Peshawar', but added that the British capital was a more civilized version of its Pakistani counterpart!

Yet it should not be forgotten that those who were involved in this kind of Islamic activism were a limited group who remained somewhat apart from the wider Muslim communities that had established themselves in Europe. Indeed the vast majority of Muslims in Europe had no interest in these groups and often viewed those who were involved – both radicals and moderates alike – as individuals who had become over-indulged in politics and their religion. Although for many Muslims in Europe Islam was still part and parcel of life and although some had no quarrel with the idea of struggling against the regimes of the Middle East, they were more preoccupied with the day-to-day problems of making a living and supporting their families either in Europe or back home. Indeed the majority of Muslims in Europe did not and still do not engage in regular collective acts of worship except at religious holidays and thus the world of these Islamist groups was far removed from most ordinary Muslims.

In fact the presence of these militant groups gave rise to suspicions among some Muslims in Europe that the radicals were themselves a creation of the West. These suspicions were based on the assumption that Western governments were only giving space to these groups and individuals in order to use them as propaganda tools against governments in the Middle East and as a means of distorting Islam. These militants were often deemed to be receiving money from Western governments as well as from those Gulf states that were seen to be in league with the West. This view was articulated very clearly by one Syrian immigrant who had come seeking employment advice from the Naples offices of the Italian trades union, the Confederazione Generale Italiana del Lavoro (CGIL). From CGIL's chaotic offices in a small street off Piazza Garibaldi, just opposite one of the main *halal* restaurants in the city, he complained, 'The Islamists in Europe are in the pay of the countries of the West.'[13] He asserted that not only the Italian state but also the Saudi government was supplying money to the Islamists of the notorious Corso Lucci mosque in Naples. This mosque, which consists of little more than a couple of prayer rooms on the ground floor of a 1970s apartment block situated near the railway tracks, is affiliated to the Muslim Brotherhood, but gained a reputation for militancy after it became a base for a group of Algerians who took a more robust approach than its affable and rather portly Jordanian director, Abulharith. The Syrian in the CGIL offices was angered by the fact that while he believed the mosque was receiving money, the 'true Muslims', i.e. the ordinary Muslim immigrants such as himself, were not receiving any assistance. Yet in spite of these assumptions and suspicions the Islamist activists across the continent tried to make the most of the opportunities that being in Europe afforded in order to make their presence felt.

## Europe as propaganda centre

One of the advantages of being in Europe was that these groups could produce their own propaganda to promote their cause almost without restriction. The various groups, both militant and moderate, started producing bulletins, magazines and pamphlets highlighting the abuses of power that their own regimes were committing, which would be sold or distributed at those mosques that were prepared to take them. These publications were often little more than badly photocopied pamphlets or tracts that would be passed around the community. Some groups also faxed copies of their publications around Europe and the Middle East, where they could be copied and distributed to a wider audience. Some groups also took to publishing statements and communiqués and, as the 1990s progressed, setting up websites.

Among the more moderate organizations that issued publications in Europe were the Libyan Muslim Brotherhood, which published its *Al Muslim* magazine in the UK, and the FIS, which produced a range of publications including *Sawt Al-Jabha* and *Al-Sabil*, as well as *Al Ribat*, which was produced in Bonn. Indeed the Algerians were perhaps the most prolific producers of such literature, reflecting not only the size of the Algerian community in Europe but also the intensity of their desire to convey the message about what was happening inside their country. The more militant groups included the Al-Jama'a Al-Islamiya, which began producing the *Al-Murabitoun* magazine in Europe when its editors were forced to move to the continent. Osama Rushdi and Talaat Fouad Qassem had first produced *Al-Murabitoun* together in Afghanistan, where the group had a significant presence in camps along the Pakistani border. This publication was focused both on the Afghan jihad and on the situation back in Egypt. After the veterans were pushed out of Afghanistan in 1992, Rushdi and Qassem continued to produce *Al-Murabitoun* from their respective European bases – Qassem from Copenhagen and Rushdi from the Netherlands. It was distributed primarily among Egyptians in exile, but was also circulated around the various Islamist organizations. According to Italian counter-terrorism officials, when they raided Anwar Shaban's Milan base in 1995, they discovered a letter that had been sent to him from Albania detailing the group's efforts to distribute *Al-Murabitoun* among the personnel working for the Saudi Al-Harramain charitable organization in the Balkans.[14]

The Libyan LIFG began producing a magazine called *Al-Fajr* in London which carried news direct from the front lines. One issue published in June 1997, for example, listed the names of LIFG fighters who had been killed in operations against government forces. Another issue in May of the same year reported how some LIFG members had attacked a military post the previous month and had seized 100 machine guns for use in future operations.[15] Although *Al-Fajr*'s focus was on Libya, it also included pieces by jihadists of other nationalities, including Abu Musab Al-Suri.[16] Another important publication was *Al-Mujahidoun*, which was produced in Europe by Egyptian radicals including Hani Sib'ai and Adel Abdel Meguid Abdelbari. Like *Al-Fajr*, *Al-Mujahidoun* carried highly emotive articles about the nature of the jihad, lauding the struggle. In one issue it declared, 'The path to establish righteousness and to bring the *Ummah* to its religion is full of blood.'[17] Yet for all their talk of establishing the *ummah*, even the two men who were running the publication could not agree. In 1998 Adel Abdel Meguid Abdelbari contacted his friend and fellow Egyptian Ahmed Ibrahim Al-Najar, who was in Albania at the time, and asked him to come to claim asylum in the UK so that he could assist him in his media work and help counter Hani Sib'ai who disagreed with the support that Meguid was giving to the Algerian GIA.[18]

The most famous and probably most influential publication at this time was *Al-Ansar*, which was produced in London and edited by several well-known Islamists including the radical preacher Abu Qatada Al-Filistini and Abdullah Djazairi (also known as Rachid Ramda), a GIA representative in London. Although it involved jihadists of various nationalities *Al-Ansar* came to serve as the mouthpiece of the GIA and to be its media window to the world, proclaiming triumphs and losses fought out on the battlefields of the Algerian *maquis*. For example, a July 1995 issue reported, 'One of the GIA brigades ambushed and killed a high official in the ministry of religious affairs whose name was Mokhtar Kadri of the Kouba town. The ministry headed by the apostate Essai Lamouri is one of the biggest enemies of the *mujahideen*.'[19] The April 1995 edition claimed, 'After issuing a threat against journalists, instructing them to stop working in the information departments of the military regime, the GIA continued to carry out its threat by slaughtering the sports journalist Makhlouf Boukhdar on the night of Monday, in Constantine. His body was placed in a car boot.'[20]

The importance of Al-Ansar reflected the fact that the Algerian jihad was the great hope of many of the mujahideen who found themselves in Europe in the early 1990s. Although the jihadists were joyous about their victory in Afghanistan, they considered winning a battle and establishing an Islamic state in the Arab world to be a far sweeter prospect. The Algerian jihad had also captured the imagination of Abu Musab Al-Suri, who desperately wanted to leave his temporary home in Granada to join the Algerian mujahideen. He was told that the GIA could smuggle him into Algeria through a Belgian cell, but that while they were arranging the operation they wanted him to help the brothers in the London media outfit. In fact one of the assistants of Qaeri Said, one of the GIA's founders, called Al-Suri to the group's London headquarters to ask him to assist with their media efforts. Al-Suri was keen on the idea, noting, 'The freedom and openness and the size of the Islamist community as well as the large number of the Islamist centres of their various persuasions help a lot.'[21] The Syrian was given a regular column in Al-Ansar, which he began writing in the middle of 1994. In fact, along with Abu Qatada, Al-Suri became the most famous writer in the publication, which was able to extend its reach into the international media. As Al-Suri, displaying his vain side, noted with relish:

> During 1995 Al-Ansar ... achieved a very important position among the Islamist revivalist and jihadist movements. Even the international media became interested, and used to quote it regarding events in Algeria. Abu Qatada and I became the most influential writers. They quoted us in the international and Arabic media, including on the French TV channels. They called us the two Sheikhs of the GIA.[22]

In addition, these Islamists were able to make use of the main Arab newspapers, such as Al-Hayat and Al-Sharq Al-Awsat, which were based in London and run by the Saudis, to get their views out to a wider Arab audience.

Some individuals also set up front organizations or their own associations to produce propaganda about the situation in their countries of origin. Yasser Al-Sirri, also known as Abu Omar, a former member of Al-Jihad, set up the Islamic Observation Centre from his London home. Hani Sib'ai set up the Al-Maqreze Centre for Historical Studies, which also focused on the plight of Egyptians under the Mubarak regime. Indeed Europe had become such a hive of media activity that it was said that the peasants had been left fighting in the maquis whilst the intelligentsia were all working with the media in Europe. Even Ayman Al-Zawahiri complained about those jihadists who had settled for a comfortable life in the West. In 1999 he railed against 'the hot-blooded revolutionary strugglers who have now become as cold as ice after they experienced the life of civilization and luxury, the guarantees of the new world order, the gallant ethics of civilized Europe, and the impartiality and materialism of Western civilization'.[23]

Not only did written material circulate in Europe. Europe also offered a market for cassettes and videos from the front lines. The GIA and the AIS both made propaganda videos of attacks against Algerian military targets that were distributed in various European countries. Sometimes the videos were advertised in the pamphlets and magazines that were doing the rounds. For example, in the mid-1990s one edition of the *Al-Tabsirah* publication, reportedly run by Algerian Nadir Remli from his council flat in Southall in London, announced to its readers that a video showing the 'first ever footage of mujahideen in action' had been smuggled into the UK and that it was on sale for six British pounds.[24] One sympathizer of the Algerian cause, Abdullah Messai, was quoted in the British *Sunday Times* as saying about the video, 'We were given the footage by people in Algeria. We have shown the video at meetings and sold it outside mosques. ... The mujahideen have told us to make the truth about Algeria known in Britain. That is our job.'[25] He went on to add, 'People should not be surprised if civilians are killed because they are spies. Some of the journalists deserve to be killed.'

Although the circulation of such material was limited and reflected the limited size of the community of activists, the freedom given to these individuals to disseminate propaganda and to rally for the cause among Muslim communities in Europe provoked much anger among the regimes of the Middle East. They accused Western governments and the UK in particular of giving a free rein to their opponents. President Mubarak of Egypt, for example, told the German newspaper *Der Spiegel* shortly after the Luxor massacres of 1997, 'I do not understand, why people on whose hands there is blood, are granted asylum in England. Why are they being granted the freedom to call, in interviews and newspaper articles, for the assassination of people who think differently?'[26] In a similar vein Colonel Qadhafi repeatedly accused London of hosting Libyan militants who were bent on overthrowing his regime. In a treatise on terrorism that Colonel Qadhafi posted on his personal website shortly after the 9/11 attacks, the Libyan leader commented, 'If we believe that youths that trained in Peshawar, who entered Afghanistan, accompanied Bin Laden, and who spread across the four corners of the earth are members of the so called *Qa'ida* organization, then Britain has the lion's share.'[27]

## Europe as logistical support base

As well as a media centre, some of these groups found that Europe also served as a useful logistical support base – a centre for transiting weapons that had come from places such as the Balkans back to the front lines. The main focus of this activity was Algeria and in 1994 a group of Algerians was arrested in Naples and convicted on charges of trafficking arms back to insurgents in Algeria. The group included the Algerians Djamel Loucini and Ahmed Nacer Yacine. Yacine, who lives in Naples and who trundles around the run-down part of the city near the station in Piazza Garibaldi on his bicycle, is full of bitterness and resentment at the state of the Algerian jihad and looks like an unlikely arms trafficker.[28] In fact he looks like just any other young North African spending his time trying to make a living and hanging out in the various *halal* restaurants that have sprung up in the city.

Although information is sketchy, according to some analysts Loucini and his group relied on networks of North African drugs traffickers operating in south west Germany that helped him move the weapons through France, Spain, Morocco and into Algeria.[29] Loucini in turn allegedly used his financial operations in Europe to launder money the group had gathered from their illegal activities.[30] In January 1995 the French publication *L'Humanité* painted a picture of Loucini moving around Europe, passing through Switzerland, France, Italy and also doing a stint in the Saint-François hospital in Aachen in Germany – a key base of the Syrian Muslim Brotherhood – where he was treated for an injury reportedly sustained while he was using a pistol.[31] According to the police, Loucini had also sent dynamite, detonators, pistols and transmitter receivers to Algeria.

Loucini and his network were not the only ones accused of smuggling weapons back to Algeria. In 1994 Abdelhakim Boutrif was arrested on the outskirts of Paris and was found to have large quantities of explosives, detonators, heavy weapons and radio transmitters in the boot of his car. He was charged with smuggling arms to insurgents in Algeria.[32] The same year, French police disrupted the so-called Chalabi network, named after one of its key operatives, hardened criminal Mohamed Chalabi, who is thought to have rediscovered Islam in prison. Chalabi was condemned to death *in absentia* in Algeria in 1993 for belonging to an armed terrorist group.[33] The network, which extended into Belgium, Germany and the UK, is alleged to have set up a youth club and offered financial assistance to disadvantaged Muslim families. It is believed to have funded these activities through a mixture of legal business and the sale of forged documents, drugs and arms.[34] It was also accused of smuggling arms to support the jihad in Algeria. Chalabi was arrested in France in 1994, and other alleged members of the network were arrested in police raids in 1995 and 1996. However, the Chalabi affair was to prove something of an embarrassment for the French authorities. They had arrested 173 suspects but only pressed charges against 138 who were accused of criminal association with a terrorist enterprise, namely the GIA. Those 138 were subjected to a highly controversial mass trial held in the gym of the Fleury-Mérogis prison. Most of the defendants, who were on bail, and the defence lawyers walked out of the trial during the first week, asserting that by trying so many people at once France was denying individuals the right to justice. While the court convicted Chalabi and two other defendants to eight years in prison, of the remaining 135, there was sufficient evidence to imprison only 21 other men, who were jailed for between four and six years.

Others who were accused of weapons smuggling at this time included the Belgian Algerian Boudkhili Moulay, whose Brussels home was raided by police in 1995 and in which was found weapons and publications promoting the Algerian jihad. Weapons were also found in a vehicle being used by Moulay and his friends in a garage in the long Rue Masui, as well as in an apartment being rented by a friend of Moulay. The weapons stash consisted of explosive substances, three grenades, 16 silencers, several rifles, 20 electric guns and 6,000 rounds of ammunition.[35] Weapons destined for Algeria were also being transited through Germany and in 1995 *Der Spiegel* reported that, according to the German security services, Germany was the premier transit country for arms trafficked into Algeria from Slovakia and Chechnya.[36] Spain was another transit country, and one of the leaders of Al-Qa'ida in Saudi Arabia, Abdelaziz Ben Issa Al-Makren, spent a couple of months in the mid-1990s in Algeria where his role was to facilitate the smuggling of weapons and military equipment from Spain through Morocco and into Algeria.[37]

However, the idea that Europe was a hotbed of arms and explosives trafficking has probably been overplayed somewhat. While networks in Europe clearly were involved in some weapons smuggling, this appears to have been on a relatively small scale and was focused almost exclusively on Algeria. Indeed there are only a few concrete examples of such activities and these are repeatedly cited by journalists and analysts to demonstrate that the continent was a trafficking centre. Moreover the regimes of the region were keen to promote this idea primarily as means to legitimize their own call for militants to be returned to them, as well as their policies of repression towards their own Islamist groups. In November 1997 the Algerian authorities sentenced 20 militants to death *in absentia*, including a number of FIS members based abroad for smuggling weapons from Europe to Algeria. Likewise in 1999 the Egyptian press noted of Algeria, 'Arms deals concluded through smuggling networks that led through many European countries and may have been encouraged by certain intelligence agencies, supplied the groups with a torrent of weaponry.'[38] Whilst the GIA would have welcomed such 'torrents', the difficulties were such that the number of weapons the group received via Europe was much less in comparison to other sources, including those it took from the Algerian military and security services.

Europe did, however, prove extremely useful for other logistical support activities. Muslim communities in Europe certainly provided a valuable source of cash. In line with Islamic tradition whereby Muslims pay around 2.5 per cent percent of their income to the mosque through what is known as *zakat*, the radicals moved around their communities collecting for the cause. One British journalist described the scene in London at the time:

> As the main prayers of the week end on a Friday lunchtime, the departing congregation at Regent's Park mosque in London has to run the gauntlet of dozens of young men raising money for holy wars against foreign governments. 'Fight the Algerian junta!' A bearded man in his 20s stands besides a grisly montage of photographs portraying, he says, victims of torture by the Algerian government. One youth says he comes from Nubia and is raising money for the overthrow of the Mubarak government. 'Help the jihad in Egypt,' he cries, trying to out-shout another youth who says he is collecting for Palestine.[39]

It is very likely that in some cases those giving were not even aware of the destination of their contributions but were simply doing their bit for their brothers or more likely just contributing to collections at their local mosque – something in line with local traditions back home. One Algerian observed how Algerians living in London regularly gave money for 'their brothers' back home without knowing exactly which groups this money was destined for.[40] There was also a kind of sympathy for the Algerian cause among the wider community that arose from the fact that it was felt that the Algerian Islamists had been denied their rightful victory in the elections; as such, people were more prepared to give money without asking too many questions. Indeed, for some who contributed, they were not supporting the GIA as such but rather expressing their empathy with the Algerian cause. Others put money into the many collection boxes for Islamic charities that adorned the counters of grocery shops and cafés in immigrant neighbourhoods. This was just part and parcel of doing one's religious duty. Others gave money directly to the Islamic charities that were set up by some of the groups abroad. In Manchester, for example, a group of Libyan Islamists set up a charity that served not only to provide money for welfare projects in Africa, but which, according to one of its employees, was also a means whereby money could be collected in Europe and channelled back to the families of Islamists in Libya.[41] Some of these militant groups, however, used more persuasive tactics to access funds. GIA members, for example, allegedly coerced Algerian businessmen in France to hand over money for the cause, and in the mid-1990s a number of shop owners in the suburbs of some French cities brought charges against GIA activists for subjecting them to 'moral' pressure' unless they paid up.[42]

Islamists in Europe were also involved in other dubious ways of raising money. There was a raging racket in stolen cars, for example, allegedly run by the Algerian FIS. FIS activists used to get hold of stolen cars, buying them at rock-bottom prices, and then would drive them to Marseilles from where they would cross the Mediterranean into Algeria or Morocco. Thanks to the complicity of Algerian customs officers and police, the cars were allowed into the country and the FIS was able to sell them on at their market value.[43] Another racket in London involved radicals who gravitated around the radical preacher Abu Qatada, who had built up his own following at the various prayer halls and centres in London, including the famous Four Feathers community centre near the bustling Baker Street, where he used to preach. According to one former informant for the British intelligence services, some of these followers used stolen credit cards to buy electrical goods, furniture and clothes that were then resold on the black market.[44] Abu Qatada also used to try to convince his followers to depart with as much cash as they could afford. The source noted, 'He [Abu Qatada] would hold out a plastic box and tell his supporters that it was their duty to give as much as they could to help the jihad. He told them that God would reimburse them. There might have been 200 people there and some would give up to £50.'[45]

Another important role that Europe played for these groups was as a place where militants could access fake documentation, easing their movement both inside Europe and beyond. The trade in counterfeit passports and identity documents was and continues to be a feature of the North African illegal immigrant scene. Some of this trade was centred around a number of European mosques, these places of worship being the most obvious gathering points for migrants. Prior to 9/11, for example, North Africans were openly trading in false documents in the grimy traffic-choked street just outside the Finsbury Park mosque.[46] Indeed the word 'visa' could often be heard coming from the huddled groups of serious looking young men who were trading in such documents. For the radical elements it was easy to tap into these networks to secure the papers and documents they required. In March 1994 French police disrupted a heroin trafficking network in Lille believed to be linked to the GIA. They discovered a stash of false Algerian identity cards, new passports and attestations of military service completion

– something that was essential if one was to get back into Algeria.[47] In May 1996 French police arrested 46 Algerians in Nanterre and Marseilles on suspicion of channelling forged identity documents to the GIA. Most of the arrests in Nanterre were of men who were staying at an immigrant hostel.[48] In June 1998 Egyptian Islamists Ibrahim Eidarous and Adel Abdel Meguid Abdelbari, who were both extradited from the UK to the US because of their alleged involvement in the East African embassy bombings, were accused of facilitating the delivery of fake travel documents to members of associates of Al-Jihad who were in the Netherlands and Albania.[49]

Therefore some of these militant groups made use of the existing fake documentation networks that were already operating in the continent to ease the passage of young hopefuls coming to try to make a better living abroad. Some of those who were involved in such networks were also easy prey for the militants and it did not take much to play on their insecurities and to convince them to assist in the cause. In fact the story of one Algerian, Bakdoush Issa, illustrates how young North African men drifted into radical Islam and how the trade in fake documents is just part and parcel of life for those trying to make a living in European countries.[50] Like many young Algerian men, Issa left his country in 1992 and crossed the Mediterranean in search of work. He found a place to stay in a Paris hotel and got a job working in a market in the dreary suburb of Saint Denis where he earned a salary of just 500 French francs a month. In the summer of 1993, having saved up enough of his hard-earned cash, he went to see one of the passport traders in the famous North African Barbès quarter of Paris, where he bought a French passport for the equivalent of US$700. As Issa had a relative who was living in Dresden, he decided to use his new passport to try his luck in Germany where he ended up settling for a couple of years. He then spent a few years going between his native Algeria and various European countries, being smuggled across borders and accessing false papers and passports to smooth his way. In the mid-1990s he decided he wanted to go to the UK, so travelled to Copenhagen from where he was able to take a boat to the British port of Harwich. He made his way on to London, where he gravitated to the Finsbury Park area – the main centre for Algerians in the city. Along with the brightly lit Algerian cafés, *halal* butchers and restaurants, was Abu Hamza Al-Masri's famous mosque, which, rather ironically, used to sit next to a betting shop before the building collapsed and was converted into a block of flats.

Through the mosque Issa was introduced to Abu Qatada, who at that time was the main religious reference for the Algerian jihad. As Issa got more heavily into the radical scene he decided in 1996 to go to Afghanistan through one of the networks operating in the mosque. After receiving training in explosives and poisons in Afghanistan he returned to Europe in 1998. After getting involved in a car theft racket in Dresden, for which he spent three months in prison on forgery charges, he returned to London where he took up once again with a group of radicals, this time forging visa cards and transferring the proceeds back to Afghanistan. However, he yearned for home and risked his chances, returning to Algiers on a forged passport. But Issa's luck had run out and he was arrested by the Algerian security services, which had been tipped off about his activities.

Issa's story illustrates the sense of impermanence and vulnerability that characterizes the lives of many young migrants who arrive in Europe in search of a way to make a living. The world of fake documents or petty crime is often a means of survival for such individuals, who are generally poorly educated and highly impressionable and who often feel ashamed of the world they have got themselves tied up in. This was the case for one illegal and illiterate Moroccan immigrant in the northern Italian city of Turin who was deeply ashamed of having spent time in prison for petty offences, but who explained that he had been trying to provide for his family and his daughter back in Morocco.[51] Yet without papers and a regularized situation, life can be desperate. Added to this is the loneliness and alienation of finding oneself in a strange country and culture many miles from home. For these individuals the mosque can come to hold a special place, providing comfort, a sense of family and community and a link to one's home traditions. How reassuring to sit with a group of your fellow Muslims in the evening in the company of the imam, who often assumes a kind of father role. Indeed one of the attractions for these vulnerable, often illiterate, young men is that through getting involved in the radical Islamist scene they can have direct access to religious teachers and become part of a world that in their own country would appear to be beyond them. The fact that there are people schooled in Islam who are willing to give them time and provide them with an education of sorts is a way for some lost souls to regain their self-respect and a means by which they can achieve something that would have been unimaginable had they stayed in their country of origin. Indeed it allows them to become more than simply economic migrants who often feel humiliated and ashamed at the way in which they are having to struggle illegally to survive.

This is exactly what happened to one young Moroccan, Zakariya, who had come to London to make his fortune.[52] Zakariya was working illegally 16 to 18 hours a day in cafés and bakeries. He was illiterate, having abandoned school as a young child, and could hardly even construct a sentence in Arabic. He had a reputation for enjoying the good life and was often found enjoying the company of the eastern European girls who were working alongside him in the cafés. He also dabbled in bringing people from Morocco, organizing their fake papers and smuggling them into the UK. However, one day he drifted to the Finsbury Park mosque where he said that he suddenly felt as though he was surrounded by brothers and where he was able to relive the Islamic traditions he had grown up with. He was deeply impressed not only by the world he had entered, but also by the fact that he was suddenly in the company of scholars and religious figures who took the time to give him attention. All of a sudden Zakariya's friends noticed that he had begun using phrases in standard Arabic and expressing ideas about religion and politics, almost as if he had learned them by heart. He became increasingly religious and seemed to have found himself, as if he suddenly felt that he had become a valued individual with a purpose and role in life.

Although Zakariya was later to turn away from this new-found religiosity and revert to his old ways, his story highlights how young vulnerable men can drift into the world of radical Islam. It is people such as he who are liable to be taken advantage of by more savvy militants who are seeking a band of followers who will assist with running errands and small-scale logistical support activities. These individuals are not necessarily deeply involved in the world of militant Islam, but almost by chance have got themselves entangled in a world that they do not necessarily fully understand. For some of these individuals their foray into radical Islam ended up in disaster, as some have been arrested and prosecuted for crimes such as credit card fraud or fake documentation, shattering their hopes of finding a bright new future in Europe.

# CHAPTER 5

# EUROPE AS BATTLEGROUND

The presence of so many Islamists of different nationalities in Europe who were all working to further their own causes clearly provided an exciting environment where experiences could be compared and ideas exchanged. Yet at the same time, being in Europe also served to highlight the very different nationalistic priorities and aspirations that persisted in spite of the feelings of unity that Afghanistan had engendered. Moreover the members of these nationalist opposition groups, while freer than their brothers at home, also came under pressures of their own. Many felt frustrated at being so far from the action and at being somehow removed from the struggles being fought out in the Islamic world, not to mention feeling homesick for their own lands. They felt disappointed too that the great dream of the mujahideen who had returned home after Afghanistan – of toppling their own regimes – was looking increasingly out of reach.

It was not long therefore before the cracks started to emerge and conflicts began to break out between the various players in the European Islamist scene. These conflicts were primarily political in nature and more often than not these groups found themselves embroiled in bitter feuds and petty squabbles. Indeed while they might have dreamed about the common goal of furthering the cause of the *ummah*, the various groups, as well as the egos, on the Islamist circuit ended up investing much of their energy in trying to outdo each other and competing over who represented 'true' or 'real' Islam. It was even said that while the militants in the Islamic world were out struggling on the battlefields, those in Europe were embroiled in their own battles, not against the *kufar* but against each other.

In fact the Islamists fighting it out on the battlefields were themselves also engaged in struggles against each other. At the most extreme end these conflicts even resulted in certain factions killing members of other factions – something that characterized the Algerian jihad, but which also occurred in other places such as Egypt. But given the constraints of their environment, those in Europe confined themselves to bickering and insulting each other, often through slanging matches that appeared in the publications and leaflets they were busy producing, or more damagingly in the Arabic media. Some characters on the scene took great delight in accusing those who disagreed with them of having 'deviated from the straight path'. Others employed much stronger and more offensive language, such as labelling others as *murtad* (those who go back on their religion) or *khawaraj* (those who seceded, coming from the word *Kharajites* – a sect that revolted against Imam Ali, the fourth caliph). *Takfiri* of course was another term which some of these characters used to badmouth those whose ideas they disagreed with.

While much of this conflict was related to petty differences and clashes of egos, the age-old divisions between those who followed the moderate or Ikhwani-type path and those who advocated more radical solutions also came to the fore, provoking even greater arguments and disagreements. These kinds of divisions were commonplace across the Islamic world, as the various groups sought to find their place in the ideological pecking order. So too were they played out in Europe, with both sides trying to convince the other of the error of their ways, sometimes in the most threatening of ways. Yet, needless to say, even this division was not clear cut and both camps were themselves divided. Although small, the militant camp in particular proved to be rife with factionalism, some of it related to the nationalist aspirations of the different groups. Moreover the scene was dominated by a few larger than life characters who craved to be considered as religious or theoretical references far beyond the confines of their adopted homes. Europe it seems could not contain them.

## Abu Qatada versus Al-Suri

Two of the most important figures on the European radical scene during the 1990s were Abu Qatada Al-Filistini and Abu Musab Al-Suri. Both men advocated a militant interpretation of Islam and were devout believers in jihad. Both men were also deeply attracted to the Algerian struggle and attached themselves to the cause, backing the newly formed GIA in 1992. Al-Suri had made a connection with the GIA leadership while he was in Peshawar at the end of the 1980s and had formed a good bond with the group. The relationship continued to blossom after Al-Suri returned to Spain and the GIA had returned to try to launch jihad in Algeria. This was to prove useful for the GIA, which was clearly aware of its own limitations – while they had strong fighters and good military capabilities, they lacked intellectual capacity and had limited skills in politics and theology. As a result they turned to Al-Suri for help with strategy and tactics. However, they still lacked a sheikh who could provide the religious framework for their activities. Therefore, as well as turning to Al-Suri, they also appealed to Abu Qatada who was considered to be one of the main sheikhs of the jihadists.

Unlike Al-Suri, Abu Qatada's early forays into the world of Islamism were largely apolitical. He was a scholar of the Salafiyah-Alamiya school in Jordan – a school that shies away from politics, considering all political movements as *biddah* (innovation, i.e. not part of the Qu'ran or *hadith*), and which prefers to concentrate on spreading *dawa*. Al-Suri described Abu Qatada at this time as a Wahabist who was heavily influenced by the Saudi scholars. However, the Jordanian went to Peshawar in 1992, where he worked his way around the various camps mixing with the mujahideen. It was there that he became convinced of the importance of fighting jihad and, according to Abu Musab Al-Suri, he moved away from Salafiyah-Alamiya and took up the jihadist banner. Because of the paucity of scholars on the jihadist scene, Abu Qatada was able to make himself famous in a very short space of time and soon became regarded as a source of *fatwas* in Peshawar. It was as if he had suddenly found his role in life and with it came the opportunity to become a leader of something. His fame travelled with him to London and from there he continued to be regarded as one of the main scholars of the militant current. In fact the GIA came to adopt him with great gusto and in return he was willing to find religious justification for whatever tactics they chose to adopt in their battle against the Algerian regime.

It was not just the GIA who looked to Abu Qatada. He gained a keen following among radicals across Europe seeking religious sanction for their actions. A group of militants in Denmark, for example, appealed to Abu Qatada in the 1990s to ask whether it was Islamically permitted for them to steal money from Christian shops – something he was willing to endorse.[1] Abu Qatada was happy to make himself available to those who sought his guidance and clearly had the personal touch. As one radical in Bologna, Hammadi, explained, 'Many young people in Bologna have contacted Abu Qatada, as have hundreds of young people in all of Italy, because it was easy to reach him. ... He has a mobile phone. I took his number from some of the other brothers in the mosque. He replies immediately.'[2] However, while on the one hand Abu Qatada was busy promoting the jihad, on the other he was also willing to give advice on the most mundane of issues. Hammadi, for example, explained how he had contacted him on one occasion to ask what one should do to make oneself clean and pure for prayer if one had fallen ill and was inadvertently producing wind.[3] Yet for many immigrants from parts of the world whose cultures are essentially oral, such as North Africa, the importance of having a sheikh to look up to and to contact directly should not be underestimated.

Initially Abu Qatada and Abu Musab Al-Suri got on well and were filled with a shared enthusiasm for the Algerian project. In the middle of 1994 Al-Suri stayed in Abu Qatada's house for a month during a visit from Spain. He described Abu Qatada as a generous host who was sociable, well mannered and devoted to his family. He described how the Jordanian used to open his house and mosque to visitors and how he was in his element when he was the centre of attention at these gatherings. However, it was not long before the tensions between these two men began to surface. Al-Suri soon came to find Abu Qatada's rigidity and his hostility to other ways of thinking difficult to accept. Abu Qatada, it seems, could not bear to be challenged and he dismissed anyone who disagreed with him. He accused the Muslim Brotherhood and those who adhered to less extreme interpretations of the faith of being heretics. Indeed anyone who dared to question his ideas ran the risk not only of his wrath but also of finding themselves the subject of the next edition of his cutting weekly column 'Between Two Methods' in *Al-Ansar*.[4] Abu Qatada began accusing Al-Suri and those jihadists who were close to him of busying themselves by theorizing in politics, claiming they were not immune from the 'Brotherhood virus'. Abu Qatada showed no mercy in this respect and regularly humiliated figures such as Al-Suri in front of his young eager followers. Abu Qatada even went so far as issuing a *fatwa* against Al-Suri, declaring that he had gone off the straight path.

It was not just a personality clash that came to divide these two men. After he arrived in London to assist the GIA, Al-Suri soon began to have his misgivings about how Abu Qatada and his men were running the GIA's media outfit. He complained, 'Their work is chaotic.'[5] The Syrian also moaned that despite the fact that the London group was supposed to be running media affairs they could not stick to the task in hand and kept getting involved in logistical support activities in conjunction with cells in other parts of Europe. He was also frustrated by the lack of theological knowledge of those involved and complained of how the GIA simply brought in young Algerians who had applied for asylum in the UK or who were part of the UK's Algerian community to work with them, and he expressed his shock at the 'shallowness of their knowledge of religious affairs and of life'. He also accused the GIA and Abu Qatada in particular of having no sense of security and of acting as though no one was monitoring them. Indeed Al-Suri described Abu Qatada's centre as 'a place for the British security services to monitor the Islamists'.[6] This may have been the case, but it was also a reflection of Al-Suri's meticulous eye for detail and his love of discipline.

Despite his misgivings, Al-Suri decided to stick with the GIA not only out of a sense of loyalty to his Algerian friends from the old Afghanistan days but also because he was most likely enjoying the attention, having found a captive audience for his theorizing on the jihad. In addition he was keen to defend the jihadist cause. Yet, from the mid-1990s onwards, the Algerian jihad became increasingly difficult to defend. In 1995 the GIA leadership in Algeria was taken over by extreme hardliners under Emir Djamel Zeitouni in what amounted to almost an internal coup. Zeitouni encouraged a more brutal campaign that included targeting civilians.

The dominance of this more militant faction in Algeria was reflected in London as the more moderate jihadist elements were pushed out of the Al-Ansar team. The publication came to revolve around the militant GIA elements there and specifically around the ideas of Abu Qatada, who continued to provide religious justification for the atrocities the militants were now inflicting on the population. Famously in 1995 Abu Qatada issued a fatwa in which he stated that it was acceptable for the wives and children of the security services and those working for the authorities to be killed. These kinds of ideas were difficult to stomach for some of the jihadist elements. Al-Suri in particular had an aversion to Zeitouni, whom he described as a mere chicken seller – his father was a poultry merchant – and whom he despised for his lack of theological knowledge. Moreover there were lots of questions being raised at the time about whether the GIA had become penetrated by the Algerian security services.

The sliding of the Algerian jihad into more extreme ideas and practices did more than just divide Abu Qatada and Al-Suri: it divided the whole Islamist scene in Europe. Indeed Abu Musab Al-Suri was later to reflect how it was the Algerian cause that had sowed real division in the Islamist scene. Owing to the importance of the Algerian jihad, the majority of the Afghan veterans and the young aspiring jihadists who were in Europe supported Abu Qatada and the GIA, while the more moderate elements backed the stance of the FIS and the other factions who after the mid-1990s came to advocate a peaceful solution to the Algerian crisis. It was not that the FIS were averse to the use of violence against the Algerian state or indeed against civilians. However, it came to consider a peaceful approach as the best means of achieving its objectives. Moreover the FIS also found it increasingly difficult to defend or justify the widespread killing of civilians that the GIA was advocating. As the violence inside Algeria increased, these moderate groups in Europe began attacking the jihadists in the media and giving lectures condemning those who had followed the path of violence. Whilst the jihadists felt that the Algerian struggle was going badly wrong and were embarrassed by the excesses being committed in the name of Islam, groups such as the LIFG, Al-Jihad and individual jihadists from Morocco and Tunisia felt that they had to stick together and try to defend the Algerian mujahideen. Indeed the Algerian jihad was itself a radicalizing experience for many North African radicals in Europe who, despite their deep aversion to the Western democratic concept, were outraged that the Islamists had been robbed of their electoral victory.

At the same time, Al-Suri and Abu Qatada felt they had to try to persuade those groups who appeared less sure about whether to give their support to the GIA to rally to the cause for the sake of the jihad. On 17 June 1995 Al-Suri wrote a scathing letter to Al-Jama'a Al-Islamiya, addressing it to Talaat Fouad Qassem in Denmark. In the letter he asks why they were publishing news of the jihad in places such as Kashmir and Chechnya in their bulletins but were ignoring the Algerian struggle. It also states:

> Brother Aba Tallal, peace, mercy and blessings of Allah be upon you. I hope from Allah (SWT) that this letter will find you well, that Allah will guide us well and bring us together in what he likes and accepts. ...
> Firstly, your stance towards them [the GIA] fluctuates between shunning and ignoring their jihad. ... Secondly, your stance and the stance of other brothers, such as Osama Rushdi and brother Shoghi in Austria who defend those who have gone astray in European hotels – I mean, the group of Rabah, Haddam, Annas and Kherbane and others who are with them [the FIS] – are taking the side of the unjust banner in the Algerian case. ...
> Your public condemnation of some of the main beliefs and methods of the armed Islamic group in Algeria in lectures and forums and gatherings as well as through your articles and your direct and indirect comments, and through what is published under your group's name – our brothers and supporters understood these documents as your way of defaming them rather than advising them. ...[7]

The Syrian also accused the Al-Jama'a Al-Islamiya of taking a moderate stance simply as a means to carry on their activities in Europe and so as not to be placed on the list of terrorist groups. However, Al-Suri's protestations had little impact on the Al-Jama'a Al-Islamiya, which was far more concerned anyway about what was going on in Egypt rather than Algeria.

Yet even Al-Suri was ultimately forced to stop defending the GIA and his doing so resulted in the development of a bitter feud between him and Abu Qatada. The event that triggered this dispute was the killing in Algeria in November 1995 of two members of the less extreme current in the GIA, Sheikh Mohamed Said and Sheikh Abdelrazak Al-Rajam, who were slaughtered by the more militant GIA factions. The word on the street was that Al-Suri and Abu Qatada were to blame for the killings, as they had encouraged the kinds of takfiri ideas that had taken root in the GIA. Al-Suri was mercilessly attacked by the more moderate elements and by the Arab media. To make matters worse, some FIS leaders asserted that the two Algerian sheikhs had been killed on the basis of a fatwa that had been issued by Al-Suri and Abu Qatada. This caused great embarrassment to Al-Suri, who was acutely sensitive about how he was perceived and who had been shocked by the deaths. Abu Qatada meanwhile, despite having promised Al-Suri and other jihadists in London that he would condemn the actions, went on to justify the killings in his weekly column and asserted that it was right for the GIA emirs to have killed those who did not have proper respect for the *salafist* methods. When Al-Suri and the other jihadists questioned Abu Qatada about why he had backed the killings, he allegedly explained that the Algerian brothers had telephoned him begging him not to leave them or their cause. It seems that Abu Qatada's need to be adored and to have a following was more important than the nature of that following. For Al-Suri, however, this was the last straw, and the split between him and Abu Qatada and his GIA entourage was all but complete.

## LIFG versus GIA

Around the same time a separate crisis broke out between the GIA and the LIFG that was to sow even more discord among the European jihadists and to highlight how, despite their shared aims, they could not ultimately over-come their own ideological differences. The LIFG had developed a good rela-tionship with the Algerian jihadists in Afghanistan and in the early 1990s decided to send a delegation to Algeria to assess whether to send a contin-gent of Libyan fighters to join the Algerian jihad. According to the LIFG, the rationale behind this decision was partly that they agreed with the GIA's broad aims and objectives and also that they thought it would be a means for their fighters to keep in shape as well as a chance to get closer to the ultimate destination, which was Libya.

In 1994 the LIFG sent a delegation led by Abdelrahman Al-Hattab, a former engineering student in Libya who had made a name for himself in Afghanistan and who was one of the founders of the LIFG, to Algeria to explore possibilities for cooperation. Al-Hattab spent a few months touring Algeria, where he was surprised by the large numbers of fighters who were so well armed. However, like Abu Musab Al-Suri, he was not very impressed by the GIA's religious credentials and called them 'religiously shallow'.[8] Despite these misgivings, in the second half of 1994 Al-Hattab decided to send a group of 15 LIFG fighters into Algeria. Many of them went from Sudan, where they had relocated after the mujahideen had been pushed out of Pakistan in the early 1990s, and the group contained some of the LIFG's best fighters. However, the LIFG leadership soon began to get worried as they stopped receiving news from their men. In fact they were so concerned that they sent a fact-finding mission to Algeria to try to find out what had happened to them. This new team was headed by two key figures within the LIFG, Abdullah Al-Libbi and Abu Sakhar Al-Libbi.

It was not long before these two men also began to have their doubts about the GIA, not least because they had been unable to meet with any of the original 15 fighters whose whereabouts remained unknown. They expressed these doubts in letters to the LIFG that were written in secret ink and smuggled out of Algeria. In one letter they wrote that they did not trust the GIA leadership, which was at this time in the hands of Djamel Zeitouni. They also had their doubts about the GIA's religious credentials and wrote that the GIA contained deviant elements who 'have no religion, nor manners'.[9]

However, these letters from the second group also stopped arriving and the LIFG leadership in London became increasingly worried about the fate of its men who had gone so gallantly to assist their Algerian brothers in arms. They began to fear that they might have suffered the same fate as the Algerian sheikhs who had been killed by the GIA after they disagreed with the group's leadership. The LIFG therefore turned to the GIA's spiritual mentors in London, Abu Qatada and Abu Musab Al-Suri, as well as to representatives of the Egyptian jihad requesting that they do something to find out what had happened to their men and whether they had been killed. Shortly afterwards Noman Bin Othman, who was the LIFG's main point of contact with the GIA supporters in London, was told by someone he describes as a well-known Islamist that Abdullah Al-Libbi had been killed by the GIA because he and the other Libyans had taken the side of a faction of the GIA led by Mustafa Kartali that disagreed with the Emir Zeitouni.

The LIFG were so angered and upset by the news that they stopped publishing news about the GIA or any of their statements in their *Al-Fajr* bulletin. The LIFG also did their utmost to lobby other jihadists in Europe not to give their support to the GIA. As relations between the two groups became increasingly tense, Noman Bin Othman was informed that the GIA leadership wanted to find out why the Libyans had stopped publishing news about them and wanted to talk to the LIFG's leadership about the issue. As the LIFG's leader, Abu Munder Al-Saidi, was away in Saudi Arabia at the time, Bin Othman decided to talk to the GIA leaders himself. Bin Othman and the other Libyans in London provided the GIA with the numbers of two public telephone boxes in the north London suburb of Harlesden after they had checked that the telephones would accept incoming calls.[10]

On the agreed date a group of LIFG members, along with some of the GIA, went to the telephone boxes but were dismayed to discover that their plans were in danger of being thwarted by a young English woman who had got out of a car and run into one of the telephone boxes to make a call. Agitated about missing their call, the LIFG tried to irritate the woman into finishing her conversation, but she ignored the rather incongruous group of bearded Islamists who were gathered around the phone box. One of the men got so frustrated that he opened the door of the cabin to hassle her into leaving but was shocked to see that although the woman was talking and was putting coins into the machine there was no number showing up on the display. This led the Islamists to conclude that the woman must have been part of the British intelligence services and that she had been sent to spy on them.[11]

Luckily for the LIFG, the other telephone box eventually rang and on the other end was the GIA's mufti, Abu Buseer, who was calling on a satellite phone from Algeria. The tense conversation lasted for two hours and Abu Buseer put various people on the line including Zeitouni himself. During the conversation Bin Othman discovered that the GIA leadership were not themselves even aware of what exactly had happened to Abdullah Al-Libbi, as the news that he had been killed had come to them from a taxi driver who had been spying on Mustafa Kartali's group before it had been attacked. However, it struck Bin Othman during the conversation that the Algerians had taken to describing Abdullah Al-Libbi and his fellow Libyan fighters as *mupteda al-thilal* (those who come with *biddah* (innovation) and who are not on the straight path). Clearly such a description meant that religiously there was no obstacle to killing the men and it was a very insulting way of describing his fellow Islamists.

After this deeply unsatisfying conversation the contacts continued between Bin Othman and the GIA leadership. The GIA began insisting that neither Abdullah Al-Libbi nor Abu Sakhar Al-Libbi had been killed. Yet the LIFG were finally able to get the truth from one Algerian, Abu Khalid, who had been friends with Bin Othman in Afghanistan and who had escaped from Algeria after the GIA turned against him and accused him of being a spy for the Saudi intelligence services. Abu Khalid related how, after all the divisions and conflicts that had occurred between the Libyans and the GIA leadership, Antar Zouabri, who by this time had become the GIA's emir, accused Abu Sakhar Al-Libbi of being an agent. The GIA then tortured Abu Sakhar, during which they removed a metal rod from his hand that had been implanted to heal a wound he had received in Afghanistan before killing him. Abu Khalid also revealed that Abdullah Al-Libbi had not in fact been killed and that he had managed to escape detention and was smuggled out of Algeria and into Europe without the knowledge of either the GIA or the Algerian authorities.

The treachery of the GIA towards their men had horrified the Libyans: all the dreams of brotherhood that had accompanied their foray into the Algerian jihad were looking very thin, and the great hope of Algeria had turned into a colossal nightmare that had done nothing but breed division and discord. This incident also marked the break between Abu Qatada and the GIA. Despite Abu Qatada's loyalty to the GIA leadership, when he discovered that some of those Libyans who had been killed had in fact been his own students in Peshawar, he reportedly burst into tears and began cursing Zeitouni and the GIA. This was clearly the turning point for Abu Qatada, who, despite his uncompromising and violent stance, could not cope when the killing came closer to home. The preacher immediately issued a statement of condemnation of the GIA in the *Al-Hayat* newspaper. This was to have major repercussions for the preacher, as the following day hardcore GIA supporters in London along with the management of *Al-Ansar* went to Abu Qatada's house where they insulted him and accused him of being impure.

However, there were other radicals, keen on the limelight, who were willing to step in and fight over the spoils. Abu Qatada's deputy, Abu Walid Al-Filistini, immediately turned his back on his former boss and opened his house to the GIA supporters, happy to be a sheikh even if it was of the discredited GIA. However, Al-Filistini did not last very long and the last crumbs of the limping organization were taken up by Egyptian preacher Abu Hamza Al-Masri. Yet shortly after Al-Masri stepped in, the group's then emir, Antar Zouabri, issued a statement declaring that the entire Algerian population was *kufar*. This kind of attitude was too much even for the likes of Abu Hamza and he withdrew, calling the GIA a group of traitors to the jihadist cause. Moreover by this point the whole GIA had become discredited given the allegations that it was completely infiltrated by the Algerian security services.

## Al-Jama'a Al-Islamiya versus itself

The Egyptian Al-Jama'a Al-Islamiya was no less immune from the factionalism and internal ruptures than the other nationalist groups. Like many of the other organizations, members of the Al-Jama'a Al-Islamiya were scattered around Europe. Osama Rushdi was in the Netherlands, Talaat Fouad Qassem was in Denmark, and Anwar Shaban was in Italy, as was Osama Mustafa Hassan, also known as Abu Omar, who disappeared from Milan in 2003 when he was abducted by American intelligence agents and forcibly returned to Egypt where he suffered brutal torture until he was released in February 2007. From abroad these members of the group tried to coordinate a policy with those still in Egypt, including the famous 'historic leadership' who were imprisoned there.

Those members of the group still in Egypt had suffered a lot during the 1980s, and by the mid-1990s the historic leadership had come to the conclusion that they should abandon their policy of violence, which had not really got them anywhere apart from prison. Moreover they were becoming aware that the violent campaigns and killings in Egypt were alienating them from the population, who were becoming increasingly unsympathetic to the group. This feeling was shared by some of those who were residing in Europe who saw that their campaign against the Egyptian state had achieved little and who were getting homesick for their homeland. As a result, some elements within the Al-Jama'a Al-Islamiya began issuing ceasefires in a bid to halt the violence and take a more moderate path. However, this did not sit well with the more hardline elements within the organization who responded to these calls by launching violent attacks. The first call for a ceasefire in March 1996, for example, was followed by the massacre of 18 Greek tourists in a hotel in Cairo whom, the perpetrators explained, they had mistaken for Jews.

In July 1997, however, the group's historic leadership in prison announced a definitive ceasefire during the military trial of 98 of its members in Cairo. One of the defendants, Mohamed Amin Abdelhalim, called on the group both in Egypt and abroad to suspend all violent activities and said he was speaking on behalf of the six senior leaders who had been in the Tora prison for the past 16 years. Disagreements ensued as various factions within the group had their own ideas as to whether this was an acceptable path to take. Yet many members of the Al-Jama'a Al-Islamiya in Europe had resigned themselves to the new realities of what was happening in Egypt and they supported the ceasefire. Therefore they, like many of the leadership in prison in Egypt, were shocked when in 1997 some of the group's members carried out what was to become one of the most renowned terrorist attacks of the time.

On the morning of 17 November 1997, a group of six young Egyptians opened fire on a group of tourists who were visiting the famous Temple of Queen Hatshepsut at Luxor. Fifty-eight of the tourists were killed along with a number of Egyptians, and after a prolonged gun battle the security services killed all of the assailants. As news of the killings spread around the world, the Al-Jama'a Al-Islamiya's leadership and many of those in Europe such as Osama Rushdi were horrified by the attacks. However, certain elements with the Al-Jama'a Al-Islamiya came out in support of what had occurred. Rifai Ahmed Taha, the head of the group's Consultative Council, who was a known hardliner and who had stayed in Afghanistan where he had become increasingly close to Osama Bin Ladin, claimed responsibility for the attacks in the name of the group.

The more moderate Al-Jama'a Al-Islamiya members were angered not only by Taha's willingness to support the attacks after the leadership had issued a ceasefire, but also by the fact that he had taken it upon himself to speak on behalf of the entire group. According to Osama Rushdi, Taha did not even know the real facts of the attack and had simply heard the news on the radio and decided to claim responsibility for it.[12] Rushdi and the other more moderate elements in Europe issued a statement to the effect that Taha was only speaking as an individual and not on behalf of the group. However, the split between them and Taha became even more pronounced the following year after Bin Ladin established his World Islamic Front. Taha, full of enthusiasm for Al-Qa'ida's new project, signed up to the Front in 1998. However, those in Europe did not share Taha's zeal for Bin Ladin's vision and preferred to continue to focus their attentions on the situation inside Egypt.

Ironically being in Europe was ultimately to enable the more moderate faction to wrestle back control of the group. As Osama Rushdi described, his being in Europe, far away from the restrictions imposed upon those members of the group inside Egypt, gave him the freedom to act to counter Taha's hawkish position. He noted, 'I found myself in a good situation so I could do something.'[13] Rushdi rallied around and succeeded in getting the backing of other members of his group and together they pressurized Taha into retracting. Taha later said he had not signed the actual declaration but had simply agreed to support the Iraqi people who were suffering from American sanctions. Taha, clearly feeling his ultimate sense of loyalty had to be with Al-Jama'a rather than with Al-Qa'ida, agreed to retract his announced joining of the World Islamic Front. Bin Ladin himself also confirmed Taha's stance and in an interview with Al-Jazeera in 1998 tried rather unconvincingly to explain away what had occurred. He noted, 'they signed the *fatwa*, but there was confusion concerning an administrative matter when the *fatwa* was issued, for it was issued on the same date as the establishment of the front. People were thus confused as to whether Al-Jama'a Al-Islamiya was a part of the Global Islamic Front, and thus Al-Jama'a was forced to clarify its position – it had signed the *fatwa* but was not part of the Global Islamic Front.'[14]

This, however, did not stop the conflict between the different elements within the group. On 22 October 1998 the blind Sheikh Omar Abdel Rahman, who was in prison in the US, called for the formation of a new world Islamic front to spread and defend Islam on the basis of peaceful action, without resort to violence. A few days later the historic leadership in prison sent a handwritten statement to an Islamist lawyer expressing their full support for the call and denounced the use of force and Bin Ladin's 'anti-American front'.[15] While such statements must have pleased those such as Osama Rushdi, they certainly did not go down well with other more hardline Egyptians who were in London. Abu Hamza Al-Masri is reported to have attacked the historic leadership and accused them of 'betraying the blood of our martyrs'.[16] The Egyptian media also alleged that London-based Yasser Al-Sirri dismissed the statements as a call for 'surrender, not peace'.[17] Yet by this time, the group had become so divided that it had reached its end as a credible force. As a result it went into decline. Those members of the group who were in Europe, such as Osama Rushdi, continued their activism, but through smaller organizations and groups that they set up, and took a line that was much more akin to the stance of the Muslim Brotherhood.

Ultimately all of these nationalist movements proved themselves to be typical of opposition forces in exile. In spite of their endless calls for unity and for raising the banner of jihad, they remained disjointed and divided and could not overcome their own national differences and preoccupations. The scene had few major characters and many of those who were there proved themselves to be narrowed by their own limitations. In fact, once away from the battleground these Islamists seemed to be pulling in different directions and seeking to outdo each other, especially through the media. The 1990s were supposed to be the jihadists' heyday and the time when the tyrannical regimes of the Arab world that had exploited their own societies would be toppled and glorious Islamic rule would prevail. Yet by the end of the decade the struggle was looking as desperate as ever. As a result some of the frustration these Islamists had towards their own governments began increasingly to be directed against those European states that were backing the various regimes of the region, thus marking the next phase in the development of radical Islam in Europe.

# CHAPTER 6

# ALGERIAN RADICALISM TARGETS FRANCE

Despite the presence of so many Islamists in Europe, the battlefields of jihad had remained largely within the confines of the Islamic world. However, a string of deadly bomb attacks on the French mainland in the mid-1990s woke Europe up to the fact that the Algerian conflict had spilled over into the heart of the continent. Alarm bells began to ring, in France in particular, about the presence of so many disaffected Islamists who were living in various European countries. However, targeting Europe was not a tactic that gained currency among jihadists residing in the continent at the time, and these attacks can only be understood within the context of the highly complex and antagonistic relationship between France and Algeria, which was based on a particularly fractious shared colonial experience.

The period of French colonization in Algeria that began in 1830 was a bitter and brutal experience. This was partly because France went as far as to annex Algeria, making it an official department of the Hexagon. As such, France considered that Algeria was not simply a colonial possession but part of the Republic. The subsequent war of independence, led by the Algerian resistance, the Front de Libération Nationale (FLN), which went on to form the government after independence in 1962, was also a bloody affair that took hundreds of thousands of lives. The whole experience left a deep scar on those who lived through it. However, the legacy of this period was to have a profound impact on the Algerian psyche, leaving many Algerians with what could be described as a complex about their former colonial master. To this day, France is still repeatedly cited as the main reason for the country's ongoing ills and its inability to create a modern efficient state.

As a result, the issue of France has always been used as a rallying cry for the various forces operating in the Algerian political scene, as each faction has sought to prove that it is the real defender of Algeria against its former colonizer. The ruling FLN, despite its strong ties with the French establish-ment, embarked on an Arabization campaign shortly after coming to power and has continued to rail against French oppression throughout its rule. The various Islamist factions proved no exception either and all sought to garner popular support by demonstrating that they were the ones to rid the coun-try of French dominance and to make it pure once again. From the Front Islamique du Salut (FIS), which emerged in the 1980s, to the more militant Groupe Islamique Armée (GIA), to the Groupe Salafiste pour la Prédication et Combat (GSPC), which was formed at the end of the 1990s by a disaf-fected faction of the GIA, these groups all took on the ready-made ideology that referred to France as an enemy. They knew that such ideas would reso-nate immediately among the population at large and bring them a degree of popular support. Indeed each of these groups proved willing to use the France issue when it suited them or when they needed a rallying cry that went beyond their own immediate borders.

## France and the FIS

From the outset the FIS was keen to portray its battle against the ruling regime through the lens of Algeria's struggle against France. The FIS had been established in March 1989 and its birth was announced at the Ben Badis mosque in Algiers. Its founders encompassed a range of views, from those who espoused armed struggle to those who preferred a more moderate path that was akin to the traditional Muslim Brotherhood way of Islamicizing the population. The FIS soon grew in popularity and seemed to provide a fresh and moralistic alternative to the regime. Its members were able to impose 'Islamic values' within their own communities and created a network of preachers and intellectuals who held great sway with the populace.

Although the FIS was a movement afflicted by divisions and internal conflict, all of the currents within it played on popular sentiment by advo-cating the need to redefine what it meant to be Algerian, seeking to promote 'pure' Islamic values that could act as an antidote to the corrupt 'Westernized' influences of the former colonial power.[1] As such, France became a symbol that was used by the FIS to garner popular support. FIS leader Ali Belhadj, for example, said in an interview, 'My father and my brothers may have phys-ically expelled the oppressor France from Algeria, but my struggle, together with my brothers, using the weapon of faith, is to banish France intellec-tually and ideologically and to have done with her supporters who drank her poisonous milk.'[2] At the same time, the FIS sought to portray their real opponents, the ruling FLN, as part and parcel of the French colonial admin-istration and as the 'sons of France'. They promoted the idea that they, with

their Islamic values, were the real mujahideen who could oust France once
and for all by getting rid of the FLN, which they claimed had betrayed the
ideals of the 1954 revolution. As one analyst rightly observed, 'The great
strength of the FIS's ideology has been to adopt this feeling of betrayal as its
own and to present a single interpretation of it. According to the FIS, the
jihad for independence should have opened the way for the establishment of
an Islamic state, but was led astray by the "children of France".'[3] In fact this
became a commonly held view to explain the failures of the revolution.

The FIS leadership did their utmost to spread the message that the FLN
were simply puppets of Paris. FIS leader Abassi Madani explained, 'The
colonizers recognized Algeria's independence, but they didn't leave political decisions in the hands of the people. They put it in the hands of their
own agents.'[4] These kinds of ideas clearly struck a chord with the Algerian
population including the youth who had not witnessed the colonial period
directly. As Hassan, one young FIS member who resided in London,
explained, 'Algeria has not yet won her own independence. ... The West is
in us, and the force of the ideology that it brings prevents us from assuming
our independence. Western ideology is not compatible with Islam.'[5]

For the FIS and its supporters, France was to demonstrate its treachery
yet again when in 1992 it did not object when the Algerian army stepped
in and cancelled the elections that the FIS were poised to win. Although
French President François Mitterrand declared that the stopping of legislative elections was 'abnormal at the very least',[6] France was unwilling to take
any steps that might look as though it was exercising undue influence in
Algeria's internal affairs. Moreover at the same time the French government
was heaving a sigh of relief that it was not about to be faced with an Islamic
government just across the waters that would in turn prompt thousands
more Algerians to flee to France. Ironically, however, as the war unfolded,
the situation in Algeria meant that those who ended up fleeing to Europe
were often Islamists and sometimes Islamists of the most militant tendency,
presenting the continent with an entirely different problem.

For the Algerians, France's apparent willingness to stand by and do nothing concrete as the democratic process was cancelled was simply confirma-
tion that France was working hand in hand with a military dictatorship that
had failed to service the needs of the population. This was a theme that was
to be repeated over and over again. As Ghemati Abdelkrim, a high-ranking
member of the FIS, noted:

> France, its positions, its attitude – none of that is neutral for the Algerians.
> Each act has its repercussions, and at the moment, these are very grave. At the
> moment, for the youth which represents 75 per cent of the Algerian population,
> the reason is simple and clear: France supports a power that no one likes, a

power which has imposed itself by force, a power which is nothing other than
the worst enemy of the Algerian people. If France is the ally of this power, then
France can only be the enemy of the Algerian people.[7]

Despite this complex relationship a number of Islamists and members of
the FIS found themselves in France.[8] One such individual was Djaffar Al-
Houari, who had travelled to France in 1987 to study for a doctorate in math-
ematics. Al-Houari explained that at that time 'the Algerians were the only
ones not to have their own association'[9] and so he and a group of Algerian
students, mostly from the Cité Universitaire d'Antony in the Hauts-de-Sein,
formed their own organization. This group became the Fraternité Algérienne
de la France (FAF) and based itself in the famous Boulevard Rochechouart
in the Barbès quarter of Paris. After 1992, although not a direct branch of
the FIS abroad, the FAF became the domain of a group of FIS activists led
by Al-Houari which included Ahmed Boudjaâdar and Moussa Kraouche, the
latter of whom worked for a time for the Municipality of Argenteuil.

The official declared objectives of the FAF when it registered itself as an
organization with the French authorities were to strengthen cultural links
between Algerians and immigrants.[10] However, its real aim was to try to
promote the message of the FIS in France and to raise awareness of what
was happening in Algeria among the North African communities there.
As FIS member Ghemati Abdelkrim explained, his mission was to 'mobilize the Algerian community, to inform it regularly of events in Algeria. It
was a question of sensitizing the people to the Algerian situation, to incite
them to struggle against the dictatorship in whatever way was consistent
with their means, peacefully and within French law.'[11] In order to achieve
this, the FAF busied itself by holding meetings, organizing photographic
displays and distributing cassettes of FIS preachers from Algeria. According
to some sources, the FAF also collected money to finance a visit to Algeria
by a young French convert to Islam, Didier Guyon.[12] Guyon was arrested in
June 1991, 250km outside of the Algerian capital, on suspicion of having
smuggled arms and explosives across the Moroccan border into Algeria. He
was also charged with being part of a subversive FIS network in France. In
December 1991 he was sentenced to death by an Algerian court.

The FAF became perhaps most notorious for its publications. It began
producing a bulletin called La Critère which carried news of the jihad in
Algeria. Despite the fact that the FIS has traditionally been portrayed as the
moderate face of Islam in comparison with the more extremist groups such
as the GIA, the content of this bulletin highlighted just how blurred this
distinction could be. Issue number 49, for example, carried the following in
its regular 'News of the Jihad' column:

MOAHMMADIA (Alger)
The mujahideen slaughtered a commissioner of the *taghout* [ungodly] police 13 January 1993. ...
REGHAIA
At the beginning of this week, the mujahideen slaughtered three elements of the forces of repression.

In fact the more hawkish members of the FIS based abroad were explicit in the early days about their support for the use of violence against the Algerian regime. The FIS's main spokesman abroad, Rabah Kebir, who resided in Germany, declared to the Paris newspaper *Libération* in February 1993, 'The violence stems from the dictatorship, which has left us no alternative to reciprocal violence.'[13] Just four months later, exiled FIS member Anwar Haddam, who was in the US, is alleged to have described the fatal stabbing of psychiatry professor Mahfoud Boucebci as 'a sentence and not a crime. It is a sentence carried out by the mujahideen.'[14] Likewise another prominent FIS member, who was one of the founders of the movement, Sheikh Abdelbaki Sahraoui, who was imam of the Khaled Ibn Walid mosque in Barbès in Paris and who was later killed allegedly by GIA militants, was equally vocal about his support for violence against the Algerian regime. In an interview in the Islamist *Al-Munkidh* publication in 1993 the elderly Sheikh is reported as having asserted that the correct response to the Algerian regime's cancelling of the elections was, 'Jihad and I repeat jihad so that the word of truth becomes supreme and the word of falsehood is wiped. ... One must deny one's ego and purify his intentions, because the Mudjahid is close to death, close to paradise.'[15] He goes on to give special advice for those Algerians residing outside Algeria:

> Outside Algeria the Mudjahideen must publicize the fact that the people have the right to be free in their choice. One must expose the junta and its injustice inflicted upon people in newspapers, colloquia and international forums. This is very important. Our community outside can provide material and moral support to the brethren, the Mudjahideen. Materially [they should help every] working Algerian and morally every writer and intellectual to champion truth with one's tongue and pen.[16]

This overt support for violence against the Algerian regime should, however, be viewed in the context of the time. These FIS members, along with those in Algeria, believed they had been robbed of their rightful victory in the elections and that the military had stepped in and begun arbitrarily using violence against them. Indeed the Algerian security services employed the harshest of methods to wipe out their opponents, and members of the FIS and their suspected sympathizers were rounded up and interned in camps in the blistering deserts in the south of the country. The FIS was also furious that the regime had cheated the population out of their opportunity to install an Islamic government. Therefore taking up arms was a case of fighting back. Furthermore this was also an era where those jihadists who had triumphed over the Soviet Union in Afghanistan were looked upon as heroes who had fought in the name of Islam. Therefore resorting to violence or supporting it was perhaps considered more acceptable then, given the spirit of the time. In fact the FIS even developed their own armed wing, the Armée Islamique du Salut (AIS), which was officially declared by the FIS's executive committee abroad in July 1994. The AIS, led by Madani Merzag, came to view itself as a rival of the GIA, as both groups sought to act as the legitimate defenders of Islam and the population. As such the distinction between the moderate and militant strands of the Algerian opposition forces had not yet become clear in the way it was to in the late 1990s when each side was forced to take a stance as it came under increasing international scrutiny.

Through their La Critère bulletin, the members of the FAF residing in France demonstrated how they had carried this hatred for the former colonial power with them into their new home. Issue number 5, dated 13 March 1992, for example, carried an editorial by Moussa Abu Louqman with the headline, 'France is an accomplice in the massacres of the people and in the reign of the dictatorship in Algeria'.[17] In fact this obsession with France partly resulted in the publication being banned by the French authorities in 1993 on the grounds that it posed a threat to public order because of its violently anti-Western and anti-French tone. After being banned, La Critère re-appeared under the name La Résistance and then L'Etendard and continued to support and to try to publicize the actions of the mujahideen in Algeria against the French-backed regime in Algiers. It was also in 1993 that the French authorities launched an arrest campaign against its members and supporters, which was called 'Operation Chrysanthemum'. These arrests were carried out in Paris, Marseilles, Lyons, Nice, Toulouse, Finistère, Metz and Strasbourg. Most of the suspects were released a few days later, but some were placed under house arrest and others imprisoned, including Djaffar Al-Houari, Moussa Kraouche and Ahmed Boudjaâdar. Around 20 of those arrested, including Djaffar Al-Houari, were interned in a disused barracks in Picardy and then deported to Burkina Faso.

Despite its efforts, however, the FAF was never able to really gain a strong foothold among the Muslim communities of France who found the organization's anti-French stance and its Islamist ideology far removed from the reality of their everyday lives. According to one media report at the time, the number of committed FIS activists in France totalled only between 50 and 100 and the Algerian community in France was not really open to the aims of the Islamists.[18] This view was supported by Algerian analyst Rachid Tlemçani, who noted of the FAF, 'Their bulletin (called initially *La Critère*, then *La Résistance*, and finally *L'Etendard*) has not, however, been well received among Algerians, who do not appreciate its political stands.'[19] Likewise the *salafist* preacher Imam Abdulhadi, who resides in Marseilles, also acknowledged that the FIS was never really able to attract a strong following in France.[20]

That is not to say that the FAF did not attract some young men. Ali, a second-generation Algerian from Nanterre, described Moussa Kraouche as 'a cold and not very engaging man ... but he made an impression upon us because of his determination and his connections'.[21] Ali, like many young second-generation immigrants growing up in the French suburbs, had begun hanging around the hostels where many first-generation immigrants lived. These hostels were places where travelling preachers would do the rounds and come to talk to the dispossessed about Islam and how they could find Allah. Ali was swayed by their arguments and turned to the mosque where he came into contact with Kraouche and figures like him who persuaded him of the attractions of struggling for his brothers in Algeria. However, for many young French Muslims who were born in France and who were rediscovering their Islamic identity, the FAF's resolute focus on the Algerian jihad was unappealing. As Moussa Kraouche explained in 1993, 'The aim of the FAF is to inform Algerians in France about the Islamic movement in Algeria. Everything that touches on Islam in France and in the suburbs does not interest us in the slightest.'[22] As a result, the pull of the FAF was not as strong as that of other organizations, such as the Union des Organisations Islamiques de France (UOIF) which took a Muslim Brotherhood line and which was more adept at articulating the kinds of day-to-day problems facing young practising French Muslims living in an overtly secular society – although the UOIF was itself also limited to the realm of the minority.

## France and the GIA

The GIA had an equally negative attitude towards the former colonizing power, but whereas the FIS had sought to use France as a propaganda centre and a place of refuge from where they could try to influence events in Algeria, the GIA employed more violent methods to try to affect change and to bring down the military junta. In fact the GIA saw the value in using French Muslims of Algerian origin to carry out attacks in France to try to alter the situation on the ground in Algeria. Yet all of these efforts proved to be resounding failures, demonstrating the limited capacity of those involved to comprehend the 'poisonous enemy' they thought they knew so well.

Prior to launching attacks on the French mainland, the GIA targeted French citizens in Algeria in a bid to drive them out of the country and to force the government in Paris to realize the dangers of backing the military junta. In September 1993 militants abducted and killed two French surveyors while they were driving to work near Sidi Bel Abbès. The following month armed insurgents kidnapped three French consular officials in the centre of the capital. They were freed when the prayer hall they were being held in was stormed by Algerian security forces, but not before the kidnappers had given a note to one of the hostages that was addressed to all the foreigners residing in Algeria, who at that time numbered around 70,000, which warned, 'Leave the country. We are giving you one month. Anyone who exceeds that period will be responsible for his own sudden death. There will be no kidnappings and it will be more violent than in Egypt.'[23] The result was that an estimated 3,000 foreign nationals fled the country within days. This stunt was clearly aimed at grabbing international headlines, as well as forcing out foreign businesses, and an attempt to prove to the Algerian population that they were intent on forcing the corrupting 'enemies of Allah' out of their territory.[24]

This kidnapping, however, has not been without its share of controversy and there have been questions raised about whether the Algerian security forces may have been somehow involved and whether the event might have been staged in order to try to convince France that it should back the junta against the Islamists. The truth of this event is unlikely to ever come to the surface. However, it was this hostage taking that, according to many analysts, convinced the French government that it should resolutely back the Algerian regime in its repression of the Islamist insurgency.[25]

The attacks, however, were not solely carried out against French nationals. In fact many of the victims were from communist or socialist countries, reflecting the other obsession held by many militants about those from 'ungodly' secular societies. It was also a reflection of the fact that because Algeria had allied itself with the Soviet bloc in the Cold War, there were large numbers of eastern Europeans working in the country. Moreover the GIA, like many other jihadist groups, had a loathing for those they considered as *kufar* and employed particularly brutal methods against their victims. In December 1993, for example, 12 Croats were snatched from their living quarters, forced to strip naked, their hands were tied with steel wire and they were pushed into an empty swimming pool where they either had their throats slit or were beaten to death.[26] After the incident the GIA stated that the attack was to avenge the deaths of Muslims who had been killed in Bosnia.

For the FIS members living in exile in the West, these kinds of attacks presented difficulties. While they had been willing to support the killings of members of the regime and of secular intellectuals, the brutal attacks on foreigners did little to assist them in their struggle to plead the Islamist case in Europe. Those FIS leaders abroad who were seeking backing for their movement were keen to present an attractive and benign image of themselves and knew that such an image would be damaged if they were perceived to be endorsing the violence that was being carried out by insurgents in Algeria.[27] Some condemned the attacks, and Anwar Haddam in the US and Sheikh Sahraoui in France demanded the immediate and unconditional release of the French hostages. However, while these FIS members had to consider their position living in the West, they still had to play to their own constituencies inside Algeria where they were concerned that they were losing out to the GIA. Therefore, as the attacks continued, Haddam and Rabah Kebir began to refer to foreigners inside Algeria as combatants because by simply being there they were in league with the regime.[28] FAF member Moussa Kraouche is alleged to have warned foreigners to expect 'much tougher acts of reprisal because you cannot play with the freedom of the people'.[29]

While the GIA's tactics succeeded in pushing scores of foreigners out of Algeria, they did not have the desired effect of changing the French government's policy towards its former colonial possession. In addition French energy companies remained well protected in the deserts of the south, ensuring the regime's coffers were not badly affected by the violence. The GIA therefore decided to up its tactics to another level. Years ahead of Osama Bin Ladin, militants devised a plan to hijack an Airbus 300 and either to explode the plane in the air over Paris or to fly it into the Eiffel Tower. On Christmas Eve of December 1994 a group of militants dressed in Air Algérie uniforms boarded an Air France flight bound for Paris at Houari Boumedienne airport in Algiers. They collected the passports of all the passengers and proceeded to hijack the plane. Upon discovering the presence of an Algerian policeman on board they dragged him to the front of the plane, shot him in the back of the head and dumped his body on the runway. They then demanded the plane be allowed to take off, but when this request was denied they threatened to kill more of the passengers. After hours of negotiations, 63 women and children were released, although not before the hijackers had killed a Vietnamese diplomat and a young French diplomatic official. They also threatened to kill one passenger every half an hour until they were allowed to fly. Finally the plane took off, but the crew managed to convince the militants that they did not have sufficient fuel and that they needed to make a stopover in Marseilles. Once on the tarmac at Marseilles airport, French Special Forces stormed the plane and a 20-minute gun battle ensued. Eventually the hijackers were all shot dead and a number of Special Force commandos and passengers were injured. This attempted operation certainly shocked the French, and indeed the whole of Europe. Yet it did not have the desired effect. In fact the French authorities were so surprised by the lack of professionalism of the Algerian military in dealing with the crisis that they became convinced of the need to give their full support to the regime against the Islamist militants.

Ever frustrated by their ongoing inability to defeat the regime in Algiers, which was proving more difficult to topple than they had anticipated at the outset, the GIA, under the emirship of Zeitouni, decided to raise the stakes even higher. It took its campaign directly to the French mainland. It was perhaps here more than anywhere else that the GIA leaders demonstrated their complete inability to understand the 'enemy' they were dealing with.

In July 1995 a bomb exploded in the busy St Michel metro station in the heart of Paris, killing ten people and injuring 86. This was followed the following month by another bomb that exploded near the Arc de Triomphe and another being found that did not explode on a high-speed railway track near France's second city of Lyons. Other bombings continued into November 1995, targeting an outdoor market, a Jewish school, the Maison Blanche metro station and a suburban train. The GIA claimed responsibility for the attacks in a statement sent to a Cairo news agency that purported to be from the organization. The statement vowed to 'wage holy war into the very heart of France' in retaliation for French support of the Algerian regime.

However, the GIA's campaign on mainland France is also subject to heated debate and there are many who claim that the attacks against France, along with many of those carried out in the name of the GIA in Algeria, were in fact orchestrated by the Algerian security services in order to frighten France into standing firm in its support for the Algerian junta.[30] Among those who have backed suggestions of the regime's involvement is the French MP and judge Alain Marsaud, who was the head of the central anti-terrorist service at the Public Prosecutor's Office in Paris in the 1980s. He explained that the more the Algerian networks in France were unravelled, 'the more one finds Algerians from the official services. At one time or another, the GIA was a smokescreen used to bring the flames to France.'[31] This thesis has also been supported by former members of the Algerian security services such as Mohamed Samraoui, who asserts that French intelligence knew that the assumed ringleader of the GIA cell in France who carried out the attacks was an Algerian security services operative 'charged with infiltrating pro-Islamist cells in foreign countries'.[32]

A number of events occurring at the time certainly lend weight to this thesis. This includes the Rome Platform of 1994, an initiative by the religious community of Sant Egidio in Italy to bring all the parties together to try to forge a common stance in the name of reconciliation. The platform included key figures from the main opposition parties, including the FIS which was represented by the leaders of its executive committee abroad and which proved extremely pragmatic in agreeing to participate despite the fact that the initiative was being carried out under the auspices of an Italian Catholic organization. By January 1995 the participants had agreed on a text that called for an inquiry into the violence in Algeria, the end of the army's involvement in political affairs and the return of constitutional rule. However, alarmed at this united show of strength by opposition forces, and fearing its own position, the Algerian regime rejected the platform, accusing it of representing interference in Algeria's internal affairs. It also claimed it was a plot hatched by the Vatican. It has therefore been suggested that the Algerian generals were so worried by the Rome Platform that they manipulated Islamists in France to orchestrate the attacks to ensure that the French would not stop supporting them in their bid to quash their Islamist opponents.

The truth of these murky allegations is unlikely ever to come to light and the debate will rage on. On the one hand there are those who claim that the GIA was itself a creation of the Algerian security services which needed to vilify the Islamists following the electoral successes of the FIS. On the other hand there are those who assert that the bloody events in Algeria were all the work of depraved Islamist militants. The truth is likely to sit somewhere in between. However, with or without the manipulation of the security services, these events highlight the GIA's lack of awareness of the wider world. This may be a reflection of the fact that those who joined the rank and file of the GIA tended to come from poor backgrounds, had limited educational ability and in many cases were illiterate. It would seem that their cause and ideology outstripped their intellectual capacity. Indeed, just like the Airbus incident, this bombing campaign proved to be a gross miscalculation on the part of the GIA. Rather than pushing France into retracting its support for the Algerian regime the bombings had precisely the opposite effect and served to resolve the determination of the French authorities to back the regime in Algiers. Crucially it also prompted the French government to clamp down even harder and disrupt the Algerian support networks that were operating in France.

It is perhaps no coincidence that the attacks were carried out under the emirship of Djamel Zeitouni. It was Zeitouni's intellectual capacity that Abu Musab Al-Suri had complained about from London. In fact Al-Suri's description of the group's poor strategic, tactical and political awareness, described in Chapter 4, would appear to have been borne out by this blighted campaign. Furthermore Al-Suri even describes how the GIA had believed that the British would have no problem with their attacking France because of the age-old rivalry between the British and the French! Even the GIA's selection of operatives looked to have been a rather desperate choice. To the surprise of the French authorities, some of those accused of involvement in the attacks were French citizens of Maghrebian descent. Indeed the GIA proved more adept at appealing to French Muslim youths of Algerian origin than the FIS ever were. However, they too were able to attract only a handful of adherents and their nationalist Islamist ideology resonated primarily with young disaffected and dispossessed men of the French suburbs. These youths might have been keen, but they did not necessarily have the skills or training to conduct a successful and sustained bombing campaign in a European state. Yet the GIA sought them out nonetheless. According to FIS leader Djaffar Al-Houari, the radicals concentrated on 'recruiting disaffected second-generation Algerian immigrants in France. It's easy enough to find them.'[33]

## Unlikely militants?

Journalists David Pujadas and Ahmed Salam have described one group of disaffected young French Muslims, who were mainly of Algerian origin, who used to gather together at each other's houses on a regular basis to watch GIA videos.[34] The group comprised Farid, aged 19, and Mustafa, aged 21, who were both unemployed; Fabrizio, 22, who had just recently converted to Islam and who was also unemployed; Mourad, 18, a trainee; Kader, 21, who was a student; Hacène, 16, who was still at college; and Mouloud, 24, who was a courier and the only one among them who had a regular income. These youths were clearly excited by the violence in the videos and were hungry for any footage they could get from the front lines. The videos themselves were rather like action-man clips, showing fighters with long beards carrying big guns around the Algerian mountains and setting off explosions. They also showed close-up graphic images of slain members of the Algerian security forces. In some cases these propaganda efforts tried to rally support among those abroad. In one video, for example, a voice carries over pictures of the mujahideen battling it out in the *maquis*, 'We are addressing our appeal equally to our brothers abroad, to Algerians and non-Algerians ... we would like to tell them that the Algerian jihad does not finish at the Moroccan and Tunisian borders.'[35] The GIA also sought to play on the fact that the majority of Algerians in France still had relatives living on the other side of the Mediterranean. In one video a GIA fighter explained, 'We are addressing our brothers abroad: if you have a brother, a sister, a mother imprisoned here, you cannot remain insensitive. You must return to defend those close to you and your honour.'[36]

However, there is a gulf of difference between getting excited over propaganda videos and actually undertaking an attack on one's own country, and few heeded the call. One young man, though, who decided to take that extra step was Khalid Kelkal, whose fingerprints were found on an unexploded bomb on the Lyons to Paris TGV line and who is believed to have been involved in the St Michel metro bombing. Kelkal's life story is typical of those young men brought up in modern-day Europe who found an attraction in the radical ideology of groups such as the GIA. Kelkal was born in Algeria but came to France with his mother to live with his father when he was still a young child. He grew up in Vaulx-en-Velin, an uninspiring suburb of Lyons, where he earned the nickname Mr Smiley because of his happy disposition. Kelkal was not academically minded and whilst at lycée he drifted into a life of petty criminality and began getting into trouble with the police. He was arrested in 1989 for stealing a car and then again in 1991 for using a car as a battering ram in order to carry out a robbery. Kelkal was convicted and sentenced to prison but appealed against the decision. However, the result of the appeal was that he had his prison term increased – something that left him extremely bitter and angry. By remarkable coincidence, Kelkal was interviewed by a sociologist in 1992 as part of a research project and his responses make for telling reading. When asked about his experiences with the law, Kelkal explained, 'Frankly, as we are Arabs, we are not favoured by justice. There is a justice of two different speeds. ... For me there is no justice. What they call justice is in fact injustice.'[37] In the interview, Kelkal comes across as a frustrated young man who consistently found himself on the margins of life and who had never found his place in the world. Indeed in the interview he very clearly refers to Algeria, not France, as home.

While in prison, like many delinquents, Kelkal turned to religion after being 'reintroduced' to his faith through a fellow inmate. This inmate is believed to have been an Algerian going by the name Khelif, who is reported to have been close to Islamist militants in Algeria.[38] Kelkal's re-Islamicization provided him with a focus in life and he managed to get out of prison early for good behaviour. Once free, Kelkal went back to live with his family, but spent a dispiriting time seeking a job that matched his interest in chemistry – one of the few subjects he had excelled in at school. However, he was repeatedly unsuccessful and soon returned to a life of petty crime. This return to the criminal underworld did not prevent him from continuing to be a devout and practising Muslim and he grew a small beard and began frequenting the Bilal mosque in the Thibaude quarter of Vaulx-en-Velin. Kelkal's ability to mix crime and religion is not unusual. In fact this is a familiar pattern among some young immigrants or delinquents who see no contradiction between crime and piety. For these young men it is acceptable to commit criminal acts but to exonerate themselves by paying *zakat* or by justifying their actions by claiming that they were only stealing from Christians and heathens.

It would appear that for Kelkal, Islam somehow brought back his self-repect and enabled him to feel proud of his roots. Also instrumental in his journey down the path of radicalization appears to have been a winter spent back in his birthplace, Mostaganem, in north west Algeria from 1994 to 1995. Shortly after his return to France he and his childhood friend, Karim Koussa, who had also turned to Islam, used to spend their time watching GIA videos together. They gathered a small network around themselves, comprising a handful of disenchanted young men from the same streets in which they had grown up. Among their 'brothers' in the cause were Abdelkader Bouhadjar and Abdelkader Maameri. It is alleged that these young men who were heady with the cause used to visit an Algerian called Ben Ali Boualem Bensaid who had left Algeria for France in 1994 and who had set himself up in an apartment in the 18th arondissement of Paris. Bensaid was eventually arrested and tried for his involvement in the bombings. At his trial Bensaid, who had initially refused to acknowledge his membership of the GIA, declared, 'I was more than a member of the GIA, I was a fighter. I was willing to die for my cause.'[39] Bensaid is believed to have acted as a link and focal point for these young mainly second-generation would-be jihadists in France, finding a way to use them in his bid to topple the Algerian regime. Indeed Bensaid's lawyer, Jamil Youness, is reported to have said of his client, 'He acted in order to punish France. ... He believes the death of innocent victims was justified in the context of a global campaign by the GIA.'[40] Presumably under the leadership of Bensaid, by the summer of 1995 Kelkal and his network set about turning their heroic fantasies about 'doing something' for the jihad into reality.

However, Kelkal's dreams of jihad turned into a sad and most unheroic ending. One of the attacks that he is believed to have carried out was against a Jewish school in the Villeurbanne suburb of Lyons on 7 September 1995. The whole thing appears to have been a highly amateur affair. Kelkal had asked to borrow a small studio flat that belonged to his friend's wife near to the school. While there he reportedly took a gas canister from the studio and used it to make a crude car bomb.[41] Kelkal had timed the bomb to go off when the children were coming out of school, but the school clock was several minutes late and so the bomb exploded in the street before the children had left the building. As a result no one was killed in the blast. Another of the attempted operations Kelkal is believed to have been involved in was equally unsuccessful, as the bomb on which his fingerprints were found on the Paris–Lyons TGV line failed to go off.

The inexperienced Kelkal was soon tracked down by police but after a shoot-out in a small village he fled into hiding in the forest of Malval, 25km west of Lyons, where his companions brought him provisions in a red car. The young men were familiar with this wood, as it was one of the places that these would-be jihadists had used for conducting their so-called training sessions, which presumably they had mimicked from the videos they had been watching. However, it was not long before Kelkal was found, and after he refused to surrender was shot dead by police on 29 September 1995. His killing sparked controversy, as camera footage of the attack showed one policeman shouting, 'Finis-le, finis-le!' (Finish him off, Finish him off!) while another kicked him to make sure he was dead. These images resulted in Kelkal becoming a potent symbol for the anti-racist movement and for non-white French youth and they sparked protests and riots across the French suburbs. Yet in spite of all the publicity, this was hardly the jihadist martyrdom Kelkal had hoped for. It was a far cry from the heady days of the mujahideen in Afghanistan or even Bosnia and was a sad and desperate ending for a sad and desperate young man.

As further evidence came to light, it emerged that Khalid Kelkal was in fact part of a network that was wider than his immediate friends from his neighbourhood. This network appears to have been run by a number of Algerians who, it has been suggested, had come to France with the aim of orchestrating the attacks. However, Kelkal appears to have been typical of the other young men in this network. Indeed after his death, Nasserdine Slimani, a French national of Algerian origin who had been part of Kelkal's gang, travelled to Paris to meet with Bensaid to discuss taking over Kelkal's role as head of the Lyons network. On an October morning the two men met at the McDonalds in St Lazare Station and spent the day walking around the French capital, stopping off at cafés along the way. Unbeknown to them, they were being tagged by French police. During his trial for his alleged involvement in the attacks in 1999 Slimani claimed that he had only met Bensaid in order to get back his passport and identity papers that he had lent another brother in need. He also asserted that he could not understand a word that Bensaid was saying because he 'spoke Algerian'. However, that did not prevent the two men from spending the day together, during which time Bensaid explained to Slimani how to make explosives. Slimani admitted that he had copied the instructions down on a piece of paper – a document that was later recovered by the police – but claimed he had not understood them. Bensaid tried to brush off the incident by declaring, 'It was in the newspapers, it was the subject of the day. It was like a cooking recipe, it was a discussion one would have over coffee.'[42] Bensaid and another defendant, Belkacem, were both sentenced to ten years in prison, although Bensaid also received an additional 30 years for a failed attack on a high-speed TGV train. The two men returned to the court in 2002 where they were convicted for the bombings and sentenced to life imprisonment.

These men were, it seems, typical of those who had got themselves involved in the campaign against the French mainland. Former French intelligence official Jean Lebeschu noted of those who were arrested after the attacks, 'I wonder about the behaviour of these young men. ... Their behaviour was childish. One would have never believed that they belonged to the GIA network.'[43] Indeed much of the campaign was strikingly amateur and those involved displayed a remarkable lack of concern for security, not realizing their telephones were being tapped or that the police were tagging them, or leaving their fingerprints on the devices that failed to go off. This surely reflects the fact that those who had got involved were mostly poorly educated young men from the suburbs with little experience of the world, let alone of conducting military campaigns. In fact they seemed to be mostly dreamers who had found a way to express their frustration and sense of alienation and a means of channelling their anger at their own situations through an ideology that had its roots in the traditions they had grown up with in the family home.

By the end of the 1990s the GIA had become almost completely discredited and had achieved little of what it had set out to do. It had failed to overthrow the Algerian regime and was being accused of having been infiltrated by the security services. Moreover the tales of the group's depravities meant that it lost its popular support base. The attacks against France that had been launched to terrorize Paris were part and parcel of the GIA's failure and its ultimate inability to 'defend' the Algerians against their own regime and against the former colonizing power.

### France, the GSPC and Al-Qa'ida in the Islamic Maghreb

In a bid to restore the fortunes and credibility of the Algerian jihad, a group of GIA militants in Algeria broke away and in 1998 formed their own group under the emirship of the former mechanic Hassan Hattab. This new group was the Groupe Salafiste pour la Prédication et Combat (GSPC), which vowed to target only members of the military and security forces. However, the GSPC proved to be singularly underwhelming in its ability to challenge the regime in Algiers and was unable to garner much popular support, as by the time it arrived on the scene the population was exhausted from the years of brutality and wanton destruction on the part of both sides in the civil war. The group's activities were mostly limited to carrying out ambushes or setting up false roadblocks to attack military convoys. In addition, like its predecessor, the GSPC was soon plagued by divisions and infighting and found itself increasingly relying on organized criminal activities, including smuggling, as a means of survival. In fact the group came to operate like mafia cells that took to small-scale criminality, such as running illegal sand supply businesses, profiting from the drugs trade and getting involved in bank robberies. It was even reported in the Algerian press in May 2005 that GSPC members had taken to raiding the Ait Oumalu post office in order to net some cash!

At its inception the GSPC was just as nationalistic as the GIA had been, and Hassan Hattab refused to join Al-Qa'ida as his focus was entirely on the Algerian jihad. In an interview with the Arab media in October 2005 Hattab explained, 'Since its inception and until the day of my resignation [in 2003], the GSPC had no links whatsoever to Al-Qa'ida.'[44] However, this nationalism did not prevent it from trying to tap into Islamist networks in Europe. It is generally assumed that after the collapse of the GIA in Algeria, the GSPC simply took over former GIA support networks abroad. However, it would appear that the GSPC was not able to muster the same degree of support, not only because its appeal among the diaspora was less after the GIA had become discredited, but also because of tightening security in Europe from the end of the 1990s onwards. Furthermore there was a widespread perception among jihadists in Europe that the GSPC, like the GIA, was heavily infiltrated by the Algerian security services.

By the end of the 1990s European security agencies were already engaged in trying to identify and dismantle these networks. Furthermore in October 2000, 11 Algerians were arrested in Italy on charges of association with terrorist groups in Algeria and of arms smuggling. These efforts intensified after 2001 and in Britain a number of Algerian suspects were arrested under anti-terrorism legislation and accused of providing support to the GSPC. For example, 'A' was accused of being an active member of the GSPC, for which, among other things, he had allegedly been involved in credit card fraud and 'procuring telecommunication equipment for the GSPC and the provision of logistical support for satellite phones by way of purchase and allocation of airtimes for those phones'.[45]

At the same time, the GSPC was struggling to maintain any real momentum inside Algeria and, to make matters worse, it was designated as a terrorist organization by the United States after 9/11. Besides in April 1999 the Algerian president had introduced an amnesty for the Islamists, offering them clemency in return for laying down their weapons, and although the GSPC rejected this offer some Islamists threw in their lot with the scheme and gave themselves up to the authorities. This new environment caused friction within the leadership of the organization and by 2003 its emir, Hassan Hattab, who had objected to stunts like the group's alleged kidnapping of a group of European tourists in the Algerian desert in 2003, withdrew and Nabil Sahraoui took over as the new emir. Under Sahraoui's new leadership, it was not long before the floundering GSPC issued a declaration of support for the various jihadist movements around the world, including Al-Qa'ida. The group announced that their loyalty was to 'all Muslims that declare that there is no God but Allah and that Mohamed is his messenger, to every mujahid who took up the banner of jihad for Allah's sake in Palestine and Afghanistan under the Emirship of Mullah Mohamed Omar, and the Al-Qa'ida movement under the Emirship of Sheikh Osama Bin Ladin.'[46] This mention of Bin Ladin's movement was seized upon immediately by the Algerian state, which since 9/11 in particular had sought to portray its domestic insurgency as being part of a wider international terrorist network. The media similarly made the most of linking the groups as if they were now part of the same organization. However, as far as the GSPC was concerned this was not a wholesale move to become part of Al-Qa'ida, but rather a way to attract some attention and to give the impression that they were part of the now world-famous jihadist scene. Indeed the tone of the statement is as if they were congratulating Al-Qa'ida as their equals.

In spite of this new interest in the outside world, the GSPC continued to focus its main attention on the battle in hand in Algeria. This was hardly surprising given that Algerian jihadists have always fiercely guarded their independence and their main aim had been to topple their own military junta. That is not to say that some of them did not go to join the Iraqi jihad, but for the hardcore GSPC elements such as Mohktar Bel Mohktar in the south, the main battle was most definitely still against the Algerian regime. In November 2004 media spokesman Abd Al-Birr made it abundantly clear in an interview posted on the jihadist website Minbar Al-Tawhed wa Jihad that for Algerians the first priority should be fighting jihad at home against the Algerian regime.[47] This call for support was not restricted to Algeria. On 15 August 2005 a rather desperate-sounding GSPC communiqué called on Muslims in France to support their brothers in Algeria, stating, 'We only wished to remind you that our brothers in the GSPC are still fighting against the enemies of Allah and his religion since the 1990s without stopping for even one moment. Therefore, brothers in faith, you should never forget that we are always in need of your support, in any form or amount.'[48]

The following month, in what was widely interpreted as a new strategic direction for the GSPC, *Le Monde* newspaper reported that the French authorities had intercepted a GSPC communiqué attributed to the group's emir that had been posted on the Internet and that made it clear that the organization now considered France its main enemy. It also reportedly urged Muslims to wage jihad in France to prevent it from returning to Algeria or wielding its influence there. Interestingly this GSPC communiqué against France does not appear to be available among the group's other statements that have appeared on various jihadist websites or to have been put on the group's own site. What is available, however, is a communiqué that the group issued in August 2005 addressed to Muslims living in France, urging them to focus their efforts not on the French but against the Algerian elite living there. This document explicitly complained about those Algerians who had 'destroyed the Algerian economy and have stolen the natural resources of the Muslim people so that they can retire in France'. It also told Muslims in France to seek out these Algerians in the 'underground centres of corruption, gambling and entertainment'.[49] The communiqué was therefore more of an attempt by the GSPC to garner support and to remind Algerians in France that they had a role to play. It was also another attempt to play on the age-old rhetoric about ridding Algeria of its corrupt elite that represent little more than the 'poisonous' sons of France.

Shortly after the alleged GSPC threat against France was made public, French security officials arrested a cell with reported links to the group. This cell was led by a young man called Safe Bourada, a second-generation Algerian and former GIA member who had recently been released from prison, where he had finished his time for his involvement in the attacks in the mid-1990s. The cell, which reportedly called itself Ansar Al-Fateh, included two French converts to Islam. According to French officials, the group was planning to carry out attacks inside France with targets including Orly airport and the Paris metro. However, these arrests appear to have come about as the result of cooperation between French and Algerian intelligence services and, according to reports in the French media, were based on the testimony of M'Hamed Benyamina, who was arrested on 9 September at Oran airport in Algeria. Despite the allegations that this group was tied to the GSPC, there is little concrete evidence to this effect. While Bourada may well have had some connections to the group through his former ties with the GIA, this does not necessarily imply that he was plotting on behalf of the GSPC. Indeed the fact that the group called itself Ansar Al-Fateh suggests that they had formed their own little cell and were working to a different agenda.

This was not the only cell arrested in Europe that was accused of having links to the GSPC. Spain arrested 11 Algerians in November 2005 on suspicion of giving logistical support to the GSPC through criminal activities. Seven Algerians were arrested at the beginning of December of the same year in the Costa del Sol and were accused of giving logistical support to the GSPC. However, it was not just Algerians who were accused of belonging to the group. Other nationalities also began to be arrested and accused of having links to the GSPC, suggesting that despite the group's relative impotence at home and its largely nationalist objective of replacing the Algerian regime with an Islamic state, it had suddenly widened its appeal beyond its own natural constituency. However, whether these men were actually part of the GSPC is another matter. It may be that they simply had loose affiliations to the group and that European security agencies found it convenient to label all North African jihadists as being part of the GSPC.

As for those in Algeria, by 2006 the situation on the ground had become increasingly desperate. The regime's amnesty to the Islamists that was now being carried out under a national reconciliation process expired at the end of August, following which the security forces moved in with particular vigour to try to finish the group off. At the same time, leading Islamists were cutting deals with the regime. This included former GIA founder Abdelhaq Layada, as well as FIS activist Rabah Kebir, who returned home in September 2006 after 14 years in exile and who urged those Islamists still fighting to lay down their weapons. As a result those jihadists of the GSPC looked weaker than ever. It is surely no coincidence then that in September 2006 the group's emir, Abu Musab Abdul Wadoud, issued a statement pledging his group's allegiance to Al-Qa'ida. The statement noted, 'We decided to give al-Baya [allegiance] to Osama Bin Ladin and we give him the achievements of our hands and the fruits of our hearts and we conduct our jihad in Algeria as soldiers under his command.' At the same time, Ayman Al-Zawahiri issued a message saying that Osama Bin Ladin had told him to announce that the GSPC had joined forces with Al-Qa'ida. By 2007 the group had announced that it was part of something called Al-Qa'ida in the Islamic Maghreb, although exactly what this new organization amounts to is still unclear. Despite the suggestions made in the international media that this is a new coordinated group that reaches across North Africa, there is no evidence as yet to suggest that those militants in Algeria have any direct links to militants in Morocco or Libya, let alone to any centralized Al-Qa'ida command structure. As one French counter-terrorism official noted about the situation in the Maghreb, 'Enormous police pressure is making plotting local strikes hard enough. Trying to synchronize multiple strikes across borders would be begging to get caught.'[50]

Given the situation on the ground in Algeria, this desire of the GSPC to fold itself under the Al-Qa'ida banner looks to have been little more than a desperate attempt to find some external support and to regain some credibility. For Al-Qa'ida it also appears to be an effort to bolster its reputation and to breathe some new life into the Al-Qa'ida organization. In fact, just prior to announcing that the GSPC had joined them, Al-Zawahiri had asserted that the Al-Jama'a Al-Islamiya had also decided to throw its lot in with Al-Qa'ida. However, the Al-Jama'a refuted this claim and it seems that it was only one member of the group, the hardline Mohamed Al-Hakaima, who had agreed to join forces. It would look as if Al-Qa'ida was itself rather desperately trying to take on dying jihadist organizations as a means of improving its own image. The announcement therefore looks to have been more of a marriage of convenience than a new carefully crafted strategy in the world of transnational jihad.

Moreover, even in its bid to become part of an international jihadist movement, the GSPC was ultimately stuck with its old colonialist enemy. In his message, Al-Zawahiri declared that the group's joining Al-Qa'ida, 'should be a source of chagrin, frustration and sadness for the apostates [of the regime in Algeria], the treacherous sons of France'.[51] He went on to urge the GSPC to become 'a bone in the throat of the American and French crusaders'. France appears to be one enemy that the Algerian Islamists cannot be imagined without.

# CHAPTER 7

# THE 9/11 EFFECT AND 'GLOBALIZED' ISLAM

It is an ongoing joke in the Arab world to ask why it is that for anything Arab to be considered worthwhile it has to be recognized in the West first. Even terrorism, it seems, cannot escape this cliché. The Islamic world has been writhing in conflict, insurgency and radicalism for years, yet it was only after the Twin Towers were hit in New York that people suddenly started talking about a new transnational globalized Islam as if it were somehow a different phenomenon now that the violence had arrived in the West. In fact people began talking about the global war on terror as though Western nations were fighting one monolithic global threat that had suddenly raised its head. Journalist Simon Jenkins had some apt words to say on this subject when he wrote, 'The truth is that global is glamorous but detail is dull. The greatest fallacy follows from globalizing the world's ills and then tying them up in single bundles. ... We are bidden to attend to global poverty, global warming, global terrorism, even global sport.'[1] It was as if the various jihadist movements fighting their diverse battles around the world suddenly had to be wrapped up into one uniform threat for them to be given real meaning.

However, talking about Islam and terrorism in global terms belies the very real differences between the various nationalistic groups that in many cases had and continue to have their own particular agendas and idiosyncrasies. As the different Islamist groups came to be officially designated as terrorist organizations, it was generally assumed that they all shared the same aims and objectives and that these objectives were broadly the same as those of Osama Bin Ladin and Al-Qa'ida. Despite the fact that what motivates an Egyptian Islamist is not necessarily the same as what motivates an Algerian Islamist or a Moroccan one, let alone one from Indonesia or India, these differences were overlooked and all the various militants and groups were spoken of as if they adhered to one homogenous ideology and one set of political aspirations. Even organizations such as Hamas and Hizbollah, which have traditionally had their own very clear-cut agendas that focused on Israel, were often portrayed as though they were fighting the same global jihad against the Western world that Bin Ladin and others had advocated. In 2006, for example, former British prime minister Tony Blair talked about an arc of extremism linking a range of conflicts and attacks as though they were all part of the same phenomenon, declaring, '9/11 in the US, 7/7 in the UK, 11/3 in Madrid, the countless terrorist attacks in countries as disparate as Indonesia or Algeria, what is now happening in Afghanistan and in Indonesia, the continuing conflict in Lebanon and Palestine, it is all part of the same thing.'[2] It was as though the Western political mindset could only tackle the problem by framing every expression of political discontent that was articulated through an Islamist rhetoric as though it was part of one global phenomenon. Yet this 'global' approach assumes a uniformity of purpose that many militants could only dream of.

At the same time as people were talking about the new global terrorist threat, they were also promoting the idea that there was a new type of Islam that had been taken up by radical Muslims in the West that had its own special characteristics. The fact that some of those militants who had been involved in terrorist atrocities had spent some time residing in the West made some assume that the West was instrumental in their radicalization. Rather than looking to the parts of the world that had been producing this strand of militant Islamism for over two decades as a means of understanding why some Muslims had turned to political violence, analysts began looking for new answers in Europe itself and some concluded that this violence was part of a new type of jihadism that was directly linked to the conditions in which Muslims found themselves in the West.[3]

Moreover after 9/11 Islamist activists and especially those who were arrested on terrorism charges suddenly had the label of Al-Qa'ida slapped on them as if all the various groups were all working to the same agenda. This was a major shift, as prior to the September 2001 attacks radical Islamists living in Europe were given minimal attention by the media and policy world. In some cases those who were particularly outspoken in their radical views were considered as something of a joke. Despite his calls for jihad, for example, the Syrian radical Omar Bakri Mohamed was widely regarded as a buffoon and even made for entertaining viewing. In 1996 a British journalist made a documentary about the Syrian preacher entitled 'The Tottenham Ayatollah' and one could not help but laugh at the scene of the oafish Bakri photocopying his jihadist propaganda leaflets in an office supply superstore just off the M25 motorway because of their 'price promise', which meant he could get them done more cheaply there than anywhere else.[4] Likewise

Abu Hamza Al-Masri, with his hook and cockney accent, was considered in some quarters as little more than a stupid joke. Furthermore, although there were arrests of groups of Islamists in Europe prior to 9/11, they did not cause much of a stir and were generally considered as part of a problem that existed elsewhere. In October 2000, 11 Algerians residing in Italy were arrested on charges of association with terrorist groups in Algeria and of arms smuggling. The arrests were not deemed sufficiently important to even receive front-page coverage in the national newspaper *Corriere della Sera*, which had relegated the story to the inside pages.[5] Militant Islam was seen primarily as a problem whose impact was felt far away from home.

After the 9/11 attacks, however, Islamists in the continent began to be regarded as a pressing security concern. Arrests were carried out in quick succession in numerous European countries including Italy, Spain and the UK. The majority of those arrested were of North African origin and were accused of either belonging to terrorist cells or of providing logistical support for terrorist activities. The various national radical groups operating in Europe that these suspects were accused of having links to also came to be associated in the media with Bin Ladin. Although the links between these groups and Al-Qa'ida was in many cases extremely tenuous, their members found themselves suddenly accused of being part of one huge terrorist network with Bin Ladin at its head. In June 2003, for example, Italian police launched dawn raids on 40 sites in and around Milan. They arrested a Moroccan imam, Mohamed el Mahfoudi, and five Tunisians who were accused of providing financial and legal assistance to the Algerian GSPC in the form of abetting and financing a terrorist organization, false accounting, involvement in illegal immigration, receiving counterfeit documents and trafficking in stolen cars. However, the case was reported in *La Repubblica* newspaper with the headline: 'Terrorism – Six Al-Qa'ida Financiers Arrested in Milan'.[6] It was as if the world was suddenly looking at these individuals through the lens of 9/11, and what had in some cases been perceived of as a type of insurgent struggle against their own regimes had now taken on a much more menacing global significance.

## The Bin Ladin effect

Prior to 9/11 the jihadist movement in all of its different hues looked to be almost on its last legs. Attempts to overthrow the secular Western-oriented regimes in the Middle East and North Africa and to replace them with Islamic states had been disastrous and had resulted in those who had fought either being exterminated, imprisoned or forced to flee abroad. By the end of the 1990s Egypt had succeeded in militarily defeating groups such as the

Al-Jama'a Al-Islamiya and Al-Jihad, and the Libyan regime had quashed the LIFG and the other smaller militant groups that had sprung up around the same time. Even the great jihadist hope of Algeria had turned out to have been a total failure, with the army-backed regime looking as strong as ever as the new century came to dawn. In addition a new generation of rulers had come to power in Jordan, Syria and Morocco who were simply carbon copies of their fathers who had ruled before them, emphasizing that despite all the hopes of the early 1990s the Islamists had failed to pull the region out of its stagnation. Those members of the various Islamist groups residing in Europe shared this sense of desperation. This was especially true of the older Afghan veterans who were feeling as though the cause they had invested so much in was slipping out of their hands.

Of course many Islamists did not express these disappointments in such terms and increasingly came to explain their own failures in the region as having been caused by the fact that their regimes had been propped up by more powerful forces working behind the scenes. Indeed they saw their own regimes as little more than puppets of Western governments. The LIFG complained on its website of the 'secular regimes that are moved by the Jews and Americans behind the scenes'.[7] Similarly Zafar Bangash of the Institute of Contemporary Islamic Thought in the UK wrote in 1997, 'The Global Islamic Movement does not have to contend only with the tyrants in the Muslim world. Their real struggle is in fact against the Western backers of unrepresentative regimes. If left alone, these regimes would collapse like a pack of cards.'[8] Interestingly these kinds of arguments that the Islamists were putting forward were not new, but had been used before by the left-wing movements in the Arab world who used the same reasoning to explain why they had not been able to come to power.

It was these kinds of sentiments that Bin Ladin hoped to tap into as a means of spreading his appeal and his message. Indeed, in spite of all his internationalist discourse and talk of the 'Far Enemy' (namely the United States), Bin Ladin was not very different to other jihadists whose main preoccupation was in freeing their own lands from foreign domination and control. It was after all the Gulf War of 1991 that prompted him to break with the Saudi establishment, as he could not stomach the idea of the kingdom relying on 'infidel' forces, namely those of the United States, to protect it from the might of the secular regimes like that of Ba'athist Iraq. Bin Ladin is reported to have offered up the services of the mujahideen to the Saudi monarchy in order to assist it in ousting Saddam Hussein's forces from Kuwait. When the Saudi regime turned down this offer and chose instead to rely on US forces to do the job Bin Ladin cut his ties with the Saudi ruling family. Things deteriorated further when Saudi Arabia sanctioned a permanent US troop presence in the kingdom – something that Bin Ladin's religiosity could not accept given that not only was Saudi Arabia his homeland but was also the site of Islam's two holiest shrines at Mecca and Medina.

Although like almost every Islamist Bin Ladin had always disdained the imperialist West, it was only after his homeland was directly affected by the American presence that he focused his attentions on the 'Far Enemy'. In 1996 he issued a *fatwa* entitled 'A Declaration of War against the Americans Occupying the Land of the Two Holy Places'. He gave the declaration an internationalist flavour, bemoaning atrocities committed against Muslims in various corners of the world, and explained, 'The latest and the greatest of these aggressions, incurred by the Muslims since the death of the Prophet (Allah's Blessing and Salutations on Him) is the occupation of the land of the two Holy Places ... by the armies of the American Crusaders and their allies.'[9] Despite its title, however, Bin Ladin used the document to launch into a general tirade against the evils of the Saudi regime and royal family, which he accused of having destroyed the country and 'torn off its legitimacy'. Although Bin Ladin advocated hitting the greater infidel, i.e. the US, he was abundantly clear that the motivation for doing so was to force it out of the 'land of the two holy places'.

Even Bin Ladin's famous declaration of February 1998 against the 'Jews and Crusaders', which is generally considered to be the launching point for Al-Qa'ida, stated:

> The ruling to kill the Americans and their allies – civilians and military – is an individual duty for every Muslim who can do it in any country in which it is possible to do it, in order to liberate the Al-Aqsa Mosque and the holy mosque [Mecca] from their grip, and in order for their armies to move out of all the lands of Islam, defeated and unable to threaten any Muslim.[10]

A few months after the statement had been issued Bin Ladin was interviewed by American journalist Johan Miller and made it clear that the main purpose behind attacking the US was to force it out of his homeland and to sabotage its alliance with the Saudi regime. He stated:

> The call to wage war against America was made because America has spearheaded the crusade against the Islamic nation, sending tens of thousands of its troops to the land of the two Holy Mosques over and above its meddling in its affairs and its politics, and its support of the oppressive, corrupt and tyrannical regime that is in control. These are the reasons behind the singling out of America as a target.[11]

The 1998 African embassy bombings and the 2000 attack on the USS

*Cole* in Yemen, which were the precursors to 9/11, were also partly an attempt by Al-Qa'ida to force the US to withdraw from Saudi Arabia. Indeed the embassy bombings occurred exactly eight years to the day after US troops were ordered on to Saudi soil.[12] Yet neither was successful in its aim. Nor indeed was 9/11 itself. In fact it would appear that Bin Ladin had grossly miscalculated what he could achieve with the dramatic events of September 2001. His famous statement in which he declared that America would not be able to sustain more than two or three painful blows indicates that he really believed that after 9/11 the US would finally withdraw from the Arabian peninsula, just as it had withdrawn from Lebanon after it was hit in 1982 and from Somalia just over a decade later.

Yet the consequences of 9/11 were to prove disastrous for Al-Qa'ida and the jihadist movement more widely. The bombing of Afghanistan not only lost Bin Ladin a base from which he could operate freely and train new recruits but also destroyed what many Islamists considered as the only true Sunni Islamic state. In addition, the attacks encouraged the regimes of the Islamic world to use the excuse of fighting against international terrorism in order to clamp down more fiercely on their own Islamists. Where once the West had been prepared to voice some criticisms of the human rights abuses committed by these regimes, this came to be replaced by an uneasy silence and in some cases loud support for the regimes' attempts to crush terrorism. In addition new anti-terrorist legislation, as well as increased scrutiny and surveillance measures introduced by various European authorities, meant that those jihadists who had previously found refuge in the continent no longer had the same degree of protection. As one former Afghan veteran said of 9/11, 'From the operational and tactical point of view, it was considered as the Achilles' heel for the whole Jihadi tendency.'[13]

Despite the tactical disaster, however, the 9/11 attacks did bring about a success on the ideological front that was to change the mood in the Islamist camp, not only in the Islamic world but also in Europe. It was not that Osama Bin Ladin had come up with anything particularly new or revolutionary. Indeed his railing against the 'crusaders and the Jews' was completely in line with the discourse that had been employed by political Islamists over decades. However, Bin Ladin's ability to attack the 'Far Enemy' had a certain appeal among those jihadists who were still frustrated by their own inabilities to topple their own regimes. Therefore it was not that attacking the 'Far Enemy' somehow represented a new globalized vision, but rather that it suddenly seemed to offer a viable, albeit desperate, way to try to effect change in the home country. Attacking those who were preventing Islamic rule in the Arab world was the next best thing to attacking the regimes themselves. As one angry Tunisian Islamist stressed, 'If you struggle against your own regime and get nowhere, you try against the West.' He went on to complain that violence against the West would continue until it 'pulls out of Tunisia and leaves us alone to get on with it'.[14] These sentiments were echoed by Omar Khyam, the British Asian accused of the fertilizer bomb plot in the UK, who complained at his trial in 2006 that the Americans, 'put up puppet regimes in Muslim countries like Saudi Arabia, Jordan and Egypt'.[15]

More importantly, Bin Ladin scored a spectacular success when he hit the US. Initially many Islamists did not believe that Muslims were capable of actually launching such a major operation and it is for this reason that many still do not believe that Al-Qa'ida was responsible for the attacks. The GSPC actually issued a communiqué after 9/11 asserting that Muslims could not have been behind the assault on the US. Yet as the evidence that Al-Qa'ida had been responsible became clearer, a kind of euphoria developed. For a movement that had been burdened by failure and disappointments, the fact that Al-Qa'ida had managed to hit a world superpower on its own soil brought a feeling of triumph that had not been experienced since the heady days when the mujahideen had ousted the Soviets from Afghanistan. Bin Ladin's success in the US therefore brought back some pride and momentum to a faltering movement, even if some disagreed with what he had done. This served to provide inspiration to a younger generation of militants who had not been through the Afghanistan experience or the trials of the 1990s, and some of those young militants claimed that it was the 9/11 attacks that reawakened their Islamic consciousness and persuaded them to get involved in radical Islamist politics.

Yet the importance of 9/11 was that it did not resonate solely within the Islamist camp but struck a far wider chord. Using the rhetoric of the 'Far Enemy', as well as arguing for the two holy cities to be free from foreign 'unclean' occupation, Bin Ladin was aware that he could tap into the grievances of Muslim populations around the entire region. He knew he could touch a raw nerve with almost every Muslim in the world. Shortly after the attacks, controversial and contested reports appeared in the media about Palestinians and Lebanese celebrating in the streets. There were even stories about how the FBI's own Arabic translators brought sweets and cakes into the office to celebrate the attacks, with one allegedly declaring, 'It's about time they got a taste of what they've been giving the Middle East.'[16] Regardless of the truth of these kinds of stories, it is undeniable that Osama became a sort of hero in the Arab world and beyond. T-shirts and other kinds of merchandise bearing his image began to appear, and demonstrators across the Islamic world took to holding posters of Bin Ladin in anti-US demonstrations such as in October 2001 when protestors in Bangladesh carried pictures of the Saudi billionaire through the streets of Dhaka. Furthermore what Bin Ladin had done had a resonance beyond the Islamic world and it was reported that after the attacks Mexican football fans were chanting their support for 'Osama! Osama!' on the terraces at football matches against US teams.

It is not that the majority of Muslims around the world applauded the killing of innocent civilians. Far from it. Most abhorred the deaths and the violence, but at the same time 9/11 served to become almost a symbol for the developing world to feel that the dominant empire had been punctured and momentarily brought down a peg or two. Syrian professor Sadik Al-Azm wrote of feeling an initial twinge of satisfaction when he first heard of the attacks but went on to explain:

> I didn't understand my own shameful response to the slaughter of innocents. Was it the bad news from Palestine that week; the satisfaction of seeing the arrogance of power abruptly, if temporarily, humbled; the sight of the jihadi Frankenstein's monsters, so carefully nourished by the United States, turning suddenly on their masters; or the natural resentment of the weak and marginalized at the peripheries of empires against the centre, or, in this case, against the centre of the centre?[17]

The reasons prompting these feelings can be found in the years of deep resentment about the pitiful situation of the Arab world and the developing world more widely that extends into migrant communities in the West. The frustration provoked by the inability to effect change, combined with a discourse that has reigned supreme for generations, which points the finger squarely at Western imperialist powers as being the root of all the real problems blighting the region, enabled many people to identify with what Bin Ladin had done as if through his twisted logic he had somehow avenged the years of humiliation suffered by Muslims. The response to the 9/11 attacks reflected the fragility of a region seeking a hero to pull it out of its misery and sense of impotence. In fact Bin Ladin is not the only figure to have attained heroic status in the region for these reasons. Saddam Hussein had achieved near epic fame when in January 1991 he launched Scud missile attacks against Israel, hitting Tel Aviv and Haifa. Likewise, despite being Shi'ite, Hizbollah leader Hassan Nasrallah became another kind of hero in the Middle East in 2006 when his movement launched attacks against Israel. It is almost as if, regardless of the consequences or political outcomes of these attacks, the very fact that these individuals had led the way in attacking the symbols of oppression meant that they had somehow taken revenge on behalf of the suffering of the entire Muslim population. As such it was Bin Ladin's ability to tap into the core grievances and hurt of the Middle

East and the developing world more widely, as well as migrant communities in Europe, that gave Al-Qa'ida its potency, regardless of whether the other individual jihadist groups sought to join it or not.

## The *ummah*

While 9/11 might have engendered feelings of shared triumph and hope, it was not sufficient to make the cherished idea of the *ummah* any more of a reality. Many analysts asserted that Islamists in the post-9/11 world now felt part of a new globalized Muslim nation. They claimed that radicals were now thinking in global rather than local terms and saw themselves as part of a bigger internationalized movement.[18] Yet this aspiration to a global Islamist ideal is nothing new and is exactly what Islamists had been striving to achieve for generations. Such aspirations, however, never succeeded in overcoming regional or even national differences. Indeed the first expression of what could be considered a transnational call to the Islamic cause in the contemporary era came with the Afghanistan conflict. How much more in tune with the idea of the *ummah* could it be to have thousands of young men travel thousands of miles to defend their fellow Muslims against the communist oppressors? Although two very different experiences, when one considers how few have gone to fight in Iraq compared to those who chose to go to Afghanistan, one would surely think that the idea of the *ummah* has in fact lost some of its appeal and currency from the early days of the 1980s. Moreover even during the Afghanistan years national differences persisted, despite the fact that the volunteers were all in it fighting together. In spite of the fact too that the *salafist* ideology that drove these mujahideen relied on a very simple purist cultural message that looked to the ancestors of the Prophet for inspiration and which was supposed to counter contaminating currents such as Arabism and nationalism that were considered to be part of the *jahiliyyah* (pagan ignorance), even the mujahideen could not overcome their own national and cultural boundaries. Not only did the Arabs not mix with the Afghans, who were viewed as inferior because of their adherence to a more Sufist interpretation of Islam, or with the Uzbeks, whose traditional form of Islam offended them, they also tended to remain mostly within their own national groupings. Each nationality had its own camp, and as one Al-Qa'ida ideologue observed of those in Afghanistan, 'Local fundamentalist organizations saw their first task as being in their home country. Generally what they wanted was to kill the leaders of their own country.'[19]

Although Bin Ladin and Al-Zawahiri used an internationalist discourse and promoted the idea that they were leading the global jihad, even they could not rise above the petty divisions and squabbling that characterized the scene. There was huge rivalry and competition between Al-Qa'ida and the Taliban after Bin Ladin's return to Afghanistan in 1996. Mullah Omar reportedly became extremely frustrated with Bin Ladin's love of the media and the international media in particular and tried to prevent him from making statements and giving interviews. There were also divisions within Al-Qa'ida itself. One of the movement's ideologues, who wrote a manuscript titled 'The Story of the Afghan-Arabs: From the Entry to Afghanistan to the Final Exodus with the Taliban', describes the tensions between the hawks and the doves in the organization and complains about Bin Ladin's authoritarian leadership style.[20] The 9/11 attacks were to divide Islamist opinion even further. In fact there was much disquiet in some jihadist circles about what Al-Qa'ida had done and what repercussions it would have on the future of their own nationalist movements. The attacks created huge fault-lines within Al-Qa'ida itself, as some of its members believed that they had hindered the campaign to bring about Islamic rule in the Middle East because they had provided the West and also the regimes in the Islamic world with the impetus to clamp down hard on Islamists.[21] Therefore despite all the talk of the global jihad, the divisions remained as deep as ever and even Al-Qa'ida could not develop into a single united movement.

If Afghanistan was unable to smooth out these national differences, it seems far-fetched to imagine that they would be overcome among radicals in Europe. Indeed, despite their talk of the *ummah*, it seems that many Islamists in Europe still cannot move far beyond their own cultural boundaries and that their thinking is still dominated by domestic and local preoccupations. It would be fair to say that a Libyan Islamist in Europe who considers himself part of the *ummah* might talk about Kashmir or Chechnya, but gets excited when he talks about issues related to the Arab world such as Palestine or Iraq, and becomes really agitated when he touches on issues related to Libya and especially when related to his own city or region. This was certainly the case for one Libyan imam in the English Midlands, for example, who, while he had a view on the various crises inflicted on the Muslim world, became most animated and excited when discussing the situation in his own city in the east of Libya. This is hardly surprising given that he is part of the first generation and the links to his homeland are still strong. Yet this attachment to the home country also often holds true for second-generation immigrants even if they have been born and raised in Europe. They might feel British, French or Belgian, on the one hand, but many still refer to the family village back in their country of origin as home, and local issues related to their family's own region are likely to resonate much more deeply than the plight of Muslims in other parts of the world.[22] As French academic Jocelyne Cesari has noted of Muslim minorities in Europe, 'Sectarian, ethnic and nationalist groupings in many cases play a more prominent role in Muslim identity than any abstract notion of a universal brotherhood of believers or *Ummah*.'[23]

Within this context of the global *ummah*, much has been made of the Internet as a key facilitator of this supposed feeling of worldwide brotherhood. Whether the Internet itself can make one more radical or really provides a sense of global brotherhood is difficult to prove. Is watching an Internet video of the mujahideen in Iraq really that different from watching a video brought back from the front lines in Bosnia or Algeria, other than the immediacy with which the image can be viewed or the fact that it can reach a wider audience? It should also be noted that Internet usage in many parts of the Arab world, and in North Africa in particular, remains very low compared to the developed world. Internet usage in countries such as Egypt or Libya is still somewhat of a luxury and the domain of the elite. In addition, those Arab countries and those of North Africa with problems of illiteracy remain primarily oral cultures where the power of the spoken word still rules supreme – this is why Islamist cassettes generally had and still have a far greater appeal than texts. The influence of a sheikh or imam is still generally much more potent than any Internet site and this is also sometimes the case among migrant communities in Europe. That is not to say that the sheikh or imam is not now making use of the Internet and downloading *khoutbas* or *fatwas* from the plethora of websites that are available. Indeed one young inarticulate, awkward and angry young Algerian imam in Naples admitted that he spent most of his time sitting in his dingy airless mosque in the back streets of the city surfing the Internet.[24] However, while second-generation migrants or those first-generation immigrants who are more educated and articulate might use the Internet, for many they still rely on other more traditional methods of communication.

Satellite television stations such as Al-Jazeera or Al-Arabia have a far greater sway and importance than the Internet. These channels have an immediacy and a sense of universal truth about them, drawn partly from the fact that they were the first Arab channels to move away from the staid state-run official media of many of the countries of the Middle East and gave many Arabs a sense of ownership of a new media that encouraged debate and criticism of some of the regimes of the region. In addition the mass communications revolution has at one level reinforced local dynamics for communities living in Europe insofar as satellite television has enabled communities to plug straight into channels from back home. Bangladeshis in the UK now have Bangladeshi stations beamed into their living rooms just as Moroccans in Belgium or the Netherlands can have their own Moroccan channels beamed into theirs. Surely this only serves to consolidate a sense of local identity.

This interest in the local does not mean that Islamists in the global age do not share a common narrative about what it means to be Muslim, how Islam is under attack and how one should defend fellow Muslims wherever they may be. Nor does it mean that they do not feel a sense of unity of purpose in their dislike of US policies or of the West more generally. This feeling has been there since the early days of political Islam and was used before by the nationalist regimes. The difference is that the success of 9/11 broadened the mindset of those launching attacks to include a wider set of targets and possibilities. In addition, the West's response to the attacks, its launching of the 'global war on terror' and the linking of many Islamist suspects to Al-Qa'ida have all served to play into this narrative and to create the impression that there is a single united Islamist front. While some at the very hardcore end of the Islamist spectrum may have been able to transcend national priorities and to make common cause with other radicals in order to carry out certain operations, this does not mean that they necessarily subscribe to a truly globalized type of Islam or that their interest in their own countries has diminished.

## Radicalization in Europe?

The fact that a number of those who perpetrated the 9/11 attacks or other terrorist operations had spent several years residing in Europe and seem to have become more religious while in the continent resulted in some commentators concluding that Europe must somehow be responsible for this radicalization. After 9/11 there was much soul searching and a lot of assumptions made about how Al-Qa'ida's ideology gave succour to young men living away from home who found it difficult to cope with the realities of everyday life in the West. One analyst wrote of 'the drift of young Algerians out of Algeria and into a precarious existence abroad, where the messianic and global vision of al-Qa'ida provides both hope and respite'.[25] This is a curious statement, as Algeria is a country that has produced an abundance of Islamic militants over the years and whose own Islamist insurgent groups, the GIA and the GSPC, had direct contacts and connections with Al-Qa'ida and Bin Ladin.

Isolation and marginalization within Europe and the individual's response to Western society are repeatedly cited as the main drivers behind the radicalization process. Farhad Khosrokhavar has written of the minority among the Muslim diaspora who aspire to the idea of a new caliphate in response to 'the fragmentation experienced by Muslims in cities that mock them with their wealth, marginalize them and make them feel a shameful loss of dignity by arrogantly displaying their affluence and offering them no way to share it'.[26] If one is to accept this description of the Western city, it is not clear why Muslims should feel this sense of fragmentation and marginalization any more than other migrant communities who were forced to settle in Europe. In a similar vein, one Western journalist talked about the city of Hamburg where some of the 9/11 hijackers lived for a while, stating:

> This turn on modernization is absolutely critical, and I don't think people understand that – that we [the modern Western countries] are both attractive and repulsive. Hamburg kind of combines both that attractive and repulsive element, and they don't know about the repulsive stuff before they go there. They only discover that when they get there, and if they find their niche, and their education goes well, and their position is good at home, and if they are fairly stable, then they are able to sort that out and go home and be productive citizens. But if they are somewhat unstable – they feel alienated, they feel shut out, they are unhappy with what is going on at home – that's a combustible combination.[27]

This highly simplistic analysis fails to take into account that figures such as the 9/11 hijackers, by the very nature of their backgrounds, already had a complex relationship with the idea of the West and were likely to have held negative preconceptions about Western culture and society before they even set foot in Hamburg or any other European city.

Some scholars have gone so far as to suggest that being in Europe meant that those who perpetrated the attacks had taken on a different kind of Islam detached from the faith of their home countries. Olivier Roy has asserted that the 9/11 hijackers became 'more a product of the Westernization of Islam than of traditional Middle Eastern politics'.[28] Roy also argues that the 'Muslims of the West are fighting the frontiers of their imaginary ummah, and are doing so because what agitates them most are the consequences of their own Westernization.'[29] While people may become attracted to radical interpretations of Islam while in Europe, one surely cannot discount the influence of their formative years that they spent in their countries of origin. To assert, for example, that the 9/11 Egyptian hijacker Mohamed Atta was more a product of Westernized Islam than that of his own country appears to ignore the fact that Atta grew up in Egypt at a time when Islamic radicalization was at its peak. Lebanese American academic Fouad Ajami wrote of how, for him, Atta was a typical product of his own country, noting, 'I almost know Mohamed Atta. ... I can almost make him out. I have known Egypt for nearly three decades, and so much of Atta's life falls neatly in place for me.'[30] Indeed Atta was, like many young Egyptians of his generation, educated and relatively bright, yet found himself shut out from the modernity and benefits of the modern Egyptian state that was the domain of the country's Westernized elite.

In fact, despite often being portrayed as a 'normal guy' who suddenly turned religious in Germany, Atta's background suggests he was more religious and politicized than he is often portrayed. Despite his father's initial denials to the media of his son's interest in politics or religion, anecdotal evidence suggests that the family was in fact religious. His middle-class lawyer father told a journalist, 'We keep our doors closed and that is why my two daughters and my son are academically and morally excellent.'[31] Moreover his father also displayed an attitude towards politics and the West that is typical of that part of the world, telling another journalist, 'Egypt is a hypocrite and the U.S. is a hypocrite. ... We are people who don't have hypocrisy. Oil companies rule the U.S. with power and [are] killing people.'[32]

Atta himself was an architecture student in the engineering department of Cairo University and reportedly joined the engineering syndicate, which like many science and engineering unions in Egypt was dominated by the Islamist movement and the Muslim Brotherhood in particular.[33] Indeed it was during this period that the Islamist movement was sweeping the universities in Egypt. After graduating, Atta went to study architecture in Germany in 1992 and right from that time friends and colleagues noted his intense religiosity. After his arrival he began working part time in an urban planning company in Hamburg and one of the firm's partners said of Atta, who used to pray regularly on the floor of the office, 'He was very, very religious.'[34] Even his choice of thesis at the Hamburg Technical University on the preservation of the Islamic quarters of old Middle East cities, especially Aleppo in Syria, suggests a man with a keen interest in the Islamic past. A fellow student from Germany who travelled with Atta to Egypt in August 1995 paints a picture of a young man unsurprisingly much more at home and comfortable in his own Cairo environment than he ever was in Europe. He also noted that Atta had strong religious convictions and that he was interested in the political situation in Egypt. In fact the fellow student Volker Hauth noted, 'That was his main topic.'[35] Other acquaintances of Atta have also noted how the young Egyptian became most animated when talking about Egypt and the tensions between its secular Western-oriented government and the Islamist movement. In addition, the will that Atta is alleged to have left displayed signs of extreme and near obsessive religiosity. It carried the instructions, 'I don't want pregnant women or a person who is not clean to come and say goodbye to me because I don't approve of it. ... I don't want women to go to my funeral or later to my grave.'[36] Therefore to suggest that Atta was more a product of some new Westernized 'deterritorialized' Islam simply because he spent a few years of his life in Germany is surely to deny the influences of his own culture and roots.

In addition, another of the hijackers, Marwan Al-Shehi, who came from a village in one of the poorer and less influential of the emirates, Ras Al-Khaimah, was in fact brought up in a very religious family. His father was reportedly the imam at his local mosque and Al-Shehi was described as a 'deeply religious child who would switch on the prayer tape at the mosque for his father'.[37] After the death of his father Al-Shehi went to Germany around 1996 on a government scholarship to study. From the limited anecdotal evidence about this young man, it would appear that he was already deeply religious before his arrival in Europe. Yet the argument that it was something in Europe that turned him to commit an act of terrorism was picked up and used by the government of the United Arab Emirates, which was keen to try to give the impression that religious fundamentalism was something that does not exist in the country. The UAE information minister said of Al-Shehi, 'He was a normal young man until he went to Germany, where it seems he met these fanatics, who have a very different understanding of Islam than we do.'[38]

The picture of Ziad Jarrah is more complex, as he appears to have been brought up in a relatively secular family in Lebanon and was educated in a Catholic school in Beirut. He moved to Germany to study and soon began dating a young Turkish woman. It would appear that it was in Europe that Jarrah's religiosity was awakened and his experiences in the continent may well have contributed to this reawakening. Yet just as in the case of Jamal Zougam, who was accused of being part of the Madrid bombings, pictures of a very secular-looking Jarrah began to be circulated in the media after the attacks. His family issued a video of Jarrah dancing at a family wedding in January 2001 and his uncle gave a long interview to the media in which he tried to clear his nephew's name, asserting the young man had never had any interest in politics or religion. However, a video released by Al-Qa'ida in 2006 clearly showed a heavily bearded Jarrah with Mohamed Atta in which they both allegedly read their wills to the camera in preparation for the 9/11 attacks.

Perhaps more importantly, one should not forget that 15 out of the 19 hijackers were Saudis and most had not spent any time in Europe at all. In fact the majority were typical of Saudi Al-Qa'ida members who presumably sought through Bin Ladin to oust the Americans from Saudi soil. Khalid Al-Mihdhar, who was on Flight 77 which crashed into the Pentagon, was brought up in Mecca and was a hardened veteran of the Bosnian jihad and had also spent time in Afghanistan. Ahmed Ibrahim Al-Haznawi, who was on Flight 93, was the son of a Saudi imam and came from one of the most desolate and underdeveloped areas of the kingdom. Ahmed Abdullah Al-Nami, who was also on Flight 93, was the *muezzin* of his local mosque in Saudi Arabia after he became extremely religious in the early 1990s. He studied *sharia* at the King Khaled University and then went off to join the mujahideen in Afghanistan. In fact the profile of most the 9/11 hijackers was of young Saudi men from the poorest and most backward part of the kingdom who, like most Saudis, had been brought up on a diet of religion and who in many cases had travelled to Afghanistan to give their lives for the jihad.

It is not just the 9/11 hijackers who, it is claimed, became radical while in Europe. It has been said of the Tunisian Sami Ben Khemais, who was convicted in Italy on terrorism charges in 2002, that he became radicalized after he began spending time at one of the mosques in Milan. While he may well have shown more outward signs of religious behaviour in Europe, this does not necessarily mean that he was not of that persuasion in Tunisia. To suggest, as some commentators have done, that he was not very religious before coming to Europe because he did not attend the mosque is to ignore the repressive nature of the Tunisian state towards anyone displaying overtly religious behaviour and the fact that in Islam one does not need to go to the mosque to pray. Moreover Ben Khemais was allegedly a veteran of the Afghanistan war – surely a factor that would have had a far greater impact on his radicalization than his being in Milan. In addition, the suggestion that some of these militants indulged in drinking and womanizing after arriving in Europe and then reacted to their 'Westernized experience' by becoming radical is to fail to understand that this is a common experience among young people in the Arab world who go through a similar rebellious hedonistic phase and then revert to their previous religious convictions. This is by no means unique to Europe.

That is not to say that these men did not become more extreme in their thinking or were not influenced at all by their time in Europe. However, to somehow disassociate the radicalism of these young men from their own roots is misleading. It is undeniable that there is a certain cultural mind-set that is present in the Islamic world that has proved prone to radicalism. This mindset has been shaped by a discourse that has regarded Western culture as decadent and corrupting. This discourse is not only the domain of the Islamists, but is common currency within the region. For example, one non-practising Libyan taxi driver from the impoverished east of the country explained how he wanted to move to Britain, but wanted to marry a British convert to Islam because he found non-Muslim women unclean. Similarly a young overtly secular Moroccan immigrant who was residing illegally in Genoa in Italy told the story of how he had had an Italian girlfriend but, despite the fact that he thought she was nice, considered her to be dirty because she was not Muslim. These kinds of ideas are partly related to limited educational opportunities and the crisis that the Islamic world has been experiencing for decades. It is this mindset that arguably makes certain individuals vulnerable to radicalization. While conditions in Europe may well have contributed to or consolidated feelings of anger against the West, or to feelings of alienation and marginalization, and may well have pushed some to immerse themselves totally in the faith of their own culture as a form of comfort, this alone is not sufficient to explain why these young men turned to such extreme measures. Indeed it is impossible to judge exactly what triggered such behaviour and it is possible that we are ignoring the power of ideology that has always captured the imagination of certain individuals. It may have been therefore that Europe was largely coincidental in the whole radicalization process.

# CHAPTER 8

# THE MADRID BOMBINGS

W hile the Algerians launched attacks against France in the mid-1990s, it took another decade before a group of Moroccans were to do the same against their former colonial masters, the Spanish, when they launched bomb attacks in Madrid.[1] Just like the Franco-Algerian relationship, Moroccan–Spanish relations have also been extremely fractious over the years and conflicts have arisen over issues such as immigration, fishing rights and the disputed territory of the Western Sahara in which Morocco accuses Spain of backing the Polisario independence movement which is seeking autonomy in the territory. Relations reached a particular crisis point in 2002 when the two states began squabbling over sovereignty of a tiny uninhabited Mediterranean island, known as Perejil (Parsley) to the Spanish and Leila to the Moroccans. Morocco sent a number of soldiers to occupy the island but met with an unexpectedly harsh response from Spanish forces who evicted the Moroccan troops. The row was only resolved when international powers stepped in. However, Spain's stance was seen as overly aggressive by many Moroccans and viewed as yet another example of Spanish arrogance and hostility towards its former colonial possession. While many Moroccans dream of going abroad to Spain to make a better life, the cultural baggage of this relationship is not always easily discarded, including by those who succeed in making it across the Mediterranean to start a new life in Europe.

The Madrid bombings of 11 March 2004 which killed 192 people and wounded 2,050 were widely interpreted as being an assault by Al-Qa'ida in its bid to force Spanish troops out of Iraq just prior to the Spanish elections. Despite the assumption that Al-Qa'ida was responsible for the attacks, it is striking to note that the vast majority of those involved were in fact young Moroccans, many of them immigrants with strong links to their country of origin. This in itself came as a surprise, as Moroccans had not tradition-ally been associated with militant Islamism or jihadism. Moreover Moroccan communities in Europe, driven out of their home country primarily for economic reasons, had a reputation for being quiet and less politicized than their Algerian counterparts. Yet these bombings, as well as those that hit Casablanca in May 2003, revealed that there was a new and destructive brand of Moroccan radicalism that, as it turned out, had been brewing below the surface in the kingdom for many years and that had Spain in its sights as a target.

## Moroccan Islamists

The Moroccan state has always achieved stability through its monarchy, which claims direct descent from the Prophet, and which bestows the title 'Commander of the Faithful' on the king. It has prided itself in following the Maliki school of Islam – a school known for its moderation and toler- ance – and has fought hard against the forces of secularism that had come in the form of the left-wing and nationalist movements of the 1950s and 1960s. Therefore Islam has always been very much part of the identity of the Moroccan state. That is not to say that the country was immune from politi- cal Islamist forces, but rather that the monarchy dealt with it in a different way to the secular regimes. King Hassan II had initially tried to eliminate the first expression of political Islam that came in the form of the Shabiba Al-Islamiya (Islamic Youth), which was set up in 1972 by Abdelkarim Moutia and which had its own armed wing, but he soon realized that repression was not necessarily the best way of dealing with the threat. Indeed, although the regime crushed the Shabiba Al-Islamiya, its members simply splintered off to form other groups. Moreover Morocco proved to be equally suscep- tible to the Islamic revivalism that was taking hold across the region in the 1980s. Aware that it could not defeat this trend, the regime took to trying to contain these forces. Under this policy two main strands developed within the Islamist opposition. The Muslim Brotherhood trend has undergone vari- ous reincarnations and currently goes under the name Hizb Al-Ahdala wa Tanmia (Justice and Development Party, or PJD). It has been permitted to take part in the elections as a political party. The other more radical strand is led by the controversial Sufist Sheikh Yassine. Yassine openly challenged the king's title of 'Commander of the Faithful' and drew a group of follow- ers to form the Al Adl wal Ihsane (Justice and Welfare). Yassine was kept under house arrest but was afforded a degree of tolerance not to be found in other more secular states such as Tunisia and Libya.

Until the Casablanca attacks of 2003, this strategy appeared to have been relatively successful and it was widely assumed that Morocco had some- how escaped the violent militant strands that had taken root elsewhere. Despite the desperate socio-economic conditions in Morocco, there were few Moroccan volunteers who chose to wage jihad in Afghanistan during the war against the Soviets in the 1980s. The number of Libyan and Tunisian mujahideen far outweighed the Moroccan contingent. The Moroccans were so few in number that when they arrived in Afghanistan they had to work under the wing of the Libyan fighters and stayed in the Libyan camps until their numbers were sufficiently large to create a camp of their own. In fact the Moroccans only began to join the war in Afghanistan in 1989 when it was almost at an end, and many of those who went were humanitarian work-ers who were there with the permission of the Moroccan authorities.[2] The Moroccans had no significant presence among the leadership of the Afghan Arabs and they were viewed by the main players in the conflict as merely low-level operatives.

However, as the Casablanca bombings revealed, from the late 1980s and 1990s there had been another more radical strand developing inside Morocco's impoverished urban slums. The roots of this trend were interest-ingly somehow of the monarchy's own making. In an effort to counter-balance its own Moroccan Islamists, as well as the left-wing movement, King Hassan II opened the doors to Saudi Arabia's propaganda efforts, allowing the Saudis to set up Qu'ranic schools and charitable organizations.[3] The Saudis also brought Moroccans to train in the kingdom, creating a new generation of radical preachers who had been schooled in a rigid purist interpretation of Islam. These included Omar Al-Haddouci, Hassan Kettani, Ahmed Al-Rafiki, Abdelkarim Chadli and Mohamed Fizazi, who were officially sanc-tioned as imams in Morocco.[4] This was not unique to Morocco, as this was exactly what the Algerian regime had tried to do in its own bid to defeat its homegrown Islamist opposition, with even more devastating results.

As was the case in Algeria, a number of these Moroccan preachers began to develop increasingly radical agendas and came to reject not only the Saudi regime that had funded them but also their own in Morocco. These preach-ers began openly criticizing the monarchy and as a result were prohibited from preaching in official mosques. Undeterred, they took to setting up their own makeshift mosques in the sprawling shanty towns around Morocco's cities, where their influence grew steadily among the poor and disenfran-chised. In keeping with the *salafist* tradition, they drew their own group of followers who were attracted to their particular hardline teachings and ideol-ogy that labelled the Moroccan regime as corrupt and that espoused jihad.

One of the most important preachers of this ideology was Mohamed Fizazi, who was based in the run-down Tchar Bendibane district of Tangiers where he lived with his two wives and gaggle of children and where he was the imam of his own mosque. Fizazi had a reputation in the neighbourhood for being a modest man who was always ready to help others, yet at the same time he was a charismatic preacher who advocated an extreme hardline

message. This was a far cry from the tamer ideology of those officially sanctioned Islamist parties such as the PJD, who, while they may have shared
many of the political objectives of the radicals, had a far less inflammatory
way of expressing it. Yet it was Fizazi's firebrand preaching that touched a
chord among certain sections of Morocco's youth. As one of his followers
noted, 'People even came from Oujda or from Fes for his lessons. Sheikh
Fizazi got angry when he preached and worked up the crowd who loved
passionate imams.'[5] Indeed, as with many of these preachers, the tone of the
delivery appears to have had a greater impact than the content.

Fizazi had developed such a reputation that he was invited to preach to
Muslim communities in various countries around the world, including in
Europe. According to his family, prior to 2001 he had visited over three
dozen countries and sometimes did so with financial support from the
Moroccan state.[6] Moroccan officials have denied that they funded Fizazi for
such ventures but did acknowledge that the government had encouraged
him to travel abroad after he had been banned from preaching in state-run
mosques.[7] In 2001 Fizazi spent some time as a preacher and imam at the
famous Al-Quds mosque in Hamburg where the 9/11 hijackers had gathered,
and his virulently anti-Western sermons were easily available at the city's Al-
Tawhid bookshop.

Another preacher who became a key figure in Morocco's radical scene
was Hassan Kettani, who was arrested in February 2003 and convicted to 20
years in prison for having influenced the Casablanca bombers, although he
maintains that he did not know them. Although Kettani, who came from a
very religious family with strong ties to Saudi Arabia, lived in a very comfortable family villa in the chic neighbourhood of Soussi in Rabat, he used to
spend his time roaming the poor districts of the Salé neighbourhood trying
to bring people back to their religion and reminding them of their moral
duties. He also sought to bring the local population to the strict *salafism* he
had been trained in in Saudi Arabia. According to a member of the religious
affairs ministry in Morocco, after 9/11, 'Surrounded by young people who
had been radicalized by misery, he started making inflammatory remarks
against America, against the anti-Afghan alliance, against impure states who
played the game and against the enemies of God.'[8] These kinds of ideas
appear to have brought him quite a following and, as he declared to the
Arabic media in 2002, 'I discovered that the young, when they support the
ideas of a scholar or a preacher, become ardent supporters to the point of
worshipping their words and ideas.'[9]

These *salafist* preachers have been accused by the Moroccan authorities of
being part of a group called Salafiyah Jihadia, which, they claim, has links to
Al-Qa'ida. However, rather than being an organization, Salafiyah Jihadia is

more akin to a current of thought that these individuals may well subscribe to and should not be confused with a specific group as such. It is also a term used primarily by Moroccan and other security agencies to label their Islamists. As another of the most prominent *salafist* preachers, Abdelwaheb Al-Rafiki, who goes by the name Sheikh Abu Hufs and whose father, Ahmed Al-Rafiki, was an Arab Afghan veteran, explained:

> This is a media and security term because I don't know anybody who claims to represent that current. There is no organization, no group that carries that name. ... We belong to the salafist current and we support jihad and mujahideen everywhere, whether in Palestine or Afghanistan, or Kashmir, or Chechnya. Wherever there is a group of Muslims who are declaring jihad and making the word of Allah higher, we support them. If this is the meaning of salafiyah jihadia, then we are salafiyah jihadia.[10]

Others have explicitly rejected this label. Sheikh Al-Haddouci, for example, reportedly called the group 'the daughter of fornication'.[11] Fizazi also rejected the term, explaining:

> I am a Muslim who prays in the mosques of Morocco. As for what is called salafiyah jihadia, this is part of the imagination of the atheist media and I wrote in a number of newspapers that we, Ahl Sunna wal Jama'a, are not salafiyah jihadia. We pray, so why don't they call us salafiyah praying, we go to pilgrimage and they don't call us salafiyah pilgrimage. We believe in jihad for the sake of Allah, like any Muslim on the earth so why do they describe us as salafiyah jihadia. ... We are Muslims and that is it.[12]

It is no coincidence that the type of hardline ideology that was promoted by these imams was able to flourish in Morocco's sprawling slums, such as Douar Sekouila on the outskirts of Casablanca, out of which many of the country's Islamists emerged. These slums are desolate fetid places with homes constructed out of wooden planks and cardboard boxes and where there is no running water, electricity or sewers. Theft and petty criminality are the mainstay for many of the inhabitants and rates of hashish use and glue-sniffing are high. The Moroccan state ignored these slums for years on end and they gradually became almost no-go areas for the country's police forces, which were allegedly too frightened to enter them. As one journalist described the shanty town of Lahraouyine near Casablanca, 'The state is absent: no schools, no dispensaries, no post office, no savings bank, no public transport. If you are lucky, the driver of a wooden cart drawn by a skinny mule will agree to take you up the road to it, but collective taxis refuse to enter it for fear of the local Salafists; the few willing to make the trip demand a risk bonus. It is fast becoming a no man's land.'[13]

Morocco's slums proved ripe for a rejectionist ideology that strips life back to basics and encourages its followers to emulate life in the time of the Prophet and rejects society on account of its being *kafir*. In addition, this extremist doctrine offers not only a way of channelling anger and frustration but also provides hope and, importantly, a justification for the miserable situation in which the inhabitants of these places find themselves. Moreover the lack of the presence of the authorities made it relatively easy for those who could quote some verses from the Qu'ran and who believed they occupied the moral high ground to impress others and to gather a following. Indeed a number of young delinquents from these slums not only followed the *salafist* preachers like Fizazi or Kettani but also appointed themselves as sheikhs or leaders and ran their own groups that operated more like criminal gangs than Islamist movements. The leaders of these groups ran little fiefdoms in their own areas and rejected all others around them, including those of rival Islamist groups who might be operating in the neighbouring area. They included young men like Zakaria Miloudi and Youssef Fikri who tried to impose their own interpretations of *sharia* law on their own communities. Miloudi is thought to have headed a group called Assirat Al-Moustakim (Straight Path) that took control over every aspect of his group's lives, even providing them with food stalls from which they could earn a living. They imposed their rigid interpretation of Islam on the local population, meting out punishments on those who refused to comply and in some cases executing those they considered depraved.[14] The young Fikri was involved in a number of 'Islamic' executions, including that of his own uncle allegedly for having homosexual and communist tendencies. At his trial he declared, 'I have only killed the enemies of Allah and at the moment I have nothing to feel reproachful about.'[15]

## The Casablanca attacks

It was in these slums that on 16 May 2003 a group of 14 young men put bags filled with explosives on their backs and went into the centre of Casablanca to blow themselves up in the name of jihad. The targets were the Spanish club Casa de España, the Farah Hotel, which was popular with tourists, an Italian restaurant called Positano, whose owner was Jewish, and a Jewish community centre. These targets encompassed a range of symbolic enemies for those who undertook the attacks. They were a means of targeting the 'debauched' Westernized Moroccan elite who frequented these sorts of places, the 'Zionists' and also the 'Spanish colonizers'. They were also an attack on the contaminating effects of tourism. Moroccan Islamists, both radical and moderate, have long railed against what they refer to as *fasad*, a word which has many meanings but which has come to encompass rottenness, corruption, decay, prostitution, nudity and alcohol. In 2000 the PJD ran a campaign in which their supporters descended on the country's beaches to hold mass prayer sessions and to urge Moroccans not to 'debauch themselves in nudity' and to repent and return to Islam. The PJD has also held tourism responsible for the spread of AIDS in the country. The objection of these Islamists is not just towards European tourists who are using Morocco as their playground, but is also aimed at Arabs, especially from the Gulf, who are known for holidaying in Morocco because of the ease and cheapness with which it is possible to find prostitutes. Indeed Morocco has the reputation for being the brothel of the Middle East.[16] The aim of the Islamists in objecting to this kind of 'tourism' is to prove that they represent pure and untainted Morocco, as opposed to the morally bankrupt and Westernized elite that has strayed from the straight path. For those who carried out the Casablanca attacks, targeting such places was not only a way to fight against the Moroccan regime and the European powers that they believed were propping it up, but was also a way to express their hostility towards the corrupting and corrosive influence of Western culture.

All of the 16 May bombers came from the Douar Sekouila and Thomas shanty towns of the Sidi Moumen slums of Casablanca, which are home to over 300,000 inhabitants, most of them poor and illiterate. These young men were no exception. They had come together through their shared attraction to a simplistic ideology that gave them a sense of identity and in some cases were friends who had grown up together. One of the bombers, Khalid Benmoussa, lived next door to the makeshift house of Adil Taich, another of the bombers. They were well known in their local neighbourhood for trying to recruit others to their *salafist* doctrine and some of their neighbours noted that they had started behaving strangely in the six months leading up to the bombings.[17] The brother of one of the bombers, Mohammed Mhani, told a journalist that he had become very conservative, especially during the last six months before the attacks. He added that he had seen his brother on several occasions secretly watching tapes on jihad with his friends, but he never thought that he would one day commit such a terrorist act.[18]

Eleven of these young men died in the attacks, one detonated his explosives but was not killed and two others changed their minds and fled at the last moment. The story of Rachid Jalil, one of the bombers who changed his mind, is telling. Jalil was one of eight children who left school at 16 to go to work to support his family. Jalil himself admitted, 'Frankly, I was never very gifted when it came to studying.'[19] After he left his studies he found work here and there, but spent a month in prison for theft after he had been discovered redirecting an electricity supply from the main public supplier into his own quarter of the shanty town. He started becoming very religious in 2002 after he began hanging around with a group of Islamists that included two of the future suicide bombers, Adil Taich and Khalid Benmoussa. He was also influenced by a radical *salafist* sheikh, Abderrazak Rtioui, who was himself arrested shortly after the Casablanca attacks but who was released after two and a half years. Just like the countless groups of jihadists around the world, Jalil's little band of militants used to gather together to watch jihadist videos, read books about the Prophet and discuss the situation of Muslims. It seems strange to think of this group of young idealists who had most likely never even been outside of their own shanty towns suddenly taking the problems of the world's Muslims – from Chechnya, to Afghanistan to Indonesia – on their shoulders. Indeed Moroccans joked that when the bombers went into Casablanca to carry out the attacks it was the first time they had ever seen the centre of their own city.

Jalil claims that on the evening before the attacks he was called to the home of one of the bombers and was shocked to see explosives and bomb-making equipment on the floor of the apartment. As it dawned upon him what his comrades planned to do, he became increasingly uncomfortable but was too afraid to say anything. The following morning he dared to express his concerns to the ringleader, Abdelfettah Bouliqdan, and explained, 'I told him that I wasn't OK, that there would be Moroccans in the places where they were going. ... I told him, "Even if they drink and they fornicate, they might also pray. It's possible."'[20] However, Bouliqdan was having none of it and Jalil claims he pretended to go ahead with the operation because he believed he would be killed if he did not. Jalil therefore accompanied the other bombers, who, after a day of praying and reciting the Qu'ran, were prepared to meet their deaths. However, when it came to his turn to explode his bomb in the Jewish community centre, Jalil dropped his bag and ran away. He was soon found by police and in August 2003 was sentenced to death.

Jalil was not the only bomber to claim that he was pushed into carrying out the attacks. The wife of Mohammed El Omari, Fatima Tarikhi, complained that it was Abdelfettah Bouliqdan who had indoctrinated her husband who, because his bomb failed to detonate properly, injured himself in the lobby of the Farah Hotel. She explained, 'One day Bouliqdan came to ask El Omari about a car which was on sale. Since then, Bouliqdan started inviting my husband to "Karyan" Thomas [Thomas shanty town] and filled his head with extremist ideas.'[21] Fatima also claimed that when the men were planning the attacks, her husband had wanted to consult a religious scholar first and as a result 'Bouliqdan had threatened to harm his family, especially our son Zoubeir, if he refused to take part.'[22]

Whether these claims are true or simply the assertions of men who have been sentenced to death for a crime that turned the stomachs of most Moroccans, their stories demonstrate the apparent amateur nature of the attacks. Despite the fact that the Moroccans have alleged that a man called Abdelhaq Bentassir, known as Moul Sebbat and who died in mysterious circumstances in police custody after his arrest, had been behind the attacks and had given the men instruction in jihad and explained to them how to make explosives, they clearly had limited skills. Those who were supposed to bomb the Positano restaurant, for example, did not manage to get beyond the doorman and had to blow themselves up in the doorway. Three of the bombers who had allegedly planned to target the Jewish cemetery mistook a fountain that was identical to the one next to the cemetery and blew themselves up in the wrong part of the medina.[23] Furthermore, according to Rachid Jalil, Abderrahim Belcaid, who had been partnered with him to attack the Jewish community centre but who ended up exploding his bomb at the Jewish cemetery, panicked when he realized that Jalil had changed his mind about going through with the bombing. Jalil recalled, 'When I told him I was going, he appeared to be completely lost, but he didn't abandon his bag like me. ... The police told me afterwards that he had turned around and around without any goal and ended up exploding himself in the medina a few streets from there, because two men wanted to take the bag away from him.'[24]

These 'jihadists' were clearly ill-educated, inexperienced young men living on the margins of a society that offered them nothing and who, like so many others who have carried out similar attacks, believed that through their actions they were securing their passage to paradise. Yet these attacks were removed from the idealism that marked the Afghanistan experience or indeed the jihad in neighbouring Algeria. The 1980s and early 1990s were a heady time where the jihadists had a strategy and ideology in which they viewed themselves as soldiers marching towards their goal of an Islamist state. The Casablanca attacks conversely appear to be more of a cry of frustration and despair and an act of wanton destruction from a group of desperate young men with little else to live for.

## From Morocco to Madrid

Less than a year after the Casablanca bombings, on 11 March 2004 a series of explosions on packed commuter trains in the Spanish capital were to place Moroccan Islamists under the spotlight once again. Although the Spanish authorities initially indicated that they believed the Spanish terrorist group ETA might be behind the deadly attacks, the discovery of a bag containing a mobile phone connected to an explosive device subsequently led police to a Moroccan immigrant who owned a telephone shop in the Lavapiés district of Madrid. This immigrant was Jamal Zougam and it turned out that his connections extended far into the world of radical Islam, not only in Spain but in Morocco, where he had links to some of those implicated in the Casablanca bombings.

Jamal Zougam was born in Tangiers in 1973. His father was the *muez-zin* of the mosque in one of the city's districts. Jamal's mother, Aicha, had a reputation in her local neighbourhood for keeping herself to herself and the little Jamal was also described as a loner. When he was 12 years old Aicha emigrated to Spain, taking Jamal and his little sisters with her. After less than two years of being in his new country Jamal left school without any qualifications. While his mother cleaned houses for a living, Jamal and his half-brother Mohamed Chaoui, who was also arrested after the Madrid attacks, took up work wherever they could find it. Jamal spent a while selling fruit at a market, but got fed up with the little money he earned from the venture. The two brothers decided instead to set up their own telephone shop in Calle Tribulete – a street bustling with immigrant shops – in the Lavapiés quarter of Madrid, selling and repairing mobile telephones. The shop, Téléphones Nuevo Siglo, also provided a money transfer and fax service and soon became a popular hub for Moroccans. According to a former member of an immigrant association in Lavapiés, the shop also became popular as a place where one could buy fake identity cards and unblock stolen mobiles.[25] Jamal's business did sufficiently well for him to provide money for his family and to return regularly to his native Tangiers.

The picture of Jamal that emerges from his friends and family is one of a Westernized, well-integrated young man who enjoyed the pleasures of life with great gusto and who was generous to all around him. There are countless stories of this strikingly good-looking young man joking around, wearing the latest Western fashions and chasing after girls and at one point cohabiting with his Spanish girlfriend. One fellow immigrant from Tangiers noted, 'He prayed, but he also went to the gym and to the disco, for the girls.'[26] After his arrest pictures emerged of a smiling, bare-chested Jamal on the beach. However, others have described him as a 'modern Muslim' and noted that he did not drink. In fact, if one is to believe anecdotal evidence, a very different picture of this young man begins to emerge. His father told of how, during the three years before the attacks, Jamal started becoming more silent and focused. He stopped going out with his friends and stopped going to the beach. He also tried to lose his sense of humour because he wanted to repent for the carefree life he had lived before and began clashing with his family because he was insistent on trying to save them and to bring them back to the straight path. One man who used to hang around with Jamal remembered that he and his friends used to spend their time moving between little Moroccan restaurants and the various makeshift mosques that were set up in the garages of the district.[27] Another former acquaintance recalled how they used to hang around in a little group, all allegedly with Bin Ladin's picture on the screens of their mobile telephones. He noted of Jamal, 'He had no knowledge of Islam, he said that wearing a tie was against the Qu'ran because it came from the West. ... He was always right, he refused to accept the ideas of others.'[28] This acquaintance also recalled how after 9/11 Jamal shaved off his beard, presumably to avoid drawing attention to himself as a practising Muslim.

In fact the picture of a fun-loving secular Jamal that has been painted in the media appears to be more of a cliché than anything else. The same has been said of countless others who got involved in terrorism, such as the 9/11 hijacker Ziad Jarrah, whose family stressed that he lived a secular lifestyle. While it may be true that Jamal, like others, enjoyed girls and nightclubbing at one stage in his life, to try to portray him as if he was not religious at all is to deny the basic religiosity that is part and parcel of life in places like Morocco and that is replicated in these communities in Europe. As one Moroccan who knew Jamal observed, 'He joked around a lot. He was religious; we're all religious.'[29] Enjoying certain pleasures that are generally equated with the West is not the same as being secular. In fact secularism has increasingly become the domain of the elite, not just in Morocco but across the entire Arab world. For the majority of populations in the region, a basic interpretation of religion that prizes morality and culture has come to fill the gap where real educational opportunities are largely absent.

It seems that despite his outwardly secularized appearance Zougam, like many ill-educated, frustrated young men, had been drawn deep into the world of radicalism. In fact he had been investigated by Spanish police in 2001 at the behest of the Moroccan authorities because of his connections with known militants, but had been released through lack of evidence. The French security services were also keen to investigate him, as his name had been found in an address book belonging to French convert jihadist David Courtailler, who was tried in Paris in 2004.[30] When Spanish police raided Jamal's apartment in 2001, along with jihadist videos they found the telephone numbers of some well-known radicals in his diary, including Syrian militant Imad Eddin Barakat Yarkas, more commonly known as Abu Dahdah, who had been part of the first wave of Islamic militants who had helped plant radical Islam in Spain, and a number of Kurdish militants who orbited around the figure of Mullah Krekar, who was a refugee in Norway. In addition in 2001 Spanish police recorded a telephone conversation between Jamal Zougam and Abu Dahdah while Jamal was in Tangiers. From the conversation it was clear that Jamal had links with the radical Moroccan preacher Fizazi. In the conversation Jamal told the Syrian, 'On Friday, I went to pray at Fizazi's place. I spoke with him and told him that if he needed any donations we could get some from the brothers.'[31]

Abu Dahdah was one of the most important men in the Spanish radical scene until he was arrested in 2001. After he arrived in Spain in the 1980s he emerged as the ringleader of a Spanish network based in Madrid that comprised mostly Syrians. Abu Dahdah's name came to become synonymous with Al-Qa'ida in Spain as he is alleged to have had the highest contacts with senior Al-Qa'ida figures, to have been a key lynchpin in the networks that sent volunteers to train in Afghanistan, Indonesia and other jihadist strongholds and to have had close links to Abu Qatada in London.[32] After Dahdah's arrest, the remnants of the network regrouped and it took on a distinctly North African flavour. One of Dahdah's followers was the Moroccan Mustafa Al-Maymouni, who drew in his own group of mostly Moroccan followers.[33] It seems that Maymouni concentrated his efforts on developing jihadist cells both in Spain and in his native Morocco until 2003, when he was arrested by the Moroccan authorities in relation to the Casablanca bombings. After Maymouni's arrest, the Madrid cell seems to have then been taken over by his Tunisian brother-in-law, Serhane bin Abdelmajid Fakhet. Fakhet had come to Spain in the 1990s on a scholarship to study economics. However, he abandoned his studies and took up work as a real-estate agent, where he soon gained a reputation for being an excellent salesman but as someone who was not keen to mix with his Spanish colleagues. While he was a student he had worked in the restaurant attached to Madrid's M30 mosque. He used to attend classes given by the mosque's imam, Moneir Mahmoud Aly el-Messery, who recalled that Fakhet began asking questions about whether the leaders of Arab countries were real believers and whether it was acceptable to use force to spread Islam.[34] According to the imam, Fakhet was becoming increasingly extreme in his views. In 2003 he married a 16-year-old Moroccan girl who wore the *niqab*. It was under Fakhet's guidance that the group turned their attentions to carrying out a deadly attack inside Spain – an attack that was followed by the alleged bombers carrying out a joint suicide in a small apartment in the bland Madrid suburb of Leganés.

## Suicide in Leganés

At the beginning of April 2004 Spanish police, in their search for the bombers, had identified a five-storey apartment block in Calle Carmen Martín

Gaite. As the police moved in, they were met with machine-gun fire. During a series of negotiations the seven men inside threatened to blow themselves up. Inside the apartment the men began preparing for death and reportedly even tried to contact Abu Qatada in Belmarsh prison.[35] By 9pm the police decided they had no option but to storm the building. After they had broken down the front door and fired tear gas into the apartment, the men detonated their explosives, ripping the apartment open, killing themselves and mortally wounding one police officer. The explosion was so violent that the body of one of the bombers was hurled into a swimming pool in the courtyard of the building.

A look at those who committed this act of joint suicide reveals a group of mostly Moroccan men not entirely dissimilar to those who undertook the Casablanca bombings. They were all young, mostly ill educated and living on the margins of society. Although some had succeeded in making a living for themselves in Spain, they all emerged out of the same society and mindset that had been open to the militant jihadist ideology of the Casablanca bombers. Apart from Fakhet, the Tunisian, and one Algerian, Allekema Lamari, who had been arrested in 1997 in Valencia for being part of an alleged GIA cell, the rest of the 'martyrs' were from the northern Moroccan city of Tétouan. Tétouan is a place that survives largely on drugs trafficking and smuggling and is also another stronghold of Moroccan Islamism, so much so that one journalist from the city, Jamal Ouahbi, commented, 'The Pakistanis have Peshawar; us, we have Tétouan.'[36]

It would appear that despite all the talk of the *ummah*, just as in so many other jihadist cells, including that of Khalid Kelkal in France, it was their shared locality and local connections that had bound these young men together. Two of them were brothers – Mohamed and Rachid Akcha – both mechanics whose family home in Tétouan was just 200 metres away from their local mosque. Another, Abdennabi Kounjaa, also came from the rundown outskirts of Tétouan, from a miserable makeshift house that was just a few metres away from the house of another of the bombers, Jamal Ahmidan. Although Kounjaa lived in Spain, where he took work as an agricultural labourer, he was very well known for being an Islamist in his local Tétouan district, where his wife and children still lived. He sported a beard and was a regular at the mosque that was right next door to his house. His antipathy towards the West and his belief that living in Europe was in itself contaminating were very clear. From the rubble of the burnt-out apartment, investigators were able to piece together a letter that Kounjaa had written to his family in Morocco. After declaring, 'I cannot bear to live this life like a weak person, humiliated in the eyes of the infidels,' he told his parents-in-law, 'If you honour your daughter and her children do not let them emigrate to the infidel countries where one doesn't know where good can be found. Protect yourselves and protect your families from hell.'[37]

Jamal Ahmidan, however, cut a very different figure. He was also well known in his local neighbourhood, but for being a drugs dealer and petty delinquent rather than for his religiosity. In fact, according to the Moroccan police, he spent two and a half years in prison for involvement in a murder linked to a drugs case.[38] After his release he decided to try his luck abroad in Spain. Once in Madrid, where his brothers owned a shop in Lapavés, he continued selling drugs but then seems to have drifted into radical circles. He was detained for drugs offences in 1999 and, according to a Spanish official, he 'set himself up as an imam and told the guards he would come back and kill them. ... No one took him seriously then, but he already had quite a following.'[39] Ahmidan was deported after this offence, but managed to get back into Spain in 2002 using a forged Belgian passport and continued selling hashish and Ecstasy. At one point this gawky-looking young delinquent must have taken the jihadist ideology to his heart and was content to channel the proceeds of his criminal activities into the cause. Just a few minutes before he blew himself up, he, like many of the others in the Leganés apartment, called his family in Morocco to say goodbye. He told his mother to pray for him. He also allegedly told her, 'Mother, I am going to paradise. I am ready.'[40]

Ahmidan's rapid taking on of Islamism is reminiscent of many young men with limited education who take on a militant ideology with extreme speed and vigour, almost as though they had been waiting for such an opportunity to come along all their lives. This was the case for some of the Casablanca bombers as well as for some of those involved in Madrid.

Just like the Casablanca bombers, those who killed themselves in Madrid appear to have carried the same attitude and anger as those who were left behind in Morocco. Despite the fact that they lived in different countries, those in Spain retained very strong links to their home towns and seem to have been as marginalized and unable to cope with their situation as those in Morocco. They also seem to have shared the same sense of hopelessness. Although perhaps somewhat exaggerated, the comments of one Moroccan analyst about Moroccan immigrants who go to Europe are pertinent. He noted:

> They leave one ghetto only to join another ... that is made up of a number of small ghettos made up from those of the same nationality and sometimes from people from the same town of origin. The same structures are there: illegal trade, electronic goods accessible to everyone, and mosques run by imams who escape all controls. If one adds to that the use of a foreign language which makes it even more difficult to control, a greater margin of freedom and space

to express oneself and a degree of financial ease, plus a degree of stability, one finds a Moroccan ghetto in Europe that is one thousand times more dangerous than a bad quarter of Casablanca.[41]

## Afghanistan, the GICM and the Al-Qa'ida connection

Immediately after the Casablanca and Madrid attacks, as investigators in Spain and Morocco began the long search to determine exactly who had been behind the crimes, the name of Al-Qa'ida was on everyone's lips. While it may well be the case that individuals linked to Bin Ladin and Al-Qa'ida were in some way involved in the attacks, the problem is that both Morocco and Spain at one point or another have cited so many different groups and individuals as being responsible that the issue has become confused. From Al-Qa'ida to the Moroccan Islamic Combatant Group (GICM), Salafiyah Jihadia, Abu Hafs Al-Masri Brigades, the Mufti Brigades and Ansar Al-Qa'ida – all these organizations have been thrown into the pot at one time or another. Likewise the names of individuals from Abu Musab Al-Suri to Abdelkarim Al-Majati to Mohamed Al-Guerbouzi, Mohamed Fizazi to Abu Musab Al-Zarqawi have also been cited. Much of the Moroccan evidence looks to have been derived from confessions extracted while individuals have been held in custody, which in some cases they have gone on to retract once in court. There certainly appears to have been an overlap in the radical networks operating in Morocco and Spain, but exactly who was responsible for the attacks remains, for the time being, an unanswered mystery. As a result both cases appear to have been muddled up somehow, with some major assumptions being made on both sides.

In the Casablanca case, while the Moroccan security services wasted no time in rounding up hundreds of local young men suspected of having Islamist sympathies, the monarchy was anxious to try to emphasize that the bombings were the work of 'outside forces' and not simply a response to conditions inside the kingdom. In July 2003 the Moroccan regime claimed that the attacks had been directly ordered by Abu Musab Al-Zarqawi and were part of a larger plan to hit several other Moroccan cities.[42] It also asserted that the attacks had been linked to a series of car bombings in Riyadh in Saudi Arabia that had occurred just days before the Casablanca attacks. One year after the bombings the head of Morocco's National Security, General Hamidou Laanigri, confirmed that Moroccan members of Al-Qa'ida were behind the attacks and that the money had come via Abu Musab Al-Zarqawi.[43]

The Moroccans also pointed to the Moroccan Islamic Combatant Group (GICM) as being responsible. Little is known about this shadowy organization, but it appears to have been formed by a group of Moroccans in Afghanistan in the 1990s, most likely the group that split off from the Libyan Islamic Fighting Group. Indeed in 1995 the *Al-Ansar* bulletin is reported to have published a statement signed by the group denying that it was simply a follower of the LIFG and asserting that it was a group in its own right. The Moroccan regime accused Mohamed Al-Guerbouzi, who has been residing in the UK for many years, of presenting the project to establish the GICM to Osama Bin Ladin and of founding the group from his base in London.[44] Indeed the movement seems to operate primarily in Europe, although Guerbouzi denies any involvement with it. However, the GICM never really gathered the strength and momentum that groups such as the LIFG, the GIA and the GSPC did. One cannot help but wonder whether the GICM has become somewhat of a free-for-all label that has been given to any Moroccan jihadist who happened to have passed through Afghanistan.

The Moroccan regime's desire to focus on the links of the GICM or of Al-Qa'ida to the Casablanca bombings is not unique to the kingdom. All of the regimes of the region have latched on to the widespread panic in the West and sought to cite international terrorism as the root cause of their own militant Islamist movements, largely as a means of deflecting attention away from the very real socio-economic and political conditions inside their own countries that fuelled support for radicalism in the first place. Indeed Libya's leader, Muammar Qadhafi, has often framed his battle with Libyan insurgents in terms of the international war on terror. Likewise the Algerian regime has sought to overplay the international dimensions of its own civil war. These regimes remain unwilling to even acknowledge their own responsibility in helping to create this radical trend. In a very telling comment, Morocco's General Hamidou Laanigri noted, 'Since the spectacular attacks on Madrid, attention has focused on the Moroccans, but it is false to assert that Morocco produces terrorism.'[45] Even the PJD Islamist party tried to claim that the ideology that spawned the attacks had nothing to do with Morocco. However, they tried to capitalize on the opportunity and claimed that they should be given greater freedom within the kingdom so that they could prevent this kind of radicalism.[46]

As for the Madrid attacks, Al-Qa'ida's involvement appeared to have been confirmed just two days after the bombings when a Spanish television station called Telemadrid was informed by an anonymous caller that there was a videotape in a rubbish bin near one of Madrid's main mosques. On the tape a man referring to himself as Abu Dujan Al-Afghani, who claimed to be Al-Qa'ida's military spokesman in Europe, announced that the Madrid attacks had been carried out because of Spain's cooperation 'with the criminal Bush and his allies'.[47] In addition, the London-based *Al-Quds* newspaper also received an e-mail from a group calling itself the Abu Hafs Al-Masri Brigades, who claimed they had attacked Spain on behalf of Al-Qa'ida. Whether these messages were really from Al-Qa'ida or indeed from anyone linked to the bombings is unclear.

At the same time much was made of a document that had appeared on a jihadist website in December 2003 which was widely assumed to have been written by Al-Qa'ida. The 42-page document, titled 'Jihadi Iraq: Hopes and Dangers', was a long, fairly mundane diatribe about the situation in Iraq which laid out the politics of the conflict and of the coalition partners. One of the sections was dedicated to Spain and asserted that it was a weak democracy that did not have the sophistication of the British. This document has been interpreted by some commentators as evidence that the authors were developing a strategy to hit Spain just ahead of the Spanish elections due on 14 March. Much was made of the phrase carried in the document, 'We think that the Spanish government cannot bear more than two or three attacks at maximum.' However, this phrase was referring directly to the possibility of attacking Spanish troops in Iraq in order to force them to withdraw, and the whole document is concerned with the ousting and attacking of foreign forces inside Iraq rather than with launching attacks elsewhere. Therefore to assert that the Madrid attacks were implicit in this document may be to overstate the case.

## The Madrid trial

After four years of gathering evidence and making arrests, the Madrid trial finally took place in 2007. There was much anticipation in the run-up to and during the trial that many questions would at last be answered about exactly what had occurred, who was involved and why the attacks had taken place at all. There was also a strong sense among some of the families of the victims that some sort of justice would be done. However, the outcome of the trial came as something of a surprise, not only because many of the sentences were much less harsh than had been expected but also because a number of the suspects were acquitted. In addition it appeared that the Spanish authorities had not been able to pinpont any of the real masterminds behind the attacks and most of those who stood trial seemed to be small players operating around the margins of jihadist activism who had limited and in some cases questionable links to the bombers. As a result the trial ended up posing more questions than it answered. Moreover, as Fred Halliday has argued, in all the disappointment it seemed to have been almost forgotten that 'of the dozen or so who committed the crime of 11 March 2004, eight are already dead (seven in confrontation with police outside Madrid three weeks later [the Leganés suicides] and an eighth reportedly going to fight in Iraq)'.[48]

Twenty-eight defendants went before the courts. Although they included an Egyptian, an Algerian, a Lebanese, a couple of Syrians and a number of Spaniards, 14 of the defendants and the vast majority of those who were found guilty were Moroccan. Indeed when the verdicts were pronounced in November 2007 six out of the eight who were acquitted were Spanish. Another of those found not guilty was the Egyptian Rabei Osman, who had been accused of being one of the architects of the attacks and who was arrested in Italy in June 2004. Osman had been living in Milan where he was a known militant and where his telephone and apartment were being bugged by the Italian authorities. The allegations about his involvement in the Madrid attacks were based largely on a recorded telephone conversation between Osman and a man called Yahia Mawad in which Osman is alleged to have acknowledged that those who had blown themselves up in Leganés were his friends and that he had been responsible for the bombings. He was accused of having boasted to Mawad, 'The operation in Madrid was prepared by me. Do you understand? ... It was my project, the group, do you understand? ... I was the thread behind the operation.'[49] However, the group of experts who examined the transcript for the Spanish courts declared that the translation by the Italian security services had been incorrect and that while Osman had stated that the men were his friends, he had said that he did not have any knowledge about what they were planning. In addition, while Spanish prosecutors claimed that Osman had visited Spain on several occasions, the court decided that there was no indication that he had been in contact with members of the cell who carried out the attacks. Osman's acquittal in particular provoked shock and indignation, in part because he had referred to those who had committed suicide in Leganés as his friends. Yet the court was unable to find any evidence that he even knew about the attacks, let alone that he ordered or coordinated them.

In the end only three of the defendants were convicted of the attacks and they were given multiple sentences for the murders and attempted murders. Among them was Jamal Zougam, who was found guilty of 191 murders and 1,856 attempted murders and sentenced to 30 years in prison for each of the former and 20 years for each of the latter. He was also sentenced to 12 years' imprisonment for belonging to a terrorist organization. Zougam continued to maintain his innocence throughout the trial and complained that he still did not know why he had been arrested on 13 March 2004 and that he had been at home at the time of the bombings. He told the court, 'On 10 March I did some sport and returned to my house and went to sleep. I woke up at ten in the morning on 11 March and contacted my brother to find out about the traffic situation.'[50] He also complained bitterly that his conviction had been based on an alleged sighting of him by a protected witness at the station just before the bombs went off.

Fellow Moroccan Otman Al-Ghanoui, who had left his native Morocco to come to Spain in 2001, was also found guilty of 191 murders and 1,856 attempted murders and received multiple sentences. Like Zougam he continued to insist on his innocence. When asked by the court why he had come to Spain in the first place Al-Ghanoui replied, 'Like all immigrants who come here. To better my situation.'[51] After his arrival he had taken on a number of casual jobs including working as a plumber and a mason before taking up some building work at the farm in Chinchon where the explosives used in the bombing are alleged to have been hidden. Al-Ghanoui insisted that he had no linkage to Jamal Ahmidan other than through the job he had taken at the farm. He admitted that he had also seen Serhane bin Abdelmajid Fakhet at Chinchon, but claimed that the Tunisian only spoke to Ahmidan.[52]

The other defendant who was given multiple sentences was the Spaniard José Emilio Suarez Trashorras, who was found guilty of supplying some of the explosives for the attacks. Trashorras is a former miner from Asturias in northern Spain who had been a police informant and a drugs trafficker with supposed ties to Jamal Ahmidan, although he was not a convert to Islam. He is known to suffer from mental illness.

The other, mainly Moroccan defendants in the trial who were found guilty were given sentences ranging from three to 23 years in prison for complicity in the attacks or more commonly for belonging to a terrorist group. Many of those given lesser sentences appear to have had only loose connections to those who were behind the attacks and seemed totally bewildered at finding themselves in court accused of being behind this heinous crime. Indeed when questioned many of them struggled to express themselves in either Spanish or Arabic, revealing in many cases their poor education and their clear despair at their own situations. In fact most looked totally overwhelmed by the experiece.[53] Unlike figures such as Mohamed Bouyeri, who when he was convicted in the Netherlands of the killing of Dutch film maker Theo Van Gogh declared that he had acted out of religious conviction and showed no remorse, all of the defendants in this trial insisted on their innocence, many of them making emotional pleas to the court. Abdelilah El Fadoual Al-Akil, who was sentenced to nine years in prison, told the court, 'Above all I would like to show to all of Spain, and to all the world, that I am totally innocent. ... And I would like to say to the families of the victims, I feel a lot for them and I still cry for them and with them. And I want to say that I am neither a terrorist, nor a delinquent. I am a Muslim, but I don't, I am not very practising.'[54] He is also reported to have said, 'I wake up every morning and I ask the mirror, Why am I here in prison?'[55]

Similarly Hassan Al-Heski, who was sentenced to 15 years in prison for belonging to the Moroccan Islamic Combatant Group, impressed upon the court, 'I don't accept any attack against innocent people and children. Islam is innocent of those kinds of actions, which go against its principles and values. Every Muslim condemns such actions. This is a crime that cannot be forgiven.'[56] He also questioned the logic of his alleged connection to the Spanish terrorist organization ETA, asking, 'How? How could I be connected to or have a relationship with a terrorist organisation like ETA? I don't speak Spanish, nor do I write it. How?'[57] Indeed in spite of the fact that many of the defendants had lived in Spain for a number of years, they chose to be questioned in Arabic, suggesting that they had limited command of Spanish.

In fact the majority of those who were convicted were young, ill-educated Moroccan immigrants whose profiles are not dissimilar to those who blew themselves up in the Leganés apartment. They were mostly legally resident in Spain, having been in the country for a number of years, and had survived by taking up various casual jobs. Some had come with their families, while others had only come to Spain recently in search of employment and a better standard of living. However, according to some reports, the vast majority were living at subsistence levels.[58]

Some have suggested that like many young immigrants who get involved in the world of radical Islam these men were consuming a diet of Saudi satellite television stations and videos of the jihad. However, the commitment of many of this group to the jihad was seemingly limited and appears to have been based mainly on their attendance at meetings where they discussed jihad, their having contacts with members of the group who had blown themselves up, or their being involved in illicit funding activities.[59] Abdelmajid Bouchar, for example, who was sentenced to 18 years in prison and who had escaped from the apartment in Leganés after warning the others that they were surrounded by police and who fled to Serbia where he was arrested in 2005, was just 20 years old at the time of the attacks and seems to have drifted into militant circles out of desperation. He had come to Spain to join his father who was working in Europe in order to send money back to his family in Morocco. When Bouchar arrived in Spain he was reportedly shocked that his father was no longer willing to give him money, as he had done in Morocco, but expected him to work. However, rather than get a job, Bouchar spent his time playing sport and used his father's house as a place to eat and sleep.[60] His father became so frustrated by his son's unwillingness to work that he eventually kicked him out of the house. It was not long before Bouchar, who had left without any money or means of making any, was picked up by the group accused of the Madrid bombings. They provided him with accommodation and looked after him, apparently able to tap into the religiosity that was just under the surface, and as a result his life soon became tied up with theirs.

In fact many of the Moroccan defendants in the trial, including Bouchar, come from two areas in Morocco that are known for being highly conservative places where religiosity is strong.[61] These areas are the northern mountainous regions of Djaballa and the Rif, both known for producing scholars of *fiqh*. As one Moroccan commentator has noted, for anyone coming from these areas, 'the storage of religiosity in the conscious and sub-conscious ... is doubled'.[62] This does not mean that those from these regions are more likely to advocate jihad, but rather that their religiosity and simplicity make them a more vulnerable target to those seeking logistical assistance in the name of Islam. Rachid Aglif, who was born in 1979 and who was sentenced to 18 years' imprisonment at the trial, came from the town of Beni Ghar in Djaballa. He claims that he simply attended a meeting that some of the bombers had been present at, and there seems to be little concrete evidence of his involvement in the actual bombings. Aglif was in fact from the same tribe, the Ait Touzin, as another of the defendants, Yousef Belhadj, who was sentenced to 12 years in prison and who the Spanish accused of being Abu Dujan Al-Afghani, the figure in the video that was released shortly after the attacks who claimed to be an Al-Qa'ida spokesman and who took responsibility for the attacks. Theo Van Gogh's killer is also reported to have come from this same tribe.[63]

In fact family ties appear to have played a major role in the arrest of some of the defendants, and many of those convicted were related to figures either in Madrid or in Morocco who had been involved in militancy in some way. Yousef Belhadj, for example, is the brother of Maymoun Belhadj, mentioned above, who is in prison in Morocco accused of being involved in the Casablanca attacks. They have another brother, Mohamed, who is believed to have joined the Iraqi jihad and who also allegedly rented the Leganés apartment. Yousef Belhadj's nephew, Mohamed Moussaten, who was born in 1984, was also charged in the trial but was ultimately acquitted. Hamid Ahmidan, meanwhile, who was sentenced to 23 years in prison, is the brother of Jamal Ahmidan, who blew himself up in Leganés and who had reportedly become radicalized in prison in Morocco.

It would appear therefore that like those who blew themselves up in Leganés, the group who stood trial were in many cases connected to one another through family or friendship ties and had drifted into jihadist circles. While some of them, such as Bouchar, may have become radicalized while they were in Spain, many of them had connections to or family members who were involved in similar types of activism in Morocco itself. Therefore, while for these individuals being in Spain may have been a factor in their radicalism, it does not explain why other members of their families who had not been in Europe were also of a militant bent. Rather it would seem more logical to suggest that their own family backgrounds and experiences at home held a far greater sway in the radicalization process than their experiences in Europe. Moreover to suggest that these individuals became radical because they were socially marginalized fails to take into account the fact that they were members of the Moroccan community in Spain and as such in many cases had strong family and social networks around them. As with many of those who become radical, they in fact shunned their own families and communities as they became increasingly drawn into the world of militancy.

The vast majority of those on trial had no experience of military training or of fighting in jihads abroad and most had seemingly led very sheltered lives. One of the main exceptions in this context, however, was Hassan Al-Heski, whose brother, Hussein Al-Heski, is wanted in Saudi Arabia and who was arrested in Belgium. Hussein is also known to have been with fellow Moroccan Abdelkarim Al-Majati who was killed by Saudi security forces in Al-Ras in 2004. The family come from a Sahrawi tribe in south west Morocco. Hassan Al-Heski, who was much older than many of the other defendants, having been in his early 40s at the time of the bombings, left Morocco for France in 1986, from where he went to Pakistan where he spent two years studying in the Islamic university of Karachi. He then moved to Syria where he spent seven years studying at the Central Islamic Institute in Damascus and where he married a Syrian woman and had a family. He also spent some time in Belgium where, like many Moroccans, he had an extended family network. He also lived for a while in the Canary Islands, a magnet for many Sahrawis, where he was arrested in 2004.

It has been alleged by the Moroccans that in 2003 Hassan Al-Heski, who was in Syria at that time, was planning to join the Iraqi jihad. However, differences allegedly broke out between him and another Moroccan, Khalid Al-Aziq, over who should be the emir of their group.[64] The falling out was such that Al-Heski did not follow Al-Aziq into Iraq but went to the Canary Islands instead. In spite of his experiences, however, at the trial Al-Heski denied that he had ever been in Afghanistan. He also denied that he had any connection to the mysterious Moroccan Islamic Combatant Group – the crime for which he was ultimately convicted. When asked in the court if he had any relation to this organization he declared, 'No, I don't have any relation with it. This group does not exist.'[65]

Given his experiences and his connections to figures such as Al-Aziq, not to mention his own brother, it would appear that Al-Heski was far more involved in the world of jihad than many of the other defendants. As such it has been alleged that he was one of the main figures involved in organizing the Madrid attacks. However, his exact role in the bombings is still not clear. As explained above, various different figures and organizations have been accused of masterminding the attacks at various times. These include Abu Dahdah, Mohamed Rabei Osman and the Syrian Mohamed Dabbas, the latter of whom was sentenced to 12 years in prison at the trial. Indeed many have suggested that while the Moroccans provided the logistical support and the brawn for the attacks, the brains behind them must have been Syrian or Egyptian. Such suggestions most likely arise from the fact that Moroccans are generally considered to be on the lowest rung of the terrorist and the immigrant ladder, in part as a result of their poor education but also because they played such a limited role in militant activity during the war in Afghanistan. Indeed the theoreticians of the jihad have tended to come from Egypt, Syria and Jordan rather than from North Africa. Moreover it is true that many Syrian Islamists who settled in Spain, including those who fled in the 1980s when the Al-Assad regime suppressed the Muslim Brotherhood, were from the middle classes and were well educated. A similar pattern is reflected in the broader Islamic community in Spain that continues to be dominated by Syrians in spite of the fact that the vast majority of the community is now Moroccan. Indeed one of the most important Muslim organizations in Spain, the Unión de Comunidades Islámicas de España (UCIDE), is run by the Syrian Riay Tatari, and the mosque, La Gran Mezquita de Valencia, is run by a group of Syrians in spite of the fact that the community in Valencia is made up mostly of Moroccans and increasingly Algerians. Therefore, although it seems that the Moroccans were involved in the Madrid bombings at the operational end, it would not be surprising if those from other communities were responsible for the planning and coordination of the Madrid attacks in some capacity.

However, there is still no ultimate proof of exactly who or which group was responsible. In spite of all the talk of Al-Qa'ida, the trial was not able to pinpoint any evidence of the defendants' links to this organization. Even Yousef Belhadj, whom the Spanish authorities claimed had referred to himself in the video as an Al-Qa'ida spokesman in Europe, appeared to have no real contacts with Al-Qa'ida, but rather was tied into Moroccan networks through his family. As such, rather than being depicted as a grand globalized attack, the trial has provided little evidence to contradict the suggestion that the Madrid bombings were largely a Moroccan affair and that those involved had links, often through family ties, with militants inside Morocco itself or within the Moroccan community in Belgium, another centre where there is increasing evidence of Moroccan Islamist activism. Indeed one of the defendants, Mohamed Larbi Ben Salam, who was sentenced to 12 years in prison for facilitating the fleeing of Mohamed Aflah to Iraq after the bombings, is still wanted by the Moroccan authorities for being part of a *salafist* group in Morocco. When he has served his sentence in Spain it is expected that he will be handed over to Rabat to be tried there. As Fred Halliday has correctly argued, in spite of the talk of global linkages, groups in North Africa itself are 'the most likely source of inspiration and organisation' for the Madrid bombers.[66]

As for the specific motivations for the attacks, this is another area that is likely to remain a mystery. Indeed, whether the objective of the Madrid bombings was to influence the outcome of the Spanish elections of 14 March and to force Spain out of Iraq has yet to be proven. One Spanish official quoted in an article that appeared in the *Washington Post* in October 2004 on this issue noted, 'It's really an analysis more than a proven fact. ... We certainly don't have any statement that that's why they did it or anything.'[67] Spanish authorities claimed that they had discovered the remains of a video in the rubble of the Leganés apartment and when they had managed to analyse it found a farewell message seemingly recorded by Fakhet and two of the other suicide bombers, who read a statement in the name of the Al-Mufti Brigades and Ansar Al-Qa'ida in which they gave Spain one week to 'leave Muslim lands'. The statement also allegedly warned, 'You know that you are not safe, and you know that Bush and his administration will bring only destruction. We will kill you anywhere and in any manner.'[68]

However, whether the desire to force Spain out of Iraq was the key motivating factor behind the attacks remains questionable. It may have been that far from a deliberate strategy to influence the Spanish political scene, Madrid was targeted simply because the opportunity to strike raised its head. Indeed the allusion to issues such as Iraq has become part of the contemporary rhetoric of these types of militant Islamist movements who try to emulate the style and the success of Bin Ladin and Al-Qa'ida. In fact Iraq is simply another issue that has been added to the existing but very real 'shopping list' of grievances repeatedly cited by radicals and moderates alike, such as Palestine, Bosnia and Afghanistan. The case of Iraq may well have fuelled anger, but it was likely that so too did other factors, including the particularities of the Moroccan–Spanish relationship. Rabei Osman Ahmed referred to the former Spanish prime minister as 'that dog Aznar' in a recorded telephone conversation.[69] In the same vein, the brother of one of those wanted for the Madrid attacks, Said Berraj, said in an interview with a Moroccan newspaper, 'Aznar [José Maria] always wanted to harm the

Moroccans and he had even sworn to see to it that this country loses its place as one of the leaders of the Arab world and of Africa. ... Accusing the Moroccans serves the interests of Spain.'[70] In fact in the video attributed to the Leganés bombers, Fakhet even made a reference to the historic period of Islamic rule in Spain referred to as Al-Andalus. He declared, 'You know of the Spanish crusade against Muslims, and that not much time has passed since the expulsion from Al-Andalus and the tribunals of the Inquisition. ... Blood for blood! Destruction for destruction!'[71] Although nostalgia for Al-Andalus has tended to be the domain of Arab intellectuals who hark back to this time primarily for its flourishing cultural and scholarly achievements, it has come to be cited in the discourse of some contemporary radical Islamist leaders, who frame it in terms of the confrontation between Islam and the West. Even Bin Ladin picked up on this historical reference in October 2001 when, in a video-taped message, he exclaimed, 'Let the whole world know that we shall never accept that the tragedy of Al-Andalus would be repeated in Palestine.'[72] Radical preacher Mohamed Fizazi also picked up on the Al-Andalus image in some of his fiery sermons, accusing the Spanish of still occupying the territory. Pointedly he also referred to the two Spanish enclaves of Ceuta and Melia that are in Morocco as another example of Spain's occupation of Muslim lands.[73]

Despite this kind of discourse, as the Casablanca bombings showed, these individuals did not need a war in Iraq or the historical experience of Al-Andalus, or even the perceived aggression of Spain towards its former colonial possession to become radical to the point of being prepared to commit violence. Militancy had been brewing both inside Morocco and among Moroccan communities in Spain, and in Europe more widely, since the 1990s. Therefore it would seem that in fact these young Moroccans at the operational end of the Madrid attacks, just like those in Casablanca, were angry individuals who through their desperate suicide attempts sought some sort of personal salvation.

# CHAPTER 9

# THE LONDON BOMBINGS

After the 9/11 attacks, Britain, like many other European states, feared that it might become the next terrorist target. With its reputation for hosting radicals from all over the world in what had been dubbed as 'Londonistan', many believed that foreign residents such as those who had perpetrated the 9/11 attacks in the US would now turn their attention towards America's transatlantic ally. The stream of arrests of terrorist suspects in the UK after 9/11, mostly first-generation immigrants from North Africa, seemed to confirm this suspicion. However, when the London bombings occurred on 7 July 2005, it soon became clear that the attacks had in fact been perpetrated by a group of young men who had been brought up in the UK. Three of the bombers, Mohammed Siddique Khan, Hasib Mir Hussain and Shehzad Tanweer, were British nationals of Pakistani origin and the fourth, Germaine Lindsay, was a British convert to Islam.[1] As details about these men came into the public domain in the aftermath of the bombings, they appeared to have been well-integrated family men who were active members of their local communities. The attacks therefore prompted much soul searching about what could have pushed these British men to launch such savage attacks on their fellow citizens.

As these questions were grappled with, a series of assumptions turned into almost given truths about the nature of the bombers, what motivated them and what the nature of their relationship to their own communities was. It soon came to be considered by many as a given that these men were motivated by a sense of alienation and marginalization driven largely by an identity crisis arising out of their feeling that they did not belong either in mainstream white British society or in the home country of their parents, where their immersion in Western culture made them feel like outsiders. It was also assumed that these men, along with other young radical second-generation south Asians, had been pushed into the hands of extremists because of the gulf that had developed between them and their parents' generation. This gulf, it was argued, was especially acute between the youth and the mosque elders who could not relate to the challenges of being a

Muslim in contemporary British society. In addition it became common currency in some circles to cite British policy in Iraq, and Western foreign policy more widely, as responsible for the radicalization not only of these men but of others who tacitly supported the acts. Many also pointed the finger at the so-called 'covenant of security', which, it was argued, had represented a tacit agreement between radicals and the British authorities that they would coexist peacefully but which had been broken by the actions of the British state. Yet on closer inspection this set of rather simplistic assumptions tell us little about the nature of radicalization and do not get us any closer to really understanding why these young men did what they did on that July morning.

Although there are many Muslim communities in Britain originating from various countries, the new wave of 'home-grown' terrorists has emerged mostly out of the country's south Asian communities that make up around two-thirds of Britain's Muslim population. Yet it was not just any south Asian community. The majority of these young radicals have come from one community in particular. From Omar Sheikh, who was accused of killing American journalist Daniel Pearl in 2002, to the two suicide bombers Asif Mohammed Hanif and Omar Khan Sharif, who went to Israel in 2003 to undertake suicide missions, to the fertilizer plot of 2004, to the London bombers, to those accused of being behind the alleged disrupted plot to blow up flights over the Atlantic, which was uncovered in 2006 – all these have been primarily second-generation Pakistanis. This came as rather a relief to a number of Arabs in the UK who felt somehow vindicated by the fact that the terror spotlight had shifted away from them on to the Asians. As Saudi columnist for the London-based Al-Sharq Al-Awsat newspaper, Abdelrahman Rashid, noted, 'This new plot has shown that Arabs no longer hold the keys to fundamentalist terror.'[2] Rashid also explained how this generation of Pakistani militants in Britain had been the students of the first wave of radical Arab Islamists who settled in Europe in previous decades but had now come to overtake their teachers in militancy. Indeed, while the number of second-generation Pakistanis espousing militant ideas or prepared to commit an act of suicide terrorism remains an extremely small minority, the phenomenon suggests that this community merits a closer look.

## New generation

Around 70 per cent of Britain's Pakistani community originate from the impoverished rural Mirpur region of Pakistani Kashmir and are concentrated predominantly in the Midlands and northern England.[3] Most of the first-generation immigrants from this region came to Britain for work and had little or no schooling. As one journalist noted, 'they made a huge cultural and geographical leap to settle in the UK – the dislocation is hard to imagine.'[4] Like any community forced to settle in a new environment, there was a deep concern about losing their cultural values, and from the early years of their arrival these new communities did their utmost to preserve their own religion and culture within their adopted environment. As Ehsan Masood has noted, 'South Asian households (particularly Bangladeshi and Pakistani) are ones in which the practice of religion remains a serious aspect of identity and daily life.'[5] The community set up its own mosques and religious schools and continued to impress upon the younger generation the importance of Islam, not only as a faith but also as a cultural identifier. As Pakistani commentator Maruf Khwaja somewhat bitterly reflects, 'The majority of the first wave of Muslim immigrants to Britain originated among the peasantry of south Asia and Africa. ... The effects on their children can be imagined: children of a Mirpuri textile worker in northwest England had to muddle through homework without any assistance or supervision from illiterate parents, who in turn were more concerned to indoctrinate their kids with the only thing they knew – the rudiments of their religion as taught to them by the village *mullah* at home.'[6] The mosque and imam still play a hugely important social function within these communities and remain 'the hub of social power'.[7] Indeed a feature of life for many children within this community continues to be the *madrassa*. Although *madrassa* is the Arabic word for school, it is generally a place set up specifically to teach children to recite the Qu'ran by heart. Many children from south Asian families in the UK spend two hours after school in the mosque learning to recite the Qu'ran in Arabic – a language they do not understand. As Ehsan Masood has complained, 'The Qu'ran is taught across the Muslim world (including in Britain) as a set of eternal truths with little reference to its historical context. Anyone who can quote from it is looked up to with reverence in what is still a strongly oral culture.'[8] Even the family of one of the London bombers, Shehzad Tanweer, which fellow community members described as 'not very religious', dutifully tried to teach all of their children, including Shehzad, to recite the Qu'ran as a matter of course.[9]

For some of these immigrants who arrived in the UK there was a strong fear that their children would become tainted by the easy pleasures of Western culture. In order to try to prevent the younger generation from going astray, many families took their children back to the homeland at regular intervals to undergo what Maruf Khwaja describes as 'a season of Islamic indoctrination and to get the Britishness out of their system'.[10] This practice is not unique to the Pakistani community but is also common among Arab communities in Europe who fear too that their children will be somehow contaminated by Western vices and who understandably do not want their youngsters to lose the values that they themselves grew up with. Daniel Pearl's killer, Omar Sheikh, underwent such an experience. His father was allegedly so concerned about Omar's penchant for drinking, smoking and chasing after girls that he moved the family back to Lahore for three years while Omar was a teenager to try to set him back on the straight path.[11] Similarly London bomber Hasib Hussain, who was just 18 years old when he carried out the attack, had been sent to Pakistan for a period after becoming a troublesome teenager.[12]

There is a general sense within some parts of these communities, as in some Arab communities, that being introverted and quiet and going to the mosque regularly to do one's religious duty is a positive attribute. For a community, which like many others is struggling with issues related to drug and alcohol abuse among the youth and whose children are moving away and into more Westernized lifestyles, those who stay out of trouble and who dutifully attend the mosque and stay in line with their parents' traditions are often considered as exemplary. In fact in the 1990s one of the bombers, Mohammed Siddique Khan, had become part of a gang going by the name 'The Mullah Boys', which was formed to try to rid the community of its drug problems.[13] On occasions the gang would forcibly kidnap young drug addicts with the consent of their parents and hold them in a flat in Beeston where they would cleanse them of their habit. According to one ex-drug user in the area, these kinds of activities were welcomed by the older generation who were too scared to tackle the drug dealers themselves. Indeed the brother of Mohammed Siddique Khan, Gultasab, reiterated the fact that the older generation welcomed the youth becoming more religious, saying that the common wisdom was that it was 'Better them being Wahhabi than on drugs'.[14] In fact, according to Gultasab, although his brother's radicalization is often portrayed as having been a sudden enlightenment, it was a gradual change that occurred over years not months. Moreover, although Khan is often portrayed as having lived a secular lifestyle, he attended Friday prayers with his family from a young age and also fasted during Ramadan.

After the bombings, several members of the community who knew the bombers expressed their shock that these men could have committed such crimes because they were known for their sense of duty and their commitment to their faith. One man who worked in Shehzad's family fish and chip shop in Leeds said of him, 'Shehzad was very religious. He used to go to the mosque a lot. He didn't like girls. He didn't have many friends but he was a nice, quiet person.'[15] In a similar vein a former imam of the Hounslow mosque, who lived opposite Asif Mohammed Hanif and who went to Israel to commit a suicide operation, said of him, 'I found him quiet and reserved.

He was very interested in education and spent a lot of time in Syria learning Arabic. When I saw the picture in the paper I couldn't believe a person like this would be able to do such a thing.'[16] Another acquaintance at his local mosque, Suleman Chachia, said of Hanif, 'He seemed to be a very polite, well-spoken and gentle person.'[17] Indeed the same was said of Mohamed Bouyeri, Theo Van Gogh's killer. The imam at his local mosque noted, 'Everybody said he was a good boy.'[18] These types of comments are repeated over and over again by neighbours and community members when asked about those who have committed acts of violence. However, it is not clear why one should imagine that anyone going to commit an act of terrorism could not act kindly towards their own community. The repeated tales of the bombers being kind, generous young men who served their own communities, especially the ringleader, Mohammed Siddique Khan, who was known for his work as a learning mentor at the Hillside Primary School in Beeston, does not mean that they could not carry out what was primarily a political act. Indeed, for these young men, blowing themselves up was the ultimate sacrifice for their fellow Muslims and they considered martyrdom to be the highest pinnacle for a good and committed Muslim.

Therefore religious commitment has always been strong within these communities, just as it has been in Pakistan itself, and to suggest that the young have taken on a new fervour for Islam in response to living within Western society is somewhat misconstrued. Rather it would appear that the younger generation simply added a more vociferous political dimension to their religiosity, and with that dimension came an overtly strict observance of Islamic duties and a very public display of this new orthodoxy, such as adopting 'Islamic dress' as a political symbol. Within this context some of these young radicals considered themselves to be using Islam to rebel against their parents' generation, which they dismissed as being stuffed with local traditions that were not part of Islam. As one young British Pakistani noted on an Islamic forum, 'It can only be for the best when we separate ourselves from non-Islamic culture. My parents don't bother arguing with me when I give them the Islamic doctrine regarding a matter. They know I will flatly refuse their wishes. We need to make Islamic doctrine over-rule parents.'[19] Incidentally these kinds of sentiments fly in the face of the importance that Islam and the Qu'ran specifically place on respecting one's parents and family.

However, this purist attitude towards the faith is nothing new and is not unique to this community or the particular generational ruptures within it. It is exactly the approach used by revivalist Islamist movements all over the Islamic world, which seek to strip Islam of its local traditions and to bolt politics on to the faith, enabling Muslims to express their frustrations with the state through the lens of Islam. This new politicized Islamism that spread across the Islamic world from the 1980s onwards was simply reflected among Muslim migrant communities in Europe. This added political dimension was also a reflection of the failure of the left-wing movement. As Kenan Malik has explained, 'Today "radical" in an Islamic context means someone who espouses a fundamentalist theology. Twenty years ago it meant a secularist who challenged the power of the mosques. The expunging of that radical secularist tradition has played an important part in the rise of Islamic militancy in this country.' [20] This view has been endorsed by Dilwar Hussein who observed of the Bangladeshi community in the UK, 'Between the 1960s and the 1980s, Bangladeshis in London used secular, socialist ideology to combat injustice – a system of thinking that could then still lay plausible claim to the future. ... Bengali secularists appear today as archaic as the political left. ... The fight of secularists against racism and poverty appears bland compared to the ardent certainties of religion.' [21] The gap between the generations therefore is not one of religiosity but of politics. Moreover even this gap is not as clear cut as is often suggested. It should not be forgotten that those who perpetrated the London bombings were mostly children at the time of the Salman Rushdie crisis and it was their parents' generation that were out burning *The Satanic Verses* in the streets.

In fact, despite their bafflement at the actions of the likes of the London bombers, it was this generation that unintentionally fostered a youth that contains elements, albeit a tiny minority, that have embraced a new radicalism that thrives on a simplistic black and white interpretation of Islam and that lays the internal problems within the community firmly at the door of the West. That is not to suggest that these communities are not struggling with very real issues and problems related to being a minority community in modern-day Britain. Yet a minority within these communities has cultivated a mindset and sense of grievance that has its foundations in the anti-Western discourse that permeates the Islamic world, including Pakistan. As Kamran Nazeer commented, 'These are often traditional communities, in which a combination of perceived local exclusion and world events has allowed a politics of grievance to develop, a politics that refuses to address these problems, blaming them all instead on the antipathy of Britain or the West towards Muslims.' [22] Nazeer also explains how it is much easier for an imam to create a sense of unity during the Friday *khoutba* by arguing that 'all these grievances come from the West's war against Muslims' rather than challenging this perception with 'a more sophisticated critique'.[23]

These grievances have been taken to the point where many within these communities continue to assert that Muslims were not responsible for 9/11 and that the attacks were a Zionist plot to discredit Muslims. Some also

believe that 7/7 was also a contrived and deliberate policy by the government
to sow discord among Muslim communities.[24] In a survey of 500 Muslims
conducted for the UK's Channel Four News, almost 60 per cent believed
that the British government had covered up the truth about the 7/7 bombings and that the bombers were not in fact responsible for the attacks.[25] In
this context, Kamran Nazeer noted after the alleged transatlantic airline plot
was discovered in 2006, 'The conspiracy theories that you hear in Pakistan
are also widely believed by British Pakistanis.'[26]

All this would suggest that second- and third-generation communities are
less detached from the cultural values and politics of the home country than
is often suggested. One Pakistani professor concluded in a recent study that
75 per cent of Pakistanis in the UK were fully engaged with politics back
in Pakistan.[27] Although it is not clear how this variable was measured, in
spite of English becoming the primary language in which these young people
communicate, the interest and link to the home country is clearly still very
strong and the mindset has not necessarily dissolved with the new generations. This is hardly surprising. One would not assume that if European
families were pushed to settle in a country like Pakistan they would not try
to preserve their secular European values and to translate them through to
the second generation and beyond. Therefore events and developments in
Pakistan are clearly reflected among Pakistani communities in the UK.

## Pakistan and the Kashmiri connection

The 1980s saw an increase in militancy in Pakistan under the leadership of
General Muhammad Zia-ul-Haq who set about Islamicizing the country. As
a Sunni he did his utmost to prevent the rise of Pakistan's Shi'ite minority whom he feared would make common cause with Khomeini's Shi'ite
Iran after the revolution of 1979. Thus the zealous president built up excellent relations with Saudi Arabia that were to become an important source
of finance for the country. Zia-ul-Haq also played an important role in the
Afghanistan conflict, with his regime and the Pakistani intelligence services strongly supporting the Afghan mujahideen against their communist
enemies. All of this set Pakistan, despite its originally having been conceived
of as an Islamic state but which had been largely considered as a secular
nation, firmly on the path of Islamism. Just as Islamic revivalism swept
the Arab world in response to the prevailing conditions there, it also hit
Pakistan in the same way. Some have put the Islamic revivalism that was
welcomed by large parts of the population down to the ongoing poverty
and political distress that characterized the first few decades of Pakistan's
existence, where 'failure led back again and again to the assertion of the

faith'.[28] This Islamicization has persisted in Pakistan, as it has in much of the Islamic world, and despite its willingness to cooperate with the West the Pakistani regime under President Musharaf has also displayed an ambiguity in its attitude towards militant Islamist movements. As one commentator noted, 'Pakistan is a carbon copy of the Arab situation. The political system is at war with the fundamentalists, but this war is taking place on the surface. Underneath there are networks recruiting, supporting and producing propaganda outside of the authority of the regime.'[29]

One of the most influential Islamist movements that has contributed to this Islamicization of Pakistan has been the Deobandi. This revivalist Sunni movement was established in India in the late nineteenth century and was named after the seminary at Deoband. It was formed partly as a reaction against British rule and had a virulently anti-colonialist agenda. It advocated a strict puritanical interpretation of the faith that promoted segregation of the sexes and abstention from politics, as it viewed all legislative authority as belonging to Allah alone. The movement established madrassas across India and beyond as a means of educating the population into accepting its reformist ideas, and after the creation of Pakistan in 1947 Deobandi madrassas flourished in the new country. Under Zia-ul-Haq the movement gained greater influence as Deobandi preachers were afforded a great deal of space, and followers of the movement became highly influential in the administration, armed forces and judiciary. Through its madrassas the Deobandis in Pakistan had a very strong influence on the development of the Taliban as scores of young Afghan students came to study at these budding religious establishments. In addition the Deobandis worked in the Afghani refugee camps indoctrinating the young Afghans with their ideology. This Afghanistan connection also gave them strong links to Osama Bin Ladin and Al-Qa'ida, whose strict Wahabist-inspired creed was not dissimilar to their own rigid teachings. It was this combination of the most traditional, simplistic and rejectionist Islamist ideologies that was to represent the new wave of Islamist activism that came to grip the world at the start of the twenty-first century.

Some parts of the Deobandi movement were keen to promote the concept of jihad. One of the most important scholars from the region who had a huge influence on the development of the political Islamist movement more widely, Abu Al-Ala Mawdudi, who advocated taking up armed struggle, passed through a Deobandi seminary before developing his own particular ideology. The Deobandis also spawned a number of jihadist groups linked to the conflict in Kashmir. These included the Jaish-e-Mohammed and Lashkar-e-Toiba, which are still fighting to liberate Kashmir from Indian control. These groups appear to be relatively free to recruit young Pakistanis to join the Kashmiri jihad, and while the Pakistani regime might try to clamp down on them, it does so half-heartedly, enabling them to maintain a solid presence in the country. Lashkar-e-Toiba has been able to build residences, farms and schools and also has its own large complex 20 miles north of Lahore, which contains a huge mosque, factories, an iron foundry, a swimming pool and three residential colonies. The group has claimed that it trains 40,000 youth per year at its schools and military training camps.[30] According to a Pakistani Interior Ministry official the group also declared that around 800 young people had been martyred fighting the Indian army during 2002 alone.[31] The group is clearly taking advantage of the misery that much of Pakistan's population finds itself in. One Pakistani commentator explained, 'The young jihadis come from poor and middle-class families. When they fail to find any employment, they join the jihadi outfits that provide them food and shelter and promise them a passage to paradise through martyrdom.'[32] As the father of one family who had 'donated' two of his eight sons to the Kashmiri jihad explained, 'It is better for them to die for a cause and embrace martyrdom before hunger kills them.'[33]

In spite of the strength and influence of the Deobandis in Pakistan, the majority of Pakistanis in the UK originate from the more mystical Barweli tradition, which is particularly strong in Mirpur. However, the Deobandis have become increasingly prevalent among these communities in the past couple of decades. Thanks to generous funding from Saudi Arabia, Deobandi mosques began to spring up in the 1980s especially in the Midlands and north of England. At the same time, various revivalist groups close to the Deobandi also began to operate in the UK and in Europe more widely. These included the Dawa Tabligh, founded by a Deobandi cleric in the 1920s. The Tablighi is generally referred to as an apolitical movement, preferring to concentrate on religious *dawa*, although many of those who go on to take up the cause of jihad have passed through Tablighi institutions before progressing to more radical ideologies. Although details are still sketchy, it would appear that both Shehzad Tanweer and Mohammed Siddique Khan followed the typical pattern of other militants who passed through moderate organizations before moving on to more militant groups. Both men are reported to have worshipped at Tablighi mosques and Khan lived in Dewsbury, which is home to the movement's international headquarters.[34] Tanweer is alleged to have dropped out of his sports science degree at Leeds Metropolitan University to study at the *madrassa* run by the Tablighi mosque in the west Yorkshire town. However, the apolitical ideology of the Tabligh was clearly not sufficient to satisfy either man.

It was in Pakistan itself that these two young men seem to have found the hardcore ideology they were so attracted to. There are indications that Mohammed Siddique Khan and Shehzad Tanweer both spent time in

Pakistan being trained in jihad by a range of Deobandi-inspired groups. Tanweer is alleged to have had links with Jaish-e-Mohammed, having met a member of the group while attending a Deobandi mosque in Pakistan.[35] He is also believed to have spent time with the Lashkar-e-Toiba. Similarly Khan is alleged to have travelled regularly to Pakistan to attend military training camps. These men are by no means unique in this respect. They rather followed in the line of British Pakistanis who made their way to the training camps of Lashkar-e-Toiba and other groups in Pakistan in order to heed the call to jihad. In March 2006, for example, British citizen Mohammed Ajmal Khan, who was sentenced to nine years for fundraising on behalf of terrorism in Pakistan and Afghanistan, admitted that he had attended a training camp run by Lashkar-e-Toiba.[36] This is not a new phenomenon directly linked to the post-9/11 climate or to Western foreign policy, but has been ongoing since the camps were set up in the 1990s and many went through them to go on to fight in Afghanistan and Kashmir. Omar Khyam, the ringleader of the fertilizer bomb plot, went to train in Pakistan in 2000 after telling his family he was going on a visit to France. In fact in 2003 the British intelligence agency MI5 drew up a list of 100 terror suspects in the UK, out of which at least 45 were British Pakistanis who had been involved in the jihad in Kashmir.[37] Others were to meet their deaths in the process. In 2000 a young British Pakistani from Birmingham, Mohamed Bilal, blew himself up in a car bomb outside an Indian army barracks in Kashmir. At the age of 18 Bilal turned his back on the world of night clubbing and became very religious after he claimed he had dreamt about the Prophet.[38] In 1994 he went to Pakistan where he was trained in weapons and theology and the following year was sent to fight in Kashmir where he is thought to have remained until his suicide attack. In the same year another British Muslim from north London who had trained in Kashmir told the BBC that he had learned how to make bombs, use artillery and a Kalashnikov and that he had returned to the UK to recruit others to the cause.[39]

The link to Kashmir is no coincidence. The disputed territory continues to hold a particular importance for Pakistanis in the UK, while generating limited interest among Arab communities whose primary focus remains on Palestine, Iraq and other Arab causes. Although militants, and indeed moderates, repeatedly cite crises across the Muslim world to demonstrate the injustices perpetrated by the West against Muslims, sometimes this appears to be something of a shopping-list approach. Despite the assertion that they are part of one *ummah*, even those at the most hardcore end of the spectrum generally remain true to their roots when they can. This is why the majority of young Pakistani militants who went to fight jihad chose to do so in Kashmir. Of course there are a number of exceptions, but in general it is noticeable that the animosity of these militants is often directed as much towards Hindus and Indians as it is against Westerners and Jews. In fact this feeling is not confined to the radicals. After Mohamed Bilal blew himself up in Kashmir, Mohamed Ghalib, the president of a UK Kashmiri lobby group based in Birmingham, stated, 'The story will encourage the youth that this is a good thing and may encourage them to become more militant. ... If Indian army soldiers died in a bomb attack then most people here wouldn't mind.' [40] Indeed there is a feeling among those youth who went off to fight jihad in Kashmir that they are somehow upholding the honour of their own communities. This is partly because of the fact that the Kashmir crisis combines a nationalistic as well as an Islamist dimension, and while most of the wider Pakistani community in the UK would not advocate going to fight, the cause is able to ignite nationalistic passions. Omar Khyam, for example, was deeply affected by the Kashmir crisis. Although his family are said to have not been particularly religious, he told the court, 'Kashmir was a very big issue in my family.' After attending a training camp in Pakistan he was asked what he had learned there. He replied, 'Everything I needed for guerrilla warfare in Kashmir.' [41] Similarly another man convicted in the same plot, Salahuddin Amin, who was born in Britain but who moved back to Pakistan aged four where he spent his formative years until he returned to the UK aged 16, travelled back to Pakistan for extended stays every summer and on one occasion became captivated by speeches given by the mujahideen about the atrocities being committed in Kashmir. This appears to have been an important moment in his radicalization.

This nationalistic connection was played upon by a number of radical clerics operating in Britain who were keen to encourage young aspiring jihadists to go to fight in the lands from which they had originated. Abu Hamza Al-Masri of Finsbury Park in London reportedly encouraged British Pakistanis such as Salman Abdullah, who gravitated to the Finsbury Park mosque where he stayed after he had left his Yorkshire home following a row with his father, to go to train in Pakistan with Lashkar-e-Toiba. [42] After a short training stint Abdullah was sent to fight in Kashmir for a few months before returning to the London mosque as a hero. Likewise Omar Bakri Mohamed's group Al-Muhajiroun opened its own offices in Lahore in 2001 and in its first meeting called for the overthrow of the Musharaf government. [43] Indeed the obsession with installing a genuine Islamic state in Pakistan appears to be of the utmost importance to the members of this organization. One British Pakistani from Manchester, Sajeel Shahid, who had gone to Pakistan told a journalist that 'Al-Muhajiroun had sent them out to Pakistan because it was ripe for an Islamic revolution. If Pakistan's president Pervez Musharaf fell, other apostate rulers would follow.' [44] This comment demonstrates more than ever the bizarre and naive world of wish-ful thinking and parallel realities that these young men are living in.

The same journalist described a meeting with the group and painted a picture of an arrogant, self-righteous bunch of young men crowded into a rundown Lahore apartment block, who despite their university qualifications appear to have been caught up in a region whose complexities they did not fully understand. He observed:

> They loathed everything about the West. The values of the kufr, the infidels, were sick, corrupt, and empty, they said. Pornography, alcohol, exploitation ... they couldn't see anything in British society that was positive. ... They were drawn from all over the country. The accents were cockney, West Midlands, one sounded quite posh. Most were from Manchester or Yorkshire. Some had come from Scotland. ... They were a closed society, at odds with the world. They liked to hint that they were up to important, secret things.[45]

From what one can surmise from such anecdotal stories, these individuals appeared to be completely at home in Pakistan, where they claimed they were revered because they had given up the luxuries of living in Britain for the cause of jihad. Moreover, for those who are deeply religious, the comforts of being in an Islamic country should not be underestimated. In fact despite all the assertions that second-generation militants turn to radical Islam because they feel they do not fit in either in the UK or in Pakistan, this is not necessarily always the case. The former spokesman of Al-Muhajiroun in Pakistan, Hassan Butt, a second-generation Pakistani refers to the time he spent living in Pakistan as the best two years of his life.[46] Anecdotal evidence about London bomber Shehzad Tanweer would also suggest that he was more than comfortable staying with his extended family in Lahore. In fact although his family in the UK were described as not being religious, his uncle in Pakistan, Tahir Pervez, sparked controversy when he praised his nephew's actions. After a funeral service attended by around 200 people in the family village where Tanweer's remains were buried, his uncle report-edly declared, 'Tanweer did nothing wrong. He died a jihadi and that is why we wanted him buried in Pakistan, on Islamic soil. ... I have no sorrow for those who died in London. They do not take the name of Allah and look at all the innocent Muslims being killed around the world. My nephew has died – why should I worry about people dying in London.'[47] It seems that despite their having been brought up in Britain it might be jumping the gun a bit to suggest that they necessarily felt alienated in their parents' country of origin.

Radicalism within this community therefore is part of a wider phenom-enon that goes beyond Britain or Europe and is intrinsically linked to a part of the world that is suffering from the same sense of stagnation and crisis that permeates much of the Middle East.

## The role of foreign policy

Joining the jihad in Kashmir or Afghanistan is one thing, but being prepared to commit an act of suicide terrorism in the UK is another. After the London bombings debate raged in the UK about the role that Britain's foreign policy in the Middle East and in Iraq in particular had played in pushing these young men to undertake their suicide attacks. In videos they made before they blew themselves up, both Mohammed Siddique Khan and Shehzad Tanweer cited Iraq and Afghanistan as the reason why they were attacking Britain. In his broad Yorkshire accent Khan stated, 'Until you stop the bombing, gassing, imprisonment and torture of my people we will not stop this fight. ... We are at war and I am a soldier. Now you too will taste the reality of this situation.'[48] In his video, broadcast one year after the attacks, Tanweer warned that the bombings were 'only the beginning of a string of attacks that will continue and become stronger until you pull your forces out of Afghanistan and Iraq and until you stop your financial and military support to America and Israel'.

There is no doubt that the Iraq war prompted feelings of real anger among large parts of the Muslim community in the UK. The images of Iraqi civilians being killed certainly touched a chord with many people and provoked genuine feelings of frustration and rage at the West's apparent double standards and its assumption that it could just move in and re-arrange the furniture of the Middle East. However, to assert that the Iraq war created a new swathe of hatred for the US and the UK and pushed these young men to kill themselves is perhaps to misunderstand the levels of anger towards the West that existed prior to the war. For many Islamists, as for populations across the Islamic world more widely, the West has been perceived to have been responsible for a string of abuses that began with the colonial period and include the running sores of Palestine, Afghanistan, Kashmir and countless others. The West is also perceived to be propping up corrupt tyrannical regimes across the Islamic world that are abusing their own populations, as well as siphoning off the wealth of these countries. It is not surprising, for example, that when Western businesses returned to Libya after the country's rehabilitation, many ordinary Libyans who were struggling to survive despite the country's vast oil resources felt deep resentment not only towards the regime that was excluding them from the financial benefits but also towards those Western companies that moved in to make a killing out of the new situation. The bombing of Afghanistan in 2001 and of Iraq in 2003 therefore simply confirmed existing suspicions about Western intentions in the region and stoked the anger that was already present.

Indeed, as has already been discussed in previous chapters, antipathy towards the West has been a core part of the rhetoric that has prevailed in the Middle East for generations and predated the emergence of the political Islamist movement. Arab nationalists used to rail against Western foreign policy, accusing Western powers of trying to reoccupy their former colonial possessions. This kind of language is still used today by the various regimes of the region as a means of bolstering their own legitimacy, and anti-Westernism still shapes the contemporary political discourse. Such ideas have also been used by secular intellectuals who have voiced a similar message. The official media in the region is also full of condemnation at the hypocrisy and double standards of the West. In some cases this is framed in religious terms, with state newspapers on occasions carrying articles that state that martyrdom is the highest attainment for any Muslim. Therefore all that the contemporary political Islamist movement has done is to appropriate this discourse and give the rhetoric an added religious dimension, framing the debate in terms of the West's waging of a war against Islam.

This idea of the West's being at war with Islam therefore predates the war on terror and has become a populist mantra. Even many non-practising Muslims are quick to assert that the West is deliberately targeting Muslims precisely because they are Muslim.[49] As one Islamist lawyer in Pakistan, Khalid Ishaq, described, 'Our people emotionally reject the West.'[50] This of course is not true across the board and the relationship to the West is much more complex than this comment would suggest. Yet the political grievances against the West that are expressed by the radicals, the moderates and the wider community at large are broadly the same. As such, despite the abhorrence of violence among the vast majority of Muslims, there is an underlying agreement about the rights and morality of the wider cause. Moreover these kinds of suspicions about the West's intentions are more common both in the Islamic world and by extension among Muslim communities in Europe than is sometimes perceived. Back in the mid-1990s the same kind of rhetoric was doing the rounds among Islamists in Europe, although it received less attention because political Islam was not considered to be a threat to the West itself at that time. The view of one Muslim from Mauritius who was living in Britain encapsulated how many viewed the West at that time: 'Anything to do with Islam. Salman Rushdie. The Gulf War. Bosnia. You name it. Chechnya. Algeria. It's nothing new. The world is manipulated by certain individuals and certain countries for their own use.'[51]

Therefore the feeling that Western foreign policy was deliberately targeting Muslims did not come about purely as a result of the Iraq war. Rather the

Iraq invasion confirmed existing suspicions about the West's bad intentions in the Islamic world. Indeed 9/11 occurred before both Afghanistan and the Iraq war and was largely a response to the years of perceived aggression of and domination by the US in the Middle East. The UK was no less exempt from this perception. Even Abdullah Azzam himself asserted that the British were a legitimate target because in 1924 London had called for the destruction of the caliphate – the Ottoman Empire. Once Al-Qa'ida had taken the step of attacking the US on its own soil on 9/11 and more importantly had scored a spectacular success, the idea of attacking Western countries became a reality for those at the most militant end of the Islamist movement. In the days following 9/11 former Al-Muhajiroun member Hassan Butt began lauding the idea of an attack in the UK. When asked about whether such an attack would result in a backlash against his own community he responded, 'Our fathers' generation has been soft for too long. Too many of them sell alcohol and pornography. It is time they made some sacrifices for Islam. The young generation is ready.'[52] Clearly this may have been bravado in the aftermath of the 9/11 attacks, but the sentiments and desire to strike the UK were real and did not need an invasion of Iraq to set them off.

It is true that the war in Iraq might have fuelled support among some parts of the Islamist community for an attack against the UK, making it more justifiable because Britain had invaded a Muslim country. Indeed the British think-tank Chatham House observed:

> There is no doubt that the situation over Iraq has imposed particular difficulties for the UK, and for the wider coalition against terrorism. It gave a boost to the Al-Qaeda network's propaganda, recruitment and fundraising, caused a major split in the coalition, provided an ideal targeting and training area for Al-Qaeda-linked terrorists, and deflected resources and assistance that could have been deployed to assist the Karzai government and to bring bin Laden to justice.[53]

Yet while the war in Iraq might have made targeting the UK more acceptable or might have provided a set of images that might have aided recruitment, in itself it did not radicalize the young men who were already involved in the world of militant Islam long before the invasion of Iraq. As one commentator explained, 'Khan may have felt indignant about Western foreign policy, as many anti-war campaigners do, but that wasn't the reason he led a cell of young men to kill themselves and 52 London commuters.'[54] Indeed Mohammed Siddique Khan was heavily involved in the world of Islamist militancy before the war in Iraq and even before 9/11. By the late 1990s his life had already narrowed to the mosques where he prayed, the Pakistani youth clubs that he helped to run, the Iqra bookshop where he gave talks and his brother's house.[55] As such it was neither of these events that prompted his sudden radicalization. This was backed up by one former militant who explained, 'Though many British extremists are angered by the deaths of fellow Muslims across the world, what drove me and many of my peers to plot acts of extreme terror within Britain, our own homeland and abroad, was a sense that we were fighting for the creation of a revolutionary state that would eventually bring Islamic justice to the world.'[56]

Moreover there are other countries in Europe which have not been involved in the Iraq war, yet which have found themselves no less vulnerable to attacks and aggression by militants. Despite its public aversion to the Iraq invasion, France has not been immune from potential terrorist attacks. In 2006 French anti-terrorism judge Jean-Louis Bruguière announced that France had averted three significant terrorist plots in the previous 18 months.[57] Similarly Germany averted a bomb attack in July 2006 when two suitcases containing explosives were discovered on regional commuter trains in the northwestern cities of Koblenz and Dortmund. Then in September 2007 Germany arrested a group of suspects believed to have been planning major bomb attacks against facilities used by Americans, including nightclubs, pubs and airports. Therefore while the Iraq war might have fuelled existing anger at the West, it is difficult to prove that it was the driving force behind the radicalization of these militants.

In addition, Afghanistan should surely have been a far greater source of anger and radicalizing factor for militant Islamists than Iraq. Afghanistan under the Taliban was after all the closest thing that the world had to a Sunni Islamic state and Saddam Hussein's secular Ba'athist regime was considered as an anathema to Islamists, who viewed him simply as a puppet of the West. In fact as they made clear in their videos, the concerns and anger of those who committed the atrocity on 7 July 2005 went far beyond the question of British troops in Iraq. Yet it was not clear exactly what the demands of these young men were. Indeed the attacks appear to have been as much about gratifying a nihilistic lust for violence and revenge against the *kufar* as they were about trying to reconfigure Western foreign policy. In addition the bombers' claims that they were somehow acting on behalf of what Mohammed Siddique Khan arrogantly described as 'my people' prompt a number of questions. Khan clearly felt himself qualified to speak on behalf of Muslims all over the world simply because he was himself a Muslim. One assumes that when he talked about 'his people' in relation to Iraq he was referring to Iraqi Sunnis and not to the country's Shi'ite, Mandean, Yazidi or Christian populations. It is surely odd that someone such as Khan could justify the continuation of 'the resistance' in a country he had not visited and had no direct connection with other than through some notion of Muslim identity. In fact the artificial construct of the *ummah* appears to be used highly selectively. While a handful of second-generation Pakistani extremists were ready to rage against injustices being perpetrated by Israel against Shi'ite Muslims in Lebanon in 2006, it is noticeable that they remained largely silent on the killing of Shi'ites by Sunnis in Pakistan, and indeed Iraq.

## The covenant of security

It was also suggested that one of the reasons that had prompted the London bombers to undertake their attack was that the 'covenant of security' between British Islamists and the British authorities had been broken. Commentators described the covenant of security as a 'well-understood compromise' between Muslim leaders and the police and explained it to mean that 'there would be high levels of toleration in exchange for self-policing'.[58] This focus on the so-called covenant is rather curious. The concept of a covenant of security is derived from early Islamic history and refers to the agreement made between the Prophet Mohammed and the city of Medina which offered him protection after he fled Mecca in return for his not attacking it. The concept of a covenant of security in Islamic terms is generally used therefore to mean that those who have been offered refuge and protection from persecution have a contract with the country that has taken them in not to attack it. It is considered to be a state between what is referred to as *Dar al-Islam* (the House of Islam) and *Dar al-Harb* (the House of War, or sometimes referred to as *Dar al-Kufar*) and is often given the term *Dar al-Ahd* (the House of Truce).

However, the covenant of security is something over which Islamic scholars are themselves divided. Each of the four main Islamic schools of jurisprudence differ, as do individual scholars, as to what exactly constitutes *Dar al-Harb* or *Dar al-Islam*. Some scholars rule that even if a Muslim lives in a non-Muslim country, as long as he or she is allowed to carry out his or her religious duties freely then this is *Dar al-Islam*. Others, including some scholars of the Hanafi school, consider that *Dar al-Islam* can become *Dar al-Harb* if ruled by the *kufar*. Sheikh Faisal Al-Mawlawi, a prominent Muslim Brother, has asserted that *Dar al-Islam* is any country in which there is a Muslim majority even if its ruler does not completely abide by Islam and even if the government there displays some sort of anti-Islamic schemes or policies. Some elements within Hizb ut Tahrir, on the other hand, have asserted, 'The term Dar al-Harb is synonymous with Dar al-Kufar. Today it is clear that the whole world is Dar al-Kufar as no country including every single Muslim country implements Islam.'[59] The concept of *Dar al-Ahd* is equally contested. Broadly it is taken to mean a state in which non-Muslim rulers have a treaty with the Muslims living there stipulating that they will not wage war against them.

The idea of the covenant of security was promoted in particular by Omar Bakri, known particularly for his limelight grabbing and publicity-seeking stunts. In early 2005 Bakri Mohamed announced that the covenant of security had been broken because of the British government's introduction of anti-terrorist legislation. He announced, 'The whole of Britain has become Dar al-Harb [land of war] ... the kufar has no sanctity for their own life or property.'[60] While this concept might have applied to Bakri, who had fled Syria and sought asylum in Britain, the preacher took it upon himself to extend it to those Muslims who had been born in Britain. This idea was readily taken on board by the members of Al-Muhajiroun, including one second-generation Pakistani from Luton, Sayful Islam, who explained, 'It is against Islam for me to engage personally in acts of terrorism in the UK because I live here. According to Islam, I have a covenant of security with the UK, as long as they allow us Muslims to live here in peace.'[61] Sayful Islam cited this covenant of security as the reason why he could support martyrdom operations, but had to restrict himself to handing out leaflets outside his local town hall! Another leading member of Al-Ghurraba, former electrician from east London Abu Izideen, explained in his broad London accent in August 2005, 'We don't live in peace with you anymore. The covenant of security doesn't no longer exist.'[62] What these individuals failed to understand, however, was that in strict Islamic terms, if one finds oneself in Dar al-Harb, the correct response would be to emigrate from it, not to attack it!

Omar Bakri himself clearly played upon this concept as a means of political posturing and of finding an excuse for attacking the West. He used it to explain why it was acceptable for the 9/11 perpetrators to have attacked the United States, claiming that they had entered the US with fake names and were therefore excluded from the covenant.[63] Moreover, not only did the covenant idea give him a kind of status that suggested he was sufficiently important to merit having his own special agreement with the British authorities, it also made him look as though he was in control of Muslim communities in the UK. It was also a rather self-inflated way of putting himself and his followers on the same level as that of the Prophet. As one commentator noted, 'Bakri's Covenant of Security was never more than a wafer-thin lid on the pressure-cooker atmosphere his inflammatory preaching had created.'[64] However, Bakri used the covenant idea to threaten the British and asserted in 2005 that the government should repeal anti-terrorist legislation and release those detained without trial, threatening, 'The response from the Muslims will be horrendous if the British government continues in the way it treats Muslims.'[65]

It also seems strange to think that the British police would be prepared to enter into such a covenant. It is true that the authorities were willing to grant a significant degree of tolerance to radical preachers such as Bakri during the 1980s and 1990s and to turn a blind eye to their antics, but this did not represent an unwritten agreement. It was rather that they did not expect any attack against Britain to come from these quarters – the focus was elsewhere at that time, especially in counter-terrorism terms, where police time and efforts were channelled mainly into the Northern Ireland problem. Moreover it would have been very foolish of the authorities to have entered into such an agreement and to have believed this would prevent an attack – Bakri did not represent the only current of radical Islamism in the UK and there were many for whom this covenant meant nothing at all. In fact even some members of Al-Muhajiroun left the group because they did not accept Bakri's rather unorthodox ruling on the issue. This includes Hassan Butt, who claims he left the group because of it and who noted:

> There is a difference between a citizen who is born in a country and someone who is here on a visa or permit. Islamically, I agree that someone who runs from the Middle East, where people like me are persecuted, and who says, 'Britain, I want you to protect me' has entered into a covenant of security. But most of our people, especially the youth, are British citizens. They owe nothing to the government. They did not ask to be born here, neither did they ask to be protected by Britain.[66]

Indeed under the original meaning of the covenant of security it is surely the bombers in Madrid rather than London who should have adhered to such an agreement because they had come from abroad and had been allowed to stay by the Spanish authorities. To imagine therefore that by repealing anti-terrorist legislation and agreeing not to arrest Muslims, Britain could somehow protect itself from future attacks by re-entering into a covenant of security is clearly ludicrous. The attacks were not related to the breaking of any special covenant played up by Omar Bakri, but rather came about because the opportunity arose and because the momentum for attacking the West had taken off after 9/11.

## The 21/7 bombers

Just one week after the 7/7 bombings another group of individuals tried to repeat the experience but were thwarted when their bombs failed to detonate. The four men – Mukhtar Said Ibrahim, Yassin Omar, Omar Ramzi Mohamed and Hussein Osman – who took homemade bombs on to London's transport system on 21 July hoping to wreak carnage and to kill themselves in the process seemed to attract less public attention than the 7/7 bombers. Perhaps this was because they failed in their bid to blow themselves up, or perhaps it was because they were not British born and as such seemed not to capture the public's imagination in quite the same way. Indeed the men had completely different backgrounds and profiles to the 7/7 bombers. They were all first-generation immigrants from the Horn of Africa who had fled countries ravaged by war and who had struggled to make a life for themselves in their adopted home. After they hatched their plan, they had set up a makeshift bomb-making factory in a north London flat where they spent hours boiling down hair bleach to concoct the explosives they believed would take them to paradise. At their trial, which took place in 2007, all four men were found guilty of conspiracy to murder and a further two defendants were convicted in relation to the plot.

The ringleader of the group, Mukhtar Said Ibrahim, was born in Asmara, Eritrea, in 1978. He came to the UK in 1990 with his family as a child refugee escaping the war that was raging between his country and Ethiopia. According to some sources, Ibrahim was known for being a cannabis-smoking bully at school and had left his family home when he was 16, soon getting involved in the world of gang culture.[67] Perhaps predictably, Ibrahim drifted into a life of crime and in June 1993 was convicted of carrying out an indecent assault against a 15 year old.[68] He was then involved in further petty crimes before being detained for five years in Feltham Young Offender Institution after being involved in a gang-related attack. Some have suggested that Ibrahim was re-awakened to his faith while in Feltham, a place where other militants have found or converted to Islam, although this has not been confirmed. However, after his release in 1998 he certainly became increasingly involved in the radical Islamist scene in London, seemingly finding in his faith a way to turn his life around. At some point he started attending the Finsbury Park mosque where, like many other young men, he became entranced by the radical preacher Abu Hamza Al-Masri. By this point Ibrahim had clearly become attracted to the idea of fighting for the cause, as in 2003 he is alleged to have travelled to Sudan to undertake jihadi training. According to one of the witnesses in his trial, Ibrahim had told his friends that he was going there to 'do jihad'.[69] After his return he was arrested in 2004 for a public-order offence on London's Oxford Street when an altercation broke out as he tried to distribute Islamic literature. Then in 2005 Ibrahim travelled to Pakistan for four months, being searched on his way out of the UK where he was found to be carrying cold-weather gear, camping equipment and £3,000, although he was still permitted to travel. It was alleged at his trial that Ibrahim may have met with some of the 7/7 bombers when he was in Pakistan, as they were there at the same time as he, although he denies that he had any contact with them. It seems that it was after his return from Pakistan that the plot to bomb the underground was hatched.

Yassin Omar meanwhile was born in war-torn Somalia in 1981, where as a boy he attended a Qu'ranic school, there being no other form of education available. He came to the UK with his sisters as a child in the early 1990s, but was handed over to local authority care, spending time in various foster homes. One of his foster carers, Steven Lamb, who lost touch with Omar after 2001, told the court that Omar was 'not comfortable with rules and boundaries' if they were set by his partner Bernice Campbell and that as he became older he had difficulty with women telling him what to do.[70] When he was 18 Omar was classified by social services as a 'vulnerable young adult' and was given his own flat in a tower block in Southgate, north London, where he spent his time playing computer games and hanging out with his friends. He then dropped out of college, where he had been studying science, and by the late 1990s had drifted into the world of militant Islam. He attended the Finsbury Park mosque where, like Ibrahim, he was captivated by Abu Hamza Al-Masri. According to a witness in the trial who had known Omar, Omar did not believe that Osama Bin Laden had been responsible for the 9/11 attacks because 'Abu Hamza said he wasn't and Abu Hamza knew Osama Bin Ladin'.[71] As he became more devout, Omar increasingly cut himself off from his friends and began spending more and more time with Ibrahim, whom he had befriended.

Like Omar, Ramzi Mohamed was also from Somalia and was also born in 1981. His father had joined one of the warring militias, leaving Mohamed to grow up in a refugee camp. His mother was so worried for his safety that in 1998 she sent Mohamed and his brother to Britain via Kenya. After his arrival in the UK, the young Mohamed was put in the care of social services in Slough but was given his own flat in west London at the age of 18. He studied IT and worked for a while in a bar in Waterloo railway station. He met a Swedish woman of Eritrean origin and although they were not married the couple had two children. However, around 2003 Mohamed began to be increasingly drawn to Islam and his views became progressively more radical. He began frequenting Speakers' Corner at Hyde Park and a number of mosques and Islamic circles, and by 2004 he was also to be found at the Finsbury Park mosque alongside Ibrahim and Omar. He regularly attended Abu Hamza's Friday sermons on the street outside the mosque and on one occasion was filmed by a CCTV camera helping to fold up the tarpaulin on which the congregation had been sitting after they had dispersed. By this point Mohamed had given up his job in the bar out of religious considerations and had also given up other employment at an outlet of the American

Bagel Factory because he did not like working with pork. He also told the court that he had thrown away his Sony Playstation and his hip-hop compact discs because, 'It was "fuck this" and "fuck that", I couldn't listen to that anymore. It was harm, it was wrong.'[72] He had clearly decided that he was ready to martyr himself, and in spite of the bombers arguing at their trial that their attempt had been nothing more than a hoax meant to raise awareness about the Iraq war, before the bombing he wrote a suicide note which read, 'My family, don't cry for [me]. But indeed rejoice in happiness and love what I have done for the sake of Allah, for he loves those who fight in his sake.'[73]

Less is known about the fourth bomber, Hussein Osman. Osman came from Ethiopia in 1978 but moved to Italy when he was 14. In the late 1990s he decided to move to the UK and claimed on entry that he was from Somalia in order to increase his chances of being granted asylum.[74] According to Osman's girlfriend, another Ethiopian whom he had met in Italy, he liked to consider himself as a gangster, but after he moved to London he became more involved in Islam and led an increasingly devout and austere life. According to neighbours who lived near Osman's south London flat, after they moved in his girlfriend became increasingly withdrawn and began wearing the *hijab*.[75] It is not clear how Osman met with the other bombers but he was in touch with them by early 2004 and was also a follower of Abu Hamza Al-Masri.

There was supposed to be a fifth bomber on 21 July, Manfo Kwaku Asiedu, but he abandoned his bomb at the last moment and fled. He later handed himself in to the police and in November 2007 pleaded guilty to conspiracy to cause explosions. Asiedu had a somewhat different background from the other bombers. He was born into a Muslim family in Ghana in the early 1970s and seems to have come from a middle-class family that had an agricultural business. He only arrived in the UK in 2003, using a false passport to gain entry. After his arrival in Britain he sought out mosques, including the one in Finchley that was also frequented by Yassin Omar. In June 2005 he moved into Omar's flat in New Southgate and appears to have got involved in the bomb making that was going on there. Asiedu claims that he was forced into taking part in the attack by Ibrahim and that he was too scared to tell the other men that he did not want to kill himself and that was why he abandoned his bomb on the day of the supposed attacks.

Another suspect, Adel Yahya, was also tried in connection with the attacks, accused of playing a leading role in the plot. He was born in Ethiopia in 1982, but had spent some of his childhood in Yemen. He came to Britain with his sister in 1991 when he was just 11 years old and became school friends with Yassin Omar. Yahya clearly maintained his links in Yemen, as in 2004 he got married there. He studied for a degree in computer networking at London Metropolitan University where he is alleged to have altered two bank statements in order to qualify for special student funding.[76] Along with Omar, Yahya began attending sermons by Abu Hamza Al-Masri and became increasingly immersed in the world of militant Islamist politics. Yahya left Britain for Ethiopia six weeks before the planned attack and was arrested on his return to the UK at Gatwick airport in December 2005 after he had been extradited. Although the charges of conspiracy to murder were dropped he was eventually convicted after he admitted collecting information that was useful to a person preparing an act of terrorism.

This group of seemingly desperate, young, first-generation immigrants, each with their own tragic life story, appear to have followed the pattern of many other militants, increasingly isolating themselves from their friends and families and from the real world, seeking some kind of certainty in their ideology. In the months leading up to the attacks, they spent almost all their time together or at the mosque and would gather in each other's flats to watch videos of the Iraq war and of beheadings, as well as sharing extremist literature. As such they seemed to have found some kind of salvation or meaning to their lives through militant Islam. They were also dreamers and only Ibrahim had any real experience of training for jihad, although even this was limited to a few months in Pakistan and Sudan. The men also seem to have been brought together to some degree by their shared backgrounds and the fact that they all came from the Horn of Africa, mostly without family or support structures. Surely it is these men, rather than the 7/7 bombers, who were forced to flee their own countries as children or young adults and who struggled to find their own way in Britain, that one could point to as being truly alienated and marginalized.

This group were clearly captivated by Abu Hamza Al-Masri, who with his simple black and white interpretation of Islam was able to attract those with limited education or who were facing some kind of crisis in their lives. However, it was not only Abu Hamza Al-Masri who provided inspiration for the group. They were also in close contact with another influential militant, Mohamed Hamid, who was convicted in the UK and in March 2008 was sentenced to seven and a half years in prison. Hamid was a stalwart of militant Islamism and a well-known face on the British radical scene. He was born in 1957 in Tanzania to an Indian Muslim family. He came to the UK as a child and grew up in Yorkshire, although he moved to London when he was 12. As he grew up he became a drop-out and got involved in a life of petty crime that landed him in and out of borstal and prison on various charges. After his first marriage broke down he became addicted to crack cocaine and was living at rock bottom selling everything he owned in order to feed his addiction. However, a chance visit to a mosque with his brother in the 1990s changed his life and he rediscovered his Islamic roots. Shortly afterwards he decided to travel to India where he met his second wife. She moved back to the UK with him and he became increasingly caught up in his religion. He opened an Islamic bookshop in Clapton in east London and also got involved with Islamic youth work. He also spoke at Hyde Park, promoting an uncompromising message advocating that young Muslims should fight for their faith. Indeed Hamid was recorded by the British security services as having said of the 7/7 bombings, 'How many people did they take out?' When given the reply '52' he responded, 'That's not even breakfast for me. That's not even breakfast for me in this country.'[77]

It is at Speakers' Corner that Hamid is believed to have first met the 21/7 bombers.[78] The bombers then began attending late-night talks in his Hackney home where he would hold court on issues related to Islam and politics. Hamid was also involved in the Oxford Street altercation in which Ibrahim had been arrested in 2004. The would-be bombers also attended some of the camping trips that Hamid organized around the country, including one in the Lake District in 2004. Ramzi Mohamed and Hussein Osman are also reported to have attended one of his paintballing trips just four days before the 7/7 bombings.[79] Clearly the charisma and crude politics of figures such as Hamid and Abu Hamza Al-Masri were sufficient to convince these individuals that giving up their lives was a worthy cause.

The very different profiles of this group of men and those who succeeded in detonating their explosives on 7/7 suggests that there is no set type of individual or specific problem that can lead to radicalism. In fact the picture in the UK was further complicated in June and July 2007 with the failed attacks on London and Glasgow that are alleged to have been carried out by a diverse group of foreign suspects, some of whom were medical practitioners. It is clear therefore that the profiles and motivations of those who have carried out attacks or planned attacks in the UK are as varied and as difficult to pin down as the individuals involved. As the number of terrorism-related arrests in the UK since 2001 demonstrates, those accused of militancy range from first-generation migrants originating from a wide range of countries, to second-generation migrants, to converts to Islam, although it appears that more of those arrested in recent years are from south Asian communities.

However, it should be noted that many of those arrested under this legislation have in fact been released without charge. According to the UK's Home Office, between 11 September 2001 and 31 March 2007, a total of 1,228 arrests were made in relation to terrorist offences. Of those people arrested only 132 were charged with terrorist offences, with a further 109 being charged with terrorist offences and other criminal offences; 669 of those arrested were released without charge.[80]

While those who have actually been charged under terrorist legislation in the UK or have actually been involved in terrorist plots come from a variety of backgrounds, as explained at the outset of this chapter, it is undeniable that radicalism among second-generation Asians in the UK is growing. Various trials have occurred since 7/7 that have implicated young second-generation Asians in attempted plots. These include the fertilizer plot in which five young militants, most of them Asian, were convicted in April 2007, and the plot to create a dirty bomb that was led by Dhiren Barot, himself a convert to Islam from Hinduism, for which six other young men were convicted in June 2007. This is clearly a difficult and complex problem that poses particular challenges for the British security services. It has also resulted in policymakers trying to grapple with how to find a way to counter radicalization inside Britain, as if young people's turning to militant interpretations of Islam is simply the result of local factors related to their being in Europe and that can be solved somehow at the local level. It is true of course that growing up in Europe must have factored somehow into the radicalization process of young British Asians, or indeed of any second-generation community in the continent, including in France or the Netherlands. Yet looking at the majority of those in the UK who have been involved in terrorism or convicted on terrorism-related charges, it would appear that their own cultural mindset and upbringing, as well as their continued links with the sub-continent, have been highly influential in shaping their worldview.

While second and third generations may have a unique experience growing up in the UK and may struggle around issues of identity, this does not necessarily mean that they do not share the same cultural values and dedication to religiosity as their parents, even if this religiosity may be expressed in different and more politicized terms. Indeed the importance of cultural values is often underestimated in debates about terrorism and radicalization, not least because of the sensitivities of the subject. Yet it is undeniable that there is a long history of suspicion between these communities and there is also a fear about Western cultural values that cannot always be easily overcome. Arguably such ideas may help to foster a mindset that may be more susceptible to radical solutions. Furthermore, although it might be being expressed more fervently among south Asian communities at the moment, this radicalism is part of a long history of political and militant Islam that evolved in the Islamic world and continues to reverberate around Muslim communities across the globe.

Therefore, while trying to find local solutions such as improving educa-

tional opportunities or housing facilities or adopting more coherent integration policies might be all well and good for the community as a whole, this
is unlikely to quash support for radical alternatives among the tiny minority
that become attracted to them. Indeed thousands of young second-generation Pakistanis in the UK are facing the same local issues and conditions,
but they do not choose the path of radicalism. The issue is clearly far more
complex and is related to a combination of factors and forces that cannot be
solved by adopting localized counter-radicalization strategies that focus on
the UK or indeed on Europe and ignore the wider, more influential context
of the Islamic world.

# CHAPTER 10

# RADICAL CONVERTS

The participation of a handful of Western converts to Islam in terrorist attacks, such as Germaine Lindsay in the London bombings or Muriel Degauque, the Belgian woman who blew herself up in Iraq in 2005, prompted much media speculation that converts were the new enemy within. It also prompted the suggestion that Al-Qa'ida was on the hunt for an army of 'blond, blue-eyed' would-be jihadists who could evade the scrutiny of Western security agencies more effectively. One analyst warned that converts 'know the local culture and blend in. They cannot be deported. They can hide their religious affiliation by avoiding mosques, lying low, even drinking alcohol and taking drugs to maintain their cover.'[1] The idea of people turning against their own societies in this way is clearly a prospect that both fascinates and frightens some within the West, and the convert issue has captured the public imagination in Europe. However, this is not the first time that such an image has been used. Experts also referred to Bosnian Muslims as posing a similar threat by virtue of their being European, issuing warnings such as, 'the next wave of terrorism could be carried out by people with fair skin, blond hair and blue eyes'.[2]

Unsurprisingly the idea of converts threatening their own societies is also something that has been taken up and used as a propaganda tool by Al-Qa'ida itself. In August 2003 Al-Qa'ida member Abu-Muhammad Al-Abaj boasted to the Arabic media that the organization had attracted 'blue eyed' members who hide their Islamic affiliations and are 'all over US institutions'.[3] In November 2005 the *Al-Sharq Al-Awsat* newspaper reported the appearance of a statement purported to be from the Global Islamic Media Front written in the name of what would seem to be a made-up character called Rakan Bin Williams. This character threatened:

> Al Qaeda's new soldiers were born in Europe of European and Christian parents. They studied in your schools. They prayed in your churches and attended Sunday mass. They drank alcohol, ate pork and oppressed Muslims, but al Qaeda has embraced them so they have converted to Islam in secret and absorbed the philosophy of al Qaeda and swore to take up arms after their brothers. They

are currently roaming the streets of Europe and the United States planning and observing in preparation for upcoming attacks.[4]

Rakan Bin Williams made another appearance in March 2006, this time also identifying himself as an undercover Al-Qa'ida soldier in the USA and posting a warning on the website of the Global Islamic Media Front threatening two major attacks.[5] Meanwhile in December 2005 Al-Qa'ida used a white Australian convert going by the name Khalid Sheikh in one of its propaganda videos. In a broad Australian accent Khalid Sheikh declared the *shahada* (declaration of faith that is said when one converts to Islam) before going on to announce, 'I thank Allah the almighty for guiding me to the only true religion of Islam. And I praise and thank him for giving me the honour to be among the mujahideen, who seek to demise all false idols, so that the word of Allah may be supreme.'[6] Using the same words that London bomber Mohammed Siddique Khan was to use in his farewell video, as if the two were reading from the same script, Sheikh also warned, 'as you kill us, you will be killed, as you bomb us, you will be bombed'.

There is of course no real proof that these messages did indeed come from Al-Qa'ida itself and it would seem strange that if this really was Al-Qa'ida's plan that it would advertise it so explicitly However, this use of white Western converts would appear to be more of a scare-mongering tactic than anything else. It is as if having converts signed up to the cause somehow gives the movement more clout. However, the idea of having an army of blond converts lining up to join them may be little more than wishful thinking on the part of Al-Qa'ida or other radical groups. Moreover it is surely ironic that some of those converts who have carried out terrorist acts or attempted or planned terrorist acts in the West have come from ethnic-minority backgrounds such as London bomber Germaine Lindsay and shoe-bomber Richard Reid, who were both of Afro-Caribbean parentage, or José Padillo, a Latino, who was arrested in 2002 and accused of plotting a dirty-bomb attack.

Some analysts have argued that converts have worked as Al-Qa'ida foot soldiers and that some, such as German convert Christian Ganczarski and French Pierre Antoine Richard, have had direct contacts with the highest ranks of Bin Ladin's organization and were responsible for directing attacks.[7] However, the nature of these links remains tenuous and the extent to which these converts were really working on behalf of Al-Qa'ida is still unclear. It seems strange that despite their European nationality and therefore their ability to 'avoid detection' in Europe that they both allegedly were linked to attacks carried out in the Arab world – Garczanski in Djerba, Tunisia, and Richard, dubbed by the Moroccan authorities as the 'blue-eyed emir', in

Casablanca. In addition groups such as Al-Qa'ida tend to maintain a highly suspicious attitude towards converts. As one radical Irish convert, Khalid Kelly, explained, 'Extremists and terrorists don't trust us white people who convert to Islam until six years have passed at least.'[8] Kelly described how he had planned to enter Afghanistan from Pakistan in 2005 but was warned not to make the visit and was told that the Taliban might suspect him of being an American spy and kill him.

That is not to say that the skills that certain converts could potentially bring, as well as their ability to move around more freely and blend in within their own cultures, would not be useful to an organization such as Al-Qa'ida, yet the attention the issue has received in the media and policy world seems to have been rather exaggerated in relation to the limited role that converts have played in terrorism so far.

## New phenomenon?

Despite the surge in public interest in the issue of converts to Islam, conversion by Westerners to the Islamic faith dates back at least to the nineteenth century and was largely related to a fascination with 'the other' or a search for an alternative faith or lifestyle. At this time conversion was largely the domain of the elite and those who could afford the luxury of foreign travel and adventure such as Liverpool lawyer William H. Quilliam, who travelled to Morocco in 1887 where he converted to Islam and later returned to the UK to found a mosque in Liverpool. Conversions had become more popular by the 1970s, during which time there was an increase in the numbers of Europeans converting to Sufist Islam. These were sometimes dubbed 'hippy conversions' owing to the mystical elements of Sufism, and Sufist communes began to spring up in Europe. Figures such as British singer Richard Thompson, for example, converted to Sufism, along with his wife, in the 1970s and they both lived in a rustic Sufi commune in the UK. But this type of conversion was still largely the domain of the intelligentsia and was often connected to visits to the Muslim world. As Thompson explained, 'I didn't really find answers to what I was looking for in Christianity, and intellectually I thought that Sufis were where it was at. I travelled around North Africa for a long time, and it was wonderful. All I ever found was generosity and hospitality.'[9] The fact that Sufism was popular among converts in Europe during this period is largely a reflection of the fact that Islam in the Middle East had yet to take on any meaningful political dimension, and religiosity had yet to enter the political sphere.

By the 1980s and 1990s, however, a new breed of converts had appeared in Europe. These individuals were taking on a more politicized interpretation of the faith, began supporting political causes such as Bosnia and Palestine and at the most extreme end were even taking up arms in the name of jihad. This shift was directly related to the development of political Islam in the Middle East and the corresponding Islamic revivalism that was sweeping the Islamic world at the time and reflected among Muslim communities in the West. It was also related to the start of the large-scale Saudi propaganda efforts that followed the Iranian revolution and which resulted in the circulation of an abundance of Wahabist literature, some of it aimed specifically at new Muslims. This interest in new Muslims was not only about spreading Wahabism, but was also motivated by the propaganda value attached to converts. Therefore converts no longer needed to travel outside of Europe to come into direct contact with Islam, and the new politicized ideology was now very much on their doorstep. As such the type of Islamist ideology that converts came into contact with at this time was very different to that of their predecessors. This was a more simplistic black and white version of Islam stripped of its intellectual traditions, focused around a series of grievances and often based around the politics of anger. This enabled the faith to reach out to a wider range of individuals with varying backgrounds and reasons for converting, rather than just the educated elite. As French Interior Ministry official Bernard Goddard has noted, the attraction to Westerners of *salafism* is that it is 'not elitist, is more simplistic and it speaks to everyone'.[10] Directly in line with the Islamist revivalism of the Islamic world, converts began talking about aspiring to a 'pure Islam' untainted by local tradition or custom and, like some born Muslims, converts also began indulging in a nostalgia for the golden era of the time of the Prophet. Therefore, like Muslim immigrant communities in Europe, converts proved to be ultimately responsive to shifts and events occurring outside of the continent.

In fact, despite the aspiration to a pure Islam, the causes and politics that some of the more militant converts took up seem to have been directly related to the nationality of the individuals who introduced them to the faith or the group of Muslims they hung around with. It was almost as if the mood of the community they were mixing in rubbed off on them directly. French converts became noticeably interested in the Algerian jihad in a much more intense and direct way than those of other nationalities. For example, two converts, Joseph Jaime and David Vallat, were sentenced in France in 1997 to five and six years respectively after they were convicted of providing logistical support to an Algerian GIA network. Jaime, who was the son of Spanish immigrants, was born in the French town of Givors in the beautiful Rhône valley. He left school as soon as he was able and got involved in petty crime and worked on the black market. Vallat, on the other hand, had been an architecture student but dropped out and converted to Islam. Jaime turned to Islam when he met Ahtmane Saada, an Algerian from his home town who had been in Afghanistan and who was later killed fighting with the GIA in Algeria in 1994. Vallat is also believed to have been involved with Algerians before he converted. The men met each other in Afghanistan, and after they had both returned to France in 1994 shared the same dream of going to assist the jihad in Algeria, but never succeeded because of logistical difficulties. Yet the Algerian cause remained in their hearts and they were arrested in August 1995. When their lodgings in Chasse-sur-Rhône were raided, police found arms, electronic components and material that could have been used to make detonators.

As the cases of Vallat and Jaime demonstrated, the concept of going to fight jihad, which first gained currency during the Afghanistan experience of the 1980s, was also translated into convert communities in the West, and a small but steady trickle of convert recruits took it upon themselves to go to fight for the cause. Bosnia was particularly important in this respect and a number of converts went there to fight on behalf of their new-found fellow Muslims. This included figures such as British jihadist David Sinclair who, according to Azzam publications, was sacked from his job in a computer company after he announced his conversion and began turning up for work dressed in full Islamic garb. After being fired, he went off to join the Bosnian mujahideen and allegedly became so extreme that he refused even to return to the UK for a break, saying, 'What is there for me to do in the land of the *kufar?*' [11] He was allegedly shot in the heart in a battle against Croat forces. Similarly British jihadist Andrew Rowe, who converted to Islam in his late teens, is also alleged to have fought in Bosnia. The story of his recruitment is similar to that of many born Muslims who joined the Bosnian struggle. Rowe began attending a west London mosque where he heard stories about the Bosnian war that prompted him to go to support the jihad there.[12] In July 1995 he was injured when a convoy he was travelling in was attacked.

However, just as there were a limited number of jihadists from the born-Muslim community who went to fight in Bosnia, the number of converts who went also appears to have been relatively small. Despite the fact that Bosnian Muslims were European, and therefore one might assume that European converts would feel a greater affinity and desire to fight on their behalf, the struggle did not appear to attract convert fighters in particularly large numbers. However, converts from a variety of backgrounds did crop up on the various jihadist battlefields or in jihadist training camps through the 1990s, not only in Bosnia but also in places such as Chechnya, Indonesia and Afghanistan. Therefore, just as for born Muslims, some of those who had been attracted to more militant interpretations of the faith saw it as their religious duty to join the jihad to defend their fellow Muslims of the *ummah* and their conversion did not limit them to the confines of European politics or the trials of being Muslim in secular European society.

Going to fight jihad in a foreign land is one thing, but launching a suicide attack against one's own country is another. Yet converts appear again to have followed the trend in the wider Islamic world since 9/11 to engage in acts of 'martyrdom'. Failed shoe-bomber Richard Reid, for example, was willing to explode himself in mid-air for the sake of the cause. Similarly Germaine Lindsay, who converted around 2000, carried out his deadly suicide attack on the London underground in July 2007. Three of the suspects arrested for their alleged involvement in the disrupted plot to blow up transatlantic airliners, which was uncovered in the UK in August 2006, were also converts. Therefore converts have proved no less immune than born Muslims to the prevailing trend of the moment and as willing to give their lives for the cause. This would suggest that there is nothing especially different about radical converts who have taken on more extreme interpretations of the faith.

## Motivations

Pinpointing exactly what prompts an individual to convert to a new faith is extremely difficult and there are as many reasons and motivations for converting as there are converts. For many, the decision to take on Islam is related to purely practical considerations such as marriage. For others becoming Muslim is the result of a personal theological quest, and many converts have dabbled in various religions before settling on Islam as the faith for them.[13] Others found Islam while they were experiencing acute personal crises and in some cases mental breakdowns. The plethora of conversion stories posted on the Internet often appear to be artificially constructed, as do the conversion experiences that regularly appear in the Arabic media. One such story appeared in the Saudi press in August 2005 and told of how an Italian priest had watched the funeral of Saudi King Fahd on satellite television at the same time as he had witnessed a Christian funeral procession. He had been so moved by the simplicity of the Islamic burial, or so the story goes, that he converted to Islam immediately.[14] These kinds of stories are particularly prevalent during Ramadan and tend to focus around intellectuals and members of the Western elite who have converted, or around famous figures. There is a feeling in some of these stories that if a Westerner converts to the faith then Islam is somehow validated.

As for those who took on more politicized and militant forms of the faith, it is extremely difficult to ascertain what drove them to convert and, as in conversion stories more generally, the information available in the public domain is limited, largely anecdotal and often contradictory. However, a number of patterns and trends do emerge that fall broadly in line with the categories determined by Olivier Roy in his book *Globalised Islam*.[15] These categories include politicized rebels who are attracted to the anti-imperialist dimensions of Islam; former drug addicts and petty thieves who turn to Islam as an escape from their situations; and converts from ethnic minorities who are seeking a way to deal with racism.[16] Roy has labelled all these types of conversions as 'protest conversions' and has suggested that Islam has become a way for modern-day European rebels to find a cause.

It is true that owing to the fact that groups such as Al-Qa'ida have targeted the United States and voiced their general opposition to Western policies as well as to the Western way of life, Islam is being interpreted by some as the ideology that can stand up to Western imperialism and capitalism. This is an idea that some converts have been keen to play on. One convert member of the group Hizb ut Tahrir in the UK commented, 'Islam is the only ideological challenge at the moment.'[17] Clearly this is vastly over exaggerated and the number of Muslims in Europe especially who are politicized or who even seek to challenge the status quo remains extremely small. Indeed it would be wrong to overplay the protest element and to suggest that Islam has stepped in to fill the void that opened up after the demise of the left-wing protest movements of the past. This is because, while left-wing ideologies were generally open to anyone who wanted to join, the religious dimension of Islam, as well as its rules and restrictions, is always likely to have limited appeal in secular Westernized European society. In fact, just as political opposition movements in Europe have splintered into single-issue protest movements such as gay rights, women's rights or environmental matters, political Islam appears to be more of a limited-issue cause that is concerned only with the situation of Muslims. Indeed much of the political Islamist agenda appears to be focused around minority politics such as securing the right to wear the *niqab* or the *hijab* rather than broader socio-economic issues. Moreover many Islamists are also concerned with regional rather than truly international politics and focus on issues confined to the Islamic world. It is difficult to see therefore how this ideology could have a broad appeal. Therefore, while conversion might represent a way for some converts to express a rejection of societal values, it cannot be considered as a broad-based ideological movement that could challenge the fundamentals of European society in any major way. While some converts might view their taking on of Islam as a form of political statement or protest, the small numbers involved would hardly constitute a new protest movement.

Moreover, while more recent converts to the faith might be attracted to the idea that Islam is often portrayed as public enemy number one, the majority of those converts we know about who have been involved in terror-ist-related activity actually converted in the 1980s and 1990s. While there were certainly concerns among Western intelligence agencies about Islamic activism during the 1990s, radical Islam has only really been considered to pose a major threat to the Western world following the attacks of 9/11. As such converting to Islam in the early 1990s might have been considered as a way to rebel against one's culture or society, but it would not have been regarded as a major statement against Western imperialism. Indeed, consid-ering that the West had allied itself with the fighters in Afghanistan in the 1980s, those who converted at that time could even be considered to have been on the same side fighting against the same communist enemy. This includes figures such as Christian Ganczarski, who converted around 1986, and French convert Joseph Jaime, who took on his new faith in the mid-1980s. The vast majority of others who were involved in terrorist-related activity converted in the 1990s, including the young German Thomas Fischer, who met his death in Chechnya, and British shoe-bomber Richard Reid. Therefore for these individuals, Islam may have represented a way to live out some sort of personalized protest related to their own particular situations or beliefs, but at the time they converted their new faith did not necessarily constitute a blatant challenge to the West.

However, some converts are clearly motivated by the romantic notion of helping the oppressed and of championing populations in the developing world. The Frenchman Lionel Dumont, the youngest of eight children who was brought up in a modest part of Tourcoing, a former textile centre in the north of France, had always dreamed of foreign travel and, like many young people, undertook casual jobs before going to university to fund this dream. He ended up serving with a French peace-keeping force in Djibouti and Somalia in the early 1990s and returned to France embittered and angered by Western policies in the region. He converted to Islam and set about find-ing a way to assist the Muslims; it was this that prompted him to go to Bosnia where he undertook humanitarian work but also reportedly under-took to fight. After his arrest in 2003 Dumont recounted, somewhat roman-tically, about his Bosnia experience, 'When we foreigners arrived we were welcomed with open arms, like Messiahs. For me this war was a humanitar-ian war.' [18] In a similar vein, another French convert, Christophe Caze, also appears to have had romantic ideas about going to help the oppressed. Caze was a medical student who, after completing five years of his course, went to Bosnia where he worked in a hospital in Zenica treating the wounded mujahideen. While he was there Caze also took up arms alongside the Arab fighters. Some reports have suggested that he travelled to Bosnia to assist the Muslims and converted there, although other reports claim that he was already a Muslim before he went. However, if one is to believe the reports that Caze had indulged himself in playing football with the severed heads of Serbian fighters, he was also clearly already inclined towards violence. The Bosnian experience appears to have radicalized both men: when they returned to France they set up the Roubaix gang and carried out a series of violent armed robberies with the aim of channelling the proceeds to the GIA in Algeria. The gang also tried to explode a car bomb in front of the main police station in Lille two days before the G7 summit in 1996, but the bomb did not go off properly. According to French police reports the two converts even received money from radical preacher Abu Hamza Al-Masri in London.[19] However, the gang was so amateur that French police were soon on to them and Caze was killed in crossfire in 1996 during a police chase on the Lille–Gand autoroute. More than anything else, Caze and Dumont appear to have been hot-headed loose canons who had become involved in Algerian politics through their personal connections with Algerians both in France and in Bosnia and who got out of their depth in their jihadist activities.

Another convert who appears to have had romantic ideas about fighting on behalf of the oppressed was Yusuf Galan, the Spanish convert who set up the Ibn Taymiyyah Cultural Association in Asturias in 1996 and who was accused of involvement in the Madrid bombings. Galan had dabbled a little in Basque separatist politics before he turned to Islam and championed the cause of oppressed Muslims and the Palestinians in particular after a trip to the Middle East. Galan was the son of a highly influential Spanish military officer and, like Dumont and Caze, had some level of education. For these men, the idea of championing a cause appears to have influenced their decision to convert to Islam. As such it would appear that the attraction for these individuals was more to do with Third World politics and with adopting an ideology or worldview outside of their own societies and cultures.

This interest in Third World politics appears to be an important motivating factor for those more educated converts who join groups such as Hizb ut Tahrir. Many cite issues such as Palestine as one of the things that pushed them to join the faith.[20] For some of these converts there is also an attraction to another culture, and their conversion often occurred after a visit to a Muslim country. One senior Hizb ut Tahrir member explained that he went to Jordan and was so moved by the generosity of the population and the sense of community that this started him on the path towards converting to Islam.[21] It seems, however, that these converts do not always distinguish between Islam and the cultural values of the places they are visiting. Moreover in some cases they appear to take a very idealistic and surface impression of the cultures that they aspire to belong to. As British convert Abdur-Raheem

Greene, who has two wives and who is famous for his fiery preaching in London's Speakers' Corner, said of what moved him to convert while he was in Egypt: 'Egyptians were poor, suffered hardships, yet were happy. They left everything in the hands of Allah and forget their miseries when they return home. ... But in England I found people shallow, materialistic. They try to be happy but happiness is superficial. Their prayers combined songs, dances, clapping but no humility, nor intimacy with God.' [22]

Therefore some converts who have adopted their new faith to the point of being prepared to take up arms to defend it are clearly motivated by a romantic sense of helping those who are less fortunate than themselves or by a yearning for an idealized alternative to their own lives and societies. This, however, tends to be primarily the domain of the educated and those who are attracted to politics, and their views about Western society are shaped more by political concerns than their own marginalization from it.

## Conversion as an escape

For the majority of converts who got involved in violence or who came to espouse more radical views, however, they appear to have been seeking a way out of the various difficulties they found themselves in rather than seeking a romantic cause. In fact the majority of converts we know about who ended up getting involved in radical Islam came from poor or deprived backgrounds. Many came from broken homes, including Richard Reid, Germaine Lindsay and Jason Walters of the Hofstaad group, to name but a few. Many did badly at school or dropped out of education altogether. Christian Ganczarski, who grew up in Muelheim in Germany after his Polish parents had settled there in 1976, did not get any further than the seventh grade at school. He became a welder in a factory and was allegedly introduced to Islam by his colleagues. He went to Saudi Arabia in the early 1990s where he became more extreme in his views. From there he is alleged to have travelled around the various jihadist hot spots of the world. Similarly British convert Andrew Rowe, who was convicted in the UK in 2005 on terrorism charges, left school with few qualifications. Richard Reid was also a very poor student, and Muriel Degauque left school at 16 and got into the habit of running away from home, including on one occasion getting as far as the Ardennes region 100 miles away from her home in Charleroi without her parents' knowledge.

This educational under-achievement often went hand in hand with a life of alcohol or drug abuse and often involvement in petty crime. This was the case for both Rowe, who was a petty drugs dealer, and Degauque, who often did not turn up to work at the bakery where she was employed because of her drug problem. French convert brothers David and Jerome Courtailler, who came from a working-class family which fell apart when their father's butcher's business went under, were also poor students who drifted into the drugs scene. They found Islam in the UK, to which they had travelled to try to get their lives back on track. David Courtailler's conversion to a radical interpretation of the faith was particularly striking and reminiscent of someone in deep crisis. He converted in the late 1990s in Brighton and allegedly flew to Pakistan just three days later, from where he travelled to Afghanistan to attend a training camp. Speaking about his experiences, Courtailler noted, 'This rapid chain of events is difficult to explain. I had problems. I was looking for a religion. I went into a mosque. I can't explain why.'[23] In some cases converts were encouraged into their new faith by other family members who thought that Islam could offer some kind of salvation. It was Richard Reid's father, Robin, who converted to Islam during a stint in prison and then convinced his son to do the same as a way of getting out of trouble. Jason Walters of the Hofstaad group was first taken to the mosque by his father who had himself converted from Baptism to Islam as a way of trying to defeat his alcohol problem. Both Jason and his brother Jermaine turned to radical Islam. Germaine Lindsay's mother was another convert to Islam, who was religiously radical enough to take on wearing the *niqab* and who reportedly hoped that Islam's strict codes on alcohol and sex would keep her son out of trouble.

Therefore it would appear that these unstable individuals latched their personal problems on to an imported ideology that enabled them to escape from their problems and start completely afresh. Indeed one of the attractions of Islam is that it offers the opportunity to wipe the slate clean and start again. While this could be said of taking on any new religion, for Europeans converting to Islam there is the added dimension that Islam is still considered largely as a faith external to European culture and so the change is more dramatic. Even the symbolic idea of adopting an Islamic name – something that is not obligatory when becoming Muslim – as well as wearing Islamic dress that marks one out from the rest of society offers the sense that one can be both physically and spiritually 'reborn' and become part of a new community.

In this vein many converts reject the very word 'convert' and prefer to be identified as 'reverts', as they believe that everyone was born Muslim but that some people moved away from the faith and adopted corrupt principles. As such they believe that they are reverting to their original Islamic identity. This idea is promoted by Islamic organizations set up to meet the needs of Muslims in Europe. For example, Dr Jamal Badawi, who is a member of the European Council for Fatwa and Research, explained:

I do not agree with the term 'convert'; I prefer to use the term 'revert'. Islam is the faith that resonates with pure human nature. ... It also teaches universal morality, justice and compassion. We believe as Muslims that these positive and constructive qualities are not a monopoly of Muslims but are embedded in upright human nature. So when the person accepts Islam, he or she is reverting back to his/her true spiritual self.[24]

This reversion idea fosters the comforting sense that by taking on Islam, converts are returning to their natural state and therefore do not need to be afraid of the fact that they are cutting links with their former identity and life. It emphasizes that, as non-Muslims, they were simply passing through a phase of *jahiliyyah*, which is full of licentiousness and hedonism, and that by taking on the new faith they have once again become pure and clean and can put a former life behind them.

Islam, with its routine, also provides a sense of structure and discipline as well as a direction and purpose in life that for many appeared to have been missing. Indeed many of those converts who have engaged in violence seem to be misfits who turned to Islam to find a community that would accept them. The German Thomas Fischer, for example, was an introverted boy who came from a poor unstable background and had a speech defect. He reportedly had no friends until the age of 14, when he was befriended by a Turkish man from his local mosque who gave him something to eat and told him stories about the Prophet. The mosque and his new faith soon became his entire social environment. His family recounted how when at home he would shut himself in his bedroom for hours on end studying the Qu'ran with a Turkish friend he had met at the mosque. He later moved out of his family home and into a room above a Milli Gorus-affiliated mosque in the nearby town of Ulm. When he was 21 years old, the congregation at the mosque paid for him to study in Khartoum, where he became increasingly radical in his views. In 2002 he decided to go to Chechnya, where he met his death while still in his 20s. In the same vein Richard Reid, who came from a poor background, is repeatedly described as a loner who never fitted in. One fellow pupil who had attended the same south London school as Reid said of him, 'He was someone whom everybody knew, but he was never one of the crowd.'[25] Another noted, 'He had this hard-man image he wanted to portray. But he was soft on the inside. He was quick to follow the crowd if it would give him status.'[26] Reid left school and focused his efforts on being a graffiti artist and also moved into a hostel when his family relocated to the south west of England. During a spell in Feltham Young Offender Institution, having been convicted of 24 robberies and 22 thefts, Reid converted to Islam. After his release from prison, the mosque became his entire life. As his aunt explained, 'He was so lonely, his life was so empty.

... He found solace with his Muslim brothers. With him, it became much more than a religion, they became his family.'[27]

For these loners who never felt they really fitted into their own societies, Islam clearly gives a new sense of belonging. Indeed the mosque or the new brotherhood replaces the family and social networks that were lacking for so many. For some the imam or sheikh becomes a new father figure. Indeed the experience of these kinds of individuals was aptly expressed in the words of one young uneducated British convert, Wayne Derby, who after convert-ing at the hands of Al-Muhajiroun declared, 'Going back before I decided to convert to Islam, my life wasn't any sort of life. I was drinking alcohol, lack of work, lack of family around me, didn't have no family. Now I've got one billion point ... so many brothers around me. I couldn't ask for a bigger family in my life now.'[28]

This moving away from old familiar cultures and family structures and immersing oneself completely in the new faith is sometimes actively encour-aged by born Muslims. At the radical end of the spectrum, converts are led to believe that they should consider their families as *kufar*. Indeed Omar Bakri Mohamed's protégé and the leader of Al-Ghurraba, Abu Izideen, who converted just before his 18th birthday, still refers to his father as a heathen. In the Arabic media he said, 'I still remember the day when I pronounced Al-Shahada in my father's home. He is still from the people of kufar.'[29] Interestingly this last sentence was not included in the newspaper's English edition. Abu Izideen, also known as Omar Brooks, also revealed how Omar Bakri was closer to his heart and mind than his own father. On one occa-sion he reportedly told a female audience that it was a Muslim's duty to keep apart from the rest of society and declared, 'Never mix with them. Never let your children play with their children.'[30]

However, these kinds of ideas are not only the domain of the extreme elements. During a New Muslims Study Circle on a cold Saturday afternoon in the dark basement of London's Regent's Park mosque, where converts grouped – men on one side of the hall and women on the other – to seek guidance about being a new Muslim from the moderate imams and schol-ars of the mosque, one young woman asked whether it was acceptable to continue to meet with her non-Muslim friends. She was told that it was not a bad thing as such, but that in time she would progress and no longer wish to spend time with those kinds of people.[31] Therefore, despite the strong emphasis on family and respecting one's parents, which is generally consid-ered to be part of Islam, this encouraging of converts by certain elements to isolate themselves from their cultural roots and family structures may make those who are so inclined become potentially more vulnerable to manipula-tion.

One of the ideas promoted by those giving *dawa* to new Muslims is that Western society is degenerating and falling apart because of a lack of morality, manners and family values. This clearly strikes a chord with some converts, including those of a more radical bent. The traditional basic principles in Islam, such as family values, strict punishments and respect for one's elders, appeal to certain converts who feel that Islam offers them a set of moral certainties that can hold society together. As one male convert explained, he had been attracted to Islam because of the clear-cut punishment system, which offered an antidote to the chaos of the modern-day world.[32] He explained, 'You can't run society along vague lines.' For some male converts the ideas that through Islam they would have the certainty of a faithful wife and that everything would be in its place are also strong attractions. As one French convert, Daoud, explained about his reasons for converting, 'It's very simple, I had always been looking for fidelity in a woman, but I had never found it. I went from deception to deception and my morale was at an all-time low.'[33] Daoud went on to convert and to marry an Algerian wife.

These concerns reflect that fact that many converts, both radical and moderate, were already religious beforehand or had religious upbringings. Even if they might have gone astray for a few years, religion seems somehow to have shaped their formative years. Many of those who converted to radical forms of Islam had a Catholic background and attended Catholic schools. This includes Christian Ganczarski, David and Jerome Courtailler, Thomas Fischer, Richard Belmar and Muriel Degauque. Others had religious upbringings in other denominations, such as Jason Walters of the Hofstaad group in the Netherlands who was raised as a Baptist, and Sheikh Abdullah Faisal whose family were members of the Salvation Army. Therefore many already had concerns about morality, came from conservative backgrounds and appear to have swapped one faith for another. In fact many converts say that they feel Islam is more relevant than their previous faith – while the churches are empty, the mosques are full. It would appear therefore that Islam can also provide a sense of community that seems to be lacking in other faiths.

## Ethnic minorities and Islam in the suburbs

While the media has focused its attention on the novelty of fair-skinned Europeans converting to Islam, it is among some of Europe's ethnic minority populations that Islam is enjoying a noticeable renaissance. This is as true of those converting to moderate forms of Islam as it is of those converting to more militant strands. Indeed, many of those involved in terrorist-related activity have come from non-white ethnic backgrounds. This includes Richard Reid, Andrew Rowe and Germaine Lindsay in the UK, Jason Walters in the Netherlands and French convert Willie Brigitte, who all came from Afro-Caribbean parentage, as well as Latinos such as José Padillo and those of African descent such as Xavier Joffo who was killed in Chechnya.

It may well be that for these converts purist *salafist* Islam appears to offer a non-racist creed and a new identity that allows them to reject a society in which they may not feel comfortable. Islam is often portrayed as being a religion for everyone, unlike Christianity, which is portrayed among some ethnic groups as the white man's religion. This message clearly resonates among certain communities, such as the Afro-Caribbean community in the UK, among which conversion rates are fast growing. Omar Urquhart, the imam of the Brixton mosque and himself a black convert to Islam, observed in 2005 that 60 per cent of the mosque's 500-strong community are black converts.[34] Ironically, however, it is also among Afro-Caribbean communities in the UK that Evangelical Christianity is also enjoying a revival, suggesting that this surge in religious revivalism is as much to do with the nature of these communities as it is about Islam itself.

Looking at those radical elements we know about from ethnic minorities, it seems that racism may have played a part in their conversion but was not necessarily a major factor. Indeed the attraction to Islam appears to have been more about getting out of a life of crime and drugs, as in the case of Richard Reid or Andrew Rowe, or in finding an ideology that suited what they were seeking at the time. Moreover it seems that, like born Muslims, many of those from ethnic minorities who take on Islam focus their attentions on places such as Palestine and espouse the traditional concerns of the Arab Muslim community rather than being overt about the situation of Muslims in places such as Africa or Jamaica or engaging in debates about race issues in Europe. Figures such as the Jamaican Sheikh Abdullah Faisal, a convert to Islam who went to study Islam in Guyana and in Saudi Arabia before settling in the UK where he based himself in the south London suburb of Brixton and where he attracted a predominantly Afro-Caribbean audience, focused his oratory on Israel and on minority groups in the UK such as Hindus. He allegedly gave speeches saying, 'People with British passports, if you fly into Israel, it is easy. ... Fly into Israel and do whatever you can. If you die, you are up in paradise' and 'How do you fight a Jew? You kill a Jew. In the case of Hindus, by bombing their businesses.'[35] Faisal may well have played on the race issue. Indeed he distributed a huge array of cassettes and DVDs with titles such as 'The Devil's Deception of the 21st Century House Niggers'.

However, Faisal's real attraction appears to have been his ability to play on feelings of inadequacy and marginalization. According to some media reports, in one sermon Faisal exclaimed, 'Let's speak about jihad and how to obtain the spoils. Many Muslims complain about not having the financial means to go on a pilgrimage to Mecca. ... Many are also sad because the women they want to marry rejects them because they are not wealthy enough. Do you, like many, cry because you are poor? ... If you are suffering from poverty, wage jihad and see the money pour into your hands.'[36] He also offered a simplistic interpretation of Islam that was full of certainties. One admirer posted the following on a website: 'I have several of Shaik Faisal's lectures and while I don't agree with everything he says, I do love to hear him speak. He has so much good information and he has a knack for teaching on a level we all can understand.'[37] Faisal's message clearly attracted certain types of converts including London bomber Germaine Lindsay, who is believed to have listened to and been influenced by Faisal's sermons and cassettes.[38] Therefore while Islam may offer a means for those from ethnic minorities to feel an identification with others from minority or oppressed groups, it does not appear to be acting primarily as a vehicle for anti-racism, as Roy and others have suggested.

This rise in conversions among ethnic minorities in Europe's inner city areas would seem to be rather a channel for expressing social dissatisfaction and frustration. Indeed just as there has been a rise in conversions among the Afro-Caribbean population in the UK, France has also witnessed an increase in conversions among the white working-class populations of its suburbs. These converts seem to be taking on the politics and ideology of those they are living with in poor areas where there is little hope of employment or bettering oneself. Indeed, just like the Afro-Caribbeans in the UK, those in the French suburbs are often living on the margins of society, and Islam may offer some sort of hope and sense of a broader community. A study undertaken by the French security services, Les Renseignements Généraux, in 2005, which sampled 610 French converts whom the police had detected because of their active proselytizing, their delinquent activities or their suspected links to militant elements, found that there was a concentration of converts in urbanized zones where there were large communities of practising North Africans.[39] Although 5 per cent were from the Antilles, the majority were young whites from the suburbs who were described as fragile individuals often seeking a cause. Forty-nine per cent of them had no qualifications, and in the 15–19 age group only 20 per cent were students or were attending college.[40] The report also found that unemployment among converts was more than five times higher than the general population.

Muslim organizations have sought to undertake *dawa* work specifically in these communities, as they clearly represent a pool of potential new converts.

As one young convert from the French suburbs who converted in 2002 described, 'When the Muslim brothers came to see us to call us to the faith, me and my mates we viewed it as a bit of a struggle for the brain because it often went on for a long time, but out of respect for these people who had something easy going and humble about them, we stayed and listened. Alongside that I saw Muslim mates in my circle who returned to the religion and I noticed a change in them. They seemed calmer.'[41] The Saudis in particular focused attention in these poor urban areas.[42] Representatives of the kingdom's Islamic institutions were often seen travelling around offering grants to prospective students. The competition was high and, as one French Muslim recounted, when a Saudi representative came to the mosque in the depressing Paris Mantes la Jolie suburb offering grants, 'Eighty young people wanted to sign up! ... But the selection was very difficult and only two young people were chosen.'[43] Another Muslim in France commented on the aura of those who had spent time in Saudi Arabia and noted, 'Those who came back from over there were completely transformed. They brought back *fatwas* and cassettes of recordings of the most hardline Saudi Sheikhs.'[44]

Within these suburbs it is the young who are particularly attracted to political Islam. This is not surprising given that it is generally among the youth that ideologies flourish, and the younger the recruit the more angry they tend to be. Young converts in inner city areas of the UK have described how Islam is sweeping their schools and colleges, and imams in south London have noted that each week young people of 12 or 13 years old are coming to convert to Islam.[45] For some of those young converts, however, Islam seems to have become something of a fashion statement which has spawned an array of clothing accessories and rap bands such as Mecca2Medina and Pearls of Islam, whose lyrics rail against injustice and Islamophobia. Mecca2Medina, for example, consists partly of Afro-Caribbean converts who follow the teachings of the Sufist Sudanese Sheikh Hasan Qaribullah, the Dean of Umm Durman Islamic University in the Sudan, and whose songs have titles such as 'Proud to be a Muslim', 'We Got to Pray' and 'Muslims Don't Bow' which, with their highly politicized lyrics, play on the community's sense of being under siege:

> All our phones might be bugged and we are under surveillance
> But with divine reverence, we praise the benevolence
> MI5 MI6 CIA
> We bow and pray to Allah every day.
> We give salutations to the Rasool [Messenger]
> So we don't get skanked and fooled
> Certain fraternities wanna shut down these emcees
> But we stand firm and strong like Islamic yardies.[46]

Taking on an Islamic identity for some of these young people is clearly more than simply theology or even politics, but is also a means of gaining some street credibility. Indeed among some communities it has taken on the dimension of a kind of sub- or counter-culture that represents the oppressed and challenges the authorities. Within this context certain young converts have taken to mixing Islam with gang culture, feeling that Islam can give religious justification to their criminal activities or that linking themselves to radical Islam somehow gives them more menace and greater street credibility. This linking of crime and Islam is of course not unique to this community, as North African immigrants have also shown a willingness to commit petty crimes – in many cases in order to survive – and crime is deemed acceptable by some when it has been carried out against Christians or *kufar*. In the UK this reached an extreme level when a teenage street gang calling itself the Muslim Boys appeared on the scene in south London and allegedly forced people to convert to Islam at gunpoint. According to Detective Superintendent John Coles of London's Metropolitan Police, the Muslim Boys are responsible for at least two execution-style murders as well as robberies and attempted murders.[47]

It would appear that Islam also provides these young people with a strong sense of community and brotherhood, as well as the feeling that they are part of something more solid and bigger than their immediate environment. As one community worker in south London explained, 'For many poverty-stricken kids growing up alienated on estates, often without fathers, the Muslim Boys have become a seductive, alternative family.'[48] However, this attraction is related more to criminality and delinquency than to what is generally conceived of as militant Islam and is a far cry from the days of Abu Musab Al-Suri and his theorizing about fighting jihad to overthrow corrupt regimes of the Middle East. Indeed Al-Suri and his ilk would have been horrified at what is essentially a trivializing of both Islam and the idea of jihad.

Yet these young, highly impressionable, often poorly educated individuals who operate at the margins of society can appear rather like a blank canvas ready to be moulded by those with an engaging and self-affirming ideology. Nowhere is this more the case than in prison. Apart from the fact that Islam offers the chance to start afresh, the discipline of a faith like Islam not only brings a structure that can help shape the long monotony of the prison day but can also act as a prop. As one convert inmate in Brixton prison explained, 'Islam makes me feel stronger and more in control of my own destiny.'[49] Another young inmate in the same prison explained how, after he had converted in prison, he felt more comfortable with himself.[50] Moreover the close-knit community and sense of brotherhood among Muslim prisoners clearly provides a sense of security and support to those who may be feeling particularly vulnerable, as well as much needed protection from other prison gangs.

However, the fact that a number of individuals who have been involved in terrorist-related activity converted to Islam in prison, such as Richard Reid who converted in Feltham Young Offender Institution in the UK, has given rise to the idea that Europe's prisons are hotbeds of radical Islamism and are churning out terrorists who have been converted by militant imams. It is true that religious groups, from moderate to radical movements, have sought to spread their ideology inside European prisons. This of course is not only the domain of the Islamists, as other faith groups have focused their proselytizing efforts on the prison population with equal if not more vigour. In the case of Islam, groups such as the Muslim Brotherhood have sought to work inside prisons, although their focus appears to be as much about bringing born Muslims back to the straight path as it is about converting new Muslims. One Algerian Ikhwani imam in Milan, for example, took it upon himself to visit his local prison in the hope of bringing Muslim inmates back to their faith and getting them off drugs.[51] The Saudis have also tried to extend their influence into the European prison system and have been willing over the years to spend huge amounts of money to try to influence this captive audience through organizations such as the Iqra Prisoner Welfare Trust, which carries out prison visits and provides literature to inmates. Hizb ut Tahrir has also proved itself keen to proselytize to the prison population and the group used to send out copies of its *Khilafah* publication and other literature to prisoners in the UK before the prison services began to clamp down in the aftermath of 9/11.

It is true that there were a number of imams who were espousing militant views within the prison system before 9/11, at which point the authorities woke up to what was going on. In the UK, for example, two prison imams were expelled between September and December 2001 for allegedly making 'inappropriate comments' about the attacks in the US. However, as in the Muslim community in the outside world, it is not necessarily the official imam who is the carrier of such radical messages. Indeed the prison imam is often a distant figure who visits periodically and is therefore not really considered to be part of the tight-knit community of brothers. In some cases this is partly because of a general lack of prison imams. Despite the large Muslim population in French prisons, there simply are not enough prison imams to go around. As Missoum Abdelkajid Chaoui, the imam at the Nanterre detention centre, explained, there are only eight Muslim chaplains for the 20,000 Muslim inmates in the Paris region.[52] More importantly the prison imam is often regarded by the prisoners as being part of the prison establishment and therefore is not necessarily completely trusted. This clearly depends on the character and background of the individual imam, but it means that other Muslim prisoners may be more influential, including in the conversion process. One convert inmate in a London prison explained how he had been introduced to Islam by his cell mate who came from Yemen and how he considered this cell mate to be his main source of information and guidance in Islamic matters.[53] In a similar vein, another Arab Muslim prisoner spoke of how he had succeeded in converting five inmates because people chose to come to him for advice and guidance on Islamic matters.[54] For some converts, those originating from an Arab country and, importantly, who are able to speak Arabic – the language of the Qu'ran – may make them feel they are getting a more 'authentic' version of Islam. In some instances it would also appear that those prisoners being held on terrorist-related charges may have additional clout and respect from those seeking a means through which to channel their anger and frustration. Indeed figures such as Safe Bourada in France, who had been imprisoned in the mid-1990s in relation to the attacks on France, is alleged to have created his own small group in prison that consisted of at least two converts to Islam. The group was re-arrested in 2005 on charges of planning a series of attacks on the French mainland.

Ironically in some places, this is inadvertently encouraged by the authorities. In some prisons in Italy, for example, the authorities do not allow outside imams to come into the premises, as they fear they cannot understand or contain the type of material and preaching that prisoners will be exposed to. The prison authorities of the Bollate prison in Milan prefer to allow Muslim prisoners to appoint imams from among themselves, but still complain that they do not understand much of what is happening.[55] Generally unable to place what is being told them about Islam in context, converts may be particularly susceptible to more radical influences in prison.

However, this issue should not be overplayed. If one looks more closely at those converts involved in terrorism who had converted in prison, some of them actually took on more militant ideologies after they had been released. Richard Reid, for example, was reportedly seeking a 'pure type of Islam' upon his exit from prison. He found his way to Brixton mosque before getting involved with more radical elements. Likewise American convert Auki Collins, who fought in Bosnia and Chechnya and who turned to Islam in prison, first spent time with the Dawa Tabligh at his local mosque after his release. This would suggest that while prison might offer a set of conditions that encourage conversion, converting to militant Islam is a much more complex process than simply being incarcerated behind prison walls.

Moreover the fact that like many other converts, those who turn to

Islam in prison also consider the most authentic and pure Islam to come from Arabs and the Arab world suggests that converts in prison, like those outside, still view Islam as a faith that is imported from abroad and consider that the heart of Islam still resides in the Middle East. More broadly, while some analysts have argued that the increasing number of converts who have become involved in jihadist activity from the 1990s onwards reflects the 'Westernization of Islam',[56] converts still do not appear to have developed any specific Westernized Islam of their own. They are not one homogeneous group and are as divided as born Muslims. In many cases, the interpretation of Islam that they take on depends on who introduced them to the faith in the first place. Furthermore there are few successful convert scholars in Europe, especially at the radical end of the spectrum, and those that do exist, such as Sheikh Abdullah Faisal, were trained in Saudi institutions and as such do not appear to be offering anything particularly new or Westernized to the faith. Moreover while many organizations in Europe with links to the Muslim Brotherhood are now pushing for a more Europeanized Islam that sits more comfortably with being a minority community, many European converts instead appear to be seeking something outside their own Westernized experience and prefer not to view themselves as being different because they are new to the faith.

CHAPTER **11**

# THE DANISH CARTOON ROW
# AND THE DILEMMA OF
# THE MODERATES[1]

O n 30 September 2005 a little-known Danish newspaper, *Jyllands-Posten*, published 12 cartoons depicting the Prophet Mohammed in various guises including one showing him with a ticking bomb nestling in his turban. Not only is portraying the Prophet considered to be a form of blasphemy in Islam, the likening of Mohammed to a terrorist was something that was bound to cause great offence to Muslims. However, the initial response to the cartoons, including the Islamic Society of Denmark's (Islamisk Trossamfund) demand that the newspaper apologize and the protest of around 3,000 Muslims in Copenhagen, hardly caused a ripple. In fact it was commensurate with the size of Denmark's small Muslim community, which numbers around 270,000 or just 5 per cent of the population.[2] The cartoons were reprinted in the Egyptian *Al-Fajr* newspaper just one month after their original publication in Denmark and went all but unnoticed.

Yet by February 2006 the Islamic world was burning. Violent protests had spread to Pakistan, Afghanistan, Lebanon, Syria and Libya, radicals in London were calling for the beheading of anyone who insulted the Prophet and the world's media was once again talking about the unbridgeable chasm between East and West. The images of angry Muslims in the streets of capital cities across the world burning the Danish flag were reminiscent of the scenes that erupted during the Salman Rushdie affair more than two decades before. But it was not just the protest scenes that echoed the events of the 1980s. Just as in the Rushdie affair, the internationalization of the crisis was carefully orchestrated by a number of local Islamist groups and various constituencies in the Middle East, as well as Muslim groups in Europe, who all jumped in to try to take advantage of the situation. Indeed what was ostensibly a religious affair related to blasphemy was soon taken up to suit an array of different political agendas.

The main players who shifted what was a local concern into a worldwide event were a group of Danish Islamists. Two main figures emerged as the leaders of this group. One was the Palestinian Ahmed Abu Laban, who had lived in Denmark since the early 1990s and ran the country's largest Islamic association, the Islamic Society of Denmark, until his death in February 2007. Although he was born in Jaffa in Palestine in 1946, Abu Laban was brought up in Egypt where he moved with his family in 1948 and where he trained as a mechanical engineer before going to train in Islamic theology in various Middle Eastern countries.[3] It has been alleged that during the 1990s Abu Laban had close contacts with the Egyptian Al-Jama'a Al-Islamiya who had a base in Copenhagen through Talaat Fouad Qassem. Indeed Abu Laban was at the forefront of demonstrations in Copenhagen in 1995 protesting against Qassem's disappearance in Croatia.[4] It is also alleged that Abu Laban worked as a translator for Al-Jama'a Al-Islamiya's publication, Al-Murabitoun.[5] The Palestinian had a reputation for hardline views and in August 1994, when questioned by the same Jyllands-Posten newspaper about a series of bloody attacks on foreigners in Algeria at the hands of the GIA, allegedly commented, 'Perhaps the tourists are spreading AIDS in Algeria just like the Jews are spreading AIDS in Egypt.'[6] Yet, aware that the spotlight was on the Islamist community, Abu Laban had softened his stance and had come to present a rather more mature and flexible figure in the post-9/11 climate.

The other prominent figure in the group was Ahmed Akkari, a Lebanese imam in his late 20s. Akkari was brought up in a largely secular family both in Denmark and Lebanon but settled in Denmark in 1994 after he was granted a humanitarian residency permit. He went on to train as a teacher in the town of Århus. While he was doing his training he undertook an apprenticeship in the town's Muslim private school. During this posting, in a clear indication of his strong religious convictions, it is reported that he beat up one of the pupils at the school after the 11-year-old boy had tried to pull off the hijab of Akkari's sister. Akkari had laid into the boy so ferociously that the police were notified and the imam was sentenced to 40 days in prison, although he was given a suspended sentence as it was his first offence.[7]

These two imams and a number of other Danish Islamists worked together to set the wheels in motion to ensure that the cartoons would not continue to go unnoticed. They contacted a number of Muslim embassies in Copenhagen and a group of diplomats from 12 countries including Pakistan and Egypt demanded a meeting with the Danish prime minister, Anders

Fogh Rasmussen, urging him to 'take all those responsible to task'.[8] After the prime minister declined to meet with the diplomats, Akkari formed a group calling itself the European Committee for Honouring the Prophet, which was to act as an apparently self-appointed umbrella group for the various Islamic organizations in Denmark. The group collected 17,000 signatures in a petition asking the Danish government to denounce the cartoons and filed a criminal complaint against the *Jyllands-Posten*. This complaint was investigated but was unsuccessful. Yet despite the group's activities, the affair had sparked little attention beyond the Danish borders. Even Muslims residing in other European countries had not taken up the issue in any major way and many were not even aware of the campaign.

Frustrated by the lack of action, the imams then decided to take the matter up in the Arab world where they were certain to get a reaction. Indeed, despite all the emphasis on globalized Islam and the talk about a special European Islam, the Islamist powerhouse is still firmly rooted in the various constituences that operate in the Middle East. Other Islamists in Europe were all too well aware of what the consequences of such a move would be and were unhappy about the situation. One leading member of a Muslim Brotherhood-affiliated organization in Germany, for example, explained how he and his organization had been concerned about the Danish imams going to the Middle East and stirring up the issue unnecessarily.[9] However, Abu Laban clearly was not the kind of man to take such advice. In November 2005 he told the Islamist website IslamOnline.net, 'We want to internationalize this issue so that the Danish government would realize that the cartoons were not only insulting to Muslims in Denmark but also to Muslims worldwide.'[10] Abu Laban also declared, 'We have fled our countries because we were denied freedom of expression so no one should play this tune with us.'[11] Yet ironically it was to some of the most repressive countries in the Arab world that Abu Laban and others looked to give their cause some weight.

In December 2005 Akkari and some of the other imams embarked upon a Middle East tour to promote their cause. However, the picture that the group drew of what had been happening in Denmark was not exactly true to the facts of the case. The imams had compiled a dossier containing the cartoons, some newspaper articles and the letters they had written to the Arab embassies. However, concerned that the original cartoons might not prove inflamatory enough they also included three further images that they presented as having been part of the original set. These additional images were far more offensive to Muslims than the rather bland cartoons that had appeared in the *Jyllands-Posten*. One depicted Mohammed as a paedophile, another showed a praying Muslim being raped by a dog and the third, perhaps the most controversial, was a photograph of a bearded man with a pig's snout and ears and carried the caption 'This is the true picture of Mohammed'.[12] The final image was rather bizarrely taken from a pig-squealing competition in France and the caption had been added by the imams. Such an image was clearly a shocking insult and was certain to provoke outrage in the Muslim world. The imams who compiled the dossier were very aware of exactly what response such images would provoke. When asked later about the violence the images had spawned, Abu Laban noted, 'I am an Arab, I'm a Muslim, I spent half of my life in the Middle East, I know the mood, but I don't have the crystal ball to see every detail.' [13]

The story was distorted even further by some of the imams while they were in the Middle East. Mohamed Assemha, for example, allegedly told some of his audiences in Egypt that the *Jyllands-Posten* was a newspaper that belonged to the Danish ruling party, thus fuelling the perception in the Muslim world that the European press was simply an arm of the state, as it is in many Islamic countries. The Arab media also did its bit to stoke up the crisis. The Al-Jazeera satellite channel hosted a number of Muslim commentators who focused primarily on the added pictures and some reportedly gave the impression that the pictures had come from a book that was misrepresenting Islam. The Qatari newspaper *Sharq* carried the following:

> There were around twelve cartoons published showing the messenger of Allah whilst he was wearing a turban full of bombs and missiles and it showed him whilst he was praying in a very insulting position. These pictures were published in public over several weeks with the full knowledge and consent of the Danish government so that Danish public opinion would be affected. Therefore the Islamic community there took a stance and demanded the stoppage of the publication of these cartoons, but their demands were rejected after all the Danish government comittees and organizations showed their solidarity with the newspaper.[14]

Abu Laban himself credited some hardline religious television stations based in Saudi Arabia and the United Arab Emirates, such as Al-Majd and Iqra, with having a big influence on encouraging boycotts of Danish goods in response to the affair.[15] Indeed parts of the Arab media jumped on the case almost with glee as if their worst preconceptions about Western society's disrespect for Islam had come true.

## Regimes respond

This Middle East tour that took in Egypt, Lebanon, Syria, Turkey and Qatar among others certainly prompted a reaction from the regimes and official religious establishments of the region, with each racing to take up the cause and to act as the defender of Islam and the Prophet. The official religious establishment in Egypt, Al-Azhar, issued a statement signed by its Grand Sheikh, Mohammed Tantawi, which declared, 'This has trespassed all limits of objective criticism into insults and contempt of the religious beliefs of more than one billion Muslims around the world, including thousands in Denmark.' Many criticized the response of Al-Azhar as being too weak.

The Egyptian foreign minister meanwhile is reported to have handed around the cartoon dossier on the sidelines of a December meeting of the powerful Organization of the Islamic Conference (OIC). Just as it had got involved in the Rushdie affair, the OIC took a stance on the cartoons and issued an official communiqué calling on Muslims to restrain themselves to peaceful protests but complaining that the Danish government had not condemned the drawings. For some in the Arab world, the OIC's role was a key catalyst in ratcheting up the tension. Egyptian analyst Mohamed Al-Sayed Said observed, 'It was no big deal until the Islamic conference when the OIC took a stance against it.'[16] Indeed it was shortly after the meeting that labour strikes began in Pakistan to protest at the images. The Arab League issued its own condemnation of the Danish government for their inaction and then in January Arab governments issued a joint statement demanding the Danish government 'firmly punish the authors of this offence'. It was as if these regimes could not comprehend the fact that governments in the West have limited control over what is published in their own press. However, these reactions were predictable enough, as the regimes of the region could do little else but condemn the insult to the Prophet. Indeed any regime not responding in this way would run the risk of being accused of not doing enough to honour both the Prophet and Islam.

However, just as in the Rushdie case, certain states decided to take the issue further. Saudi Arabia sought to take the lead and in January issued its own public condemnation of the cartoons and recalled its ambassador from Denmark. Saudi clerics also railed against the pictures, sometimes in the most inflammatory of ways. A recording of Sheikh Badr Bin Nader Al-Mashari, an imam of a Riyadh mosque, which was posted on an Internet site, heard him raging, 'Brothers, it's war against Islam ... grab your swords. ... To the billion Muslims: where are your arms? Your enemies have trampled on the Prophet. Rise up.'[17] Some clerics also began calling for a public boycott of Danish goods and the Danish dairy group, Arla Foods, reported that two of its staff in Saudi Arabia had been beaten by angry customers. In fact the cartoons spawned much small-scale activity inside the kingdom and many capitalized on the public mood. It was reported, for example, that some Saudi businessmen set up a competition offering $50,000 for the best study of the Prophet, while Islamists began a project to re-Islamicize people inside the kingdom, issuing DVDs calling on the young to pray five times a day. Others collected 700,000 signatures against the Danish government. Therefore, just as in the Rushdie affair more than two decades before, the Saudis, from the ruling family to the religious establishment, were looking to demonstrate that they were leading the way in defending the Prophet and Muslims everywhere. However, as in the 1980s, they were upstaged once again, although this time not by Iran.

Ironically it was the secular states of the region that made the most of the opportunity that the cartoons had thrown up. Syria and Libya, two avowedly secular regimes that have done their utmost over the years to suppress any form of Islamist activism outside of that sanctioned by the state, saw in the crisis the chance to rally domestic support and to take up the cause of Islam as a means of bolstering their own legitimacy. Indeed many regimes in the Middle East have long been content to crush their own Islamists at home while at the same time using Islam and Islamist groups abroad as a means of extending their influence.

Libya responded to the cartoons by withdrawing its ambassador from Denmark. In addition, Colonel Qadhafi used the cartoons as a means of trying to rebuild his credibility not only at home but also in the regional context, as he had been roundly accused in the Arab world of having sold out to the West when he agreed to abandon his weapons of mass destruction (WMD) programmes in December 2003 in return for restored relations with the USA. As such the cartoons presented an opportunity that was just too good for the Libyan leader to miss. Qadhafi declared that those who had published the cartoons were 'infidels' and that European school children are taught that Mohammed was a liar. In addition Qadhafi's favoured son, Saif Al-Islam, who has sought to promote himself as the Western-friendly face of the regime since its rehabilitation, told the Austrian media that the Danish cartoonists should be imprisoned. He also tried to use the events to extend Libya's influence over Muslim communities in Europe. He called upon Muslims in Austria to demonstrate against the images and revealed that he was communicating with Islamists in Italy to try to organize demonstrations there.[18]

The Libyan state also sanctioned a number of demonstrations in Libya against the cartoons and specifically against comments made by an Italian MP, Roberto Calderoli, who had announced that he intended to have the cartoons reprinted on T-shirts. Spontaneous protest is strictly prohibited in Libya, as it is in most other Middle Eastern states, so this apparent spur-of-the moment demonstration had the fingerprints of the Libyan authorities all over it. However, the protests got out of hand as demonstrators in the impoverished city of Benghazi, known for being an Islamist stronghold, started attacking the Italian consulate and also began to turn some of their anger and frustration against their own regime. Panicked Libyan security forces waded in with a typically heavy-handed approach that left at least ten people dead and many others injured. Despite the public-relations disaster of the Benghazi riots, however, by and large the cartoons had allowed the Libyan regime to promote itself as a key defender of the Muslim world.

Likewise the Syrian regime, which was feeling the pressure of the United States, tried to use the crisis to rally domestic support and strengthen its own position. At the end of January the secular Ba'athist regime of Bashar Al-Assad condemned the cartoons and the following month recalled its ambassador to Copenhagen. Then the Danish embassy in Damascus was stormed and set alight by an angry mob. Shortly afterwards the Norwegian embassy was also attacked. As in the Libyan case, these sorts of demonstrations of public anger must have been tacitly condoned by the authorities, as anyone daring to demonstrate or even hold an unauthorized public gathering in Syria would be liable to the severest punishment. Yet the regime was content to allow imams to stir the population up. Indeed one Damascus imam in his Friday *khoutba* asserted, 'The Europeans are using all their power to destroy our faith. It is our Islamic duty to boycott all goods from these countries. ... When our sanctity is oppressed we will sacrifice our souls, spirits and bodies for you, O Prophet.'[19]

It would appear therefore that, like the Libyan regime of Colonel Qadhafi, the Syrian regime was happy to tap into the public mood for its own benefit. Indeed it was the tacit encouragement given by these regimes that served to exacerbate tensions that resulted in violence and demonstrations all over the Islamic world from Nigeria to Afghanistan to Lebanon and that left scores of people dead. From the starting point of their mosques in Denmark Abu Laban and Ahmed Akarri had certainly succeeded in internationalizing their case and making the cartoons a cause célèbre across the Middle East and beyond.

## Clash of the clerics

Not only did the regimes of the Middle East see in the cartoons an opportunity to use the crisis for their own benefit, but the Islamists also saw a chance to muscle in, and it was not long before they were squabbling over who should take the lead in the affair. The Danish delegation had been sure to include the tiny Gulf state of Qatar on their Middle East itinerary. Qatar is not only the base of the Al-Jazeera channel, but also the home of the highly influential Sheikh Yusuf Al-Qaradawi who, although not part of any particular Islamist movement, is held up by the Muslim Brotherhood as their main spiritual guide. Al-Qaradawi, who among other things is the head of the International Union of Muslim Scholars, is widely considered to be the leader of the moderate Islamist camp. Many religious and political radicals, especially those of a strict *salafist* bent, consider his rulings to be far too lenient. In fact he epitomizes the Muslim Brotherhood's strategy of combining pragmatism and flexibility while maintaining an orthodox Islamic line. As a result he has succeeded in becoming one of the most important Islamic voices of the contemporary period and as such represents an important and powerful figure in the Islamic world and beyond.

After being briefed by the Danish delegation Sheikh Qaradawi called for a day of anger to protest at the cartoons and advocated boycotting Danish goods. He also stated:

> We reject the duplicity of the Western criteria with regard to the freedom of expression. Denmark refused to apologize for these cartoons that insulted the Muslims on the pretext of the freedom of expression, while British historian David Irving was sentenced to three years imprisonment in Austria on charges of denying the Jewish Holocaust. This case clearly exposes the duplicity of the Western criteria related to the freedom of expression.[20]

As these comments demonstrate, rather than choosing to focus on the specific issue of the newspaper that had published the cartoons, Qaradawi appeared keen to raise the stakes and to portray the issue as being part of a wider assault against Islam by the West.

Sheikh Qaradawi drew criticism from some Islamists who objected to his attempts to speak on behalf of the Islamic nation and to focus all Islamic authority in himself. Syrian scholar Mohammed Said Al-Bouti, for example, reminded Qaradawi that the Islamic caliphate was over and that no particular group could claim to have the power of authority.[21] Indeed there is much competition between those in the moderate camp who strive to be considered as the main religious authority on such issues. As such it was not long before Qaradawi found himself directly challenged on the cartoon issue by another popular Islamist figure who sought to take the lead.

The Egyptian Amr Khaled is a media-savvy preacher who has a particular appeal with the young. He rose to fame through his relaxed populist approach to preaching but has drawn criticism from older scholars, including Qaradawi, for not being sufficiently Islamically qualified. Amr Khaled saw in the cartoons an opportunity to spread his popularity further in Europe and called for a conference to be held in Copenhagen to show the Europeans what Islam was all about and to exchange ideas and dialogue. Indeed the young preacher explained, 'We found the cartoon crisis to be a

golden opportunity that may not occur again to introduce a true picture of
our Prophet to the West, where at least five million Danes were eager, for
the first time ever, to hear about Islam.' [22] A rather self-congratulatory Khaled
was keen to tell of his success after the conference and told the media, 'Now
I can attest to a friendly, peace-loving Danish nation which respects Muslims
and is ashamed of what happened.' [23]

Qaradawi, however, rejected Khaled's conference suggestion and instead
chose to stage his own counter-conference in Bahrain. He also accused Amr
Khaled of being too soft, explaining, 'I was surprised to see that he [Amr
Khaled] prepared for a conference in Denmark aimed at calming down the
Muslim anger and their denunciation of the Danish cartoons that insulted
their Prophet.' [24] As this squabble unfolded, the extent to which Qaradawi
sought to use the cartoons for his own political agenda became increasingly
evident. In numerous statements to the Arabic media he emphasized the
need to keep Muslim public opinion inflamed over the affair. He told *Al-
Sharq Al-Awsat* newspaper, 'I have advised him [Amr Khaled] several times
not to break the flow of the awakening of the Muslim nation for the sake
of Denmark.' [25] Indeed Qaradawi refused to meet with a Danish government
delegation that requested to see him. He said his reason for declining the
invitation was 'because I do not want to block the way of the Islamic nation
for the benefit of Denmark, as we want to stand by the Muslim institutions
in expressing denunciation of these cartoons'.[26] It would appear therefore
that Qaradawi was trying to keep public anger against the West simmering
– something that could only serve to deepen divisions between Muslims
and non-Muslims in Europe and elsewhere. As journalist Mshari Al-Zaydi
explained, 'When Qaradawi shouts, "revenge, revenge; rage, rage" he is in
fact maintaining the survival of the Islamic movement. Had the Danes apol-
ogized according to the conditions of the Muslim masses and had [they],
for example, taught the full biography of the Prophet Mohammed by Ibn
Hisham in their schools, then this would have been more of a gain than
having the masses perpetually aligned in a state of religious anger.' [27] It would
appear that Qaradawi was trying to do the same thing when the row erupted
in September 2006 about comments Pope Benedict XVI made about Islam.
The pope had quoted from a medieval Christian emperor who had asserted
that Mohammed had brought the world evil and inhuman things. Again
angry protests erupted across the Muslim world and again Qaradawi called
for a day of anger and tried to harness the crisis to his own increasingly
hawkish political agenda. He also accused the pope of providing an 'international cover for what [President] Bush is doing'.[28]

This desire to profit from the outrage held as true for Abu Laban and
the Danish clerics as it did for Sheikh Qaradawi. Despite Abu Laban's

public insistence that the whole campaign had been an attempt to stimulate 'communication and intellectual discussions ... to discuss how we can combine both values adopted by democracy: freedom of speech and freedom of faith',[29] he roundly backed Qaradawi's stance and rejected Amr Khaled's attempts to bring Islam to the West through dialogue. He was reportedly angered by the fact that Amr Khaled did not consult him about the conference, although this would appear to be more about being frustrated by the Egyptian's ability to win over hearts and minds of Danish Muslims – something he considered as his own territory. Indeed the whole affair served to highlight the deep divisions even between those who consider themselves to be part of the moderate camp. Each group was so intent on claiming the activism around the cartoons as their own that they were unable to show a united face that would hold up their assertions of being part of the *ummah*. Meanwhile the various radical groups in Europe took up the issue with great fervour, as they too competed to lead the way in defending the Prophet. The Al-Ghurraba group in the UK, for example, jumped on the bandwagon, using the cartoons as an opportunity to mobilize support and comparing them to the Crusades of centuries before. Demonstrations were held in London at which protestors expressed their anger unrestrainedly. One British Muslim, Umran Javed, was later convicted of soliciting murder after he urged the crowd to bomb Denmark and the United States.

Yet the Danish imams appeared satisfied enough with the outcome. Despite the violence and loss of life, those involved seemed pleased with what they had achieved. One of the imams who had been part of the Danish delegation to the Middle East, Sheikh Raed Hlayhel, reportedly declared in one *khoutba*, 'The Mohammed controversy was a sign from Allah and a test for the believers. The whole case has been good for the Muslims because it has revealed the infidels, hypocrites and the arrogants. It has also given us, the Muslims, an opportunity to profile ourselves.'[30] Abu Laban stated that although 'these riots were not on our agenda ... it might be good for the West to know what happens when you insult Mohammed'.[31] In a similar vein, Ahmed Akkari said, 'I don't know what result we'll see out of this, but I'm very positive. ... In the future ... maybe we'll get a little more respect.'[32]

A number of other Islamist groups in Denmark were outraged at the whole affair and sought to distance themselves from the actions of Abu Laban and his group. One Iranian living in Denmark complained, 'It is an irony that I am today living in a European democratic state and have to fight the same religious fanatics that I fled from in Iran many years ago.'[33] In response a group of Muslims set up an organization called Demokratiske Muslimer (Democratic Muslims) – a group Abu Laban and his entourage reportedly referred to as rats.[34] However, the damage had already been done,

and by taking the issue to the Middle East the group of imams had ultimately worked to aggravate tensions and sow discord between Muslims and
non-Muslims, not only in Denmark but across all of Europe.

## War against Islam

Many of the complaints made about the cartoons by the various Islamist
organizations in Europe were framed in the context of their being part of
a wider war against Islam being waged by the West. For example, a spokesman from the Muslim Association of Britain stated, 'The latest controversy
has arisen out of a period in which the Muslim world has felt vilified and
targeted beyond reason. ... While Britain and the US have generally shown
restraint on the cartoon issue, they remain the target of considerable anger
because they are seen as spearheading the "war on terror", which seems to
have mutated into a war against Islam and its followers.'[35] This same organization, along with other prominent Islamic organizations in the UK, staged
a one-day rally in the heart of London to protest against the cartoons. They
also issued a press statement, which commented, 'The Islamophobic attitudes
which have been pervading across the European continent for a sustained
period have come to a head over these cartoons. There is an understandable anxiety among Muslims about where this kind of portrayal will lead.'[36]
This Islamophobia argument was also taken up by Islamists in the Middle
East. For example, Hamas member of parliament Aziz Duwaik, who is also a
professor of urban planning at Nablus University, declared, 'These cartoons
are a reflection of rampant Islamophobia in Europe, which is very similar
and nearly as virulent as the anti-Semitism that existed in Europe, especially
in Germany, prior to World War II.'[37]

The cartoon affair therefore was transformed into a discourse that
has increasingly sought to amplify the issue of Islamophobia. The Islamic
Human Rights Commission, which is based in the UK, now holds annual
Islamophobia awards which it advertises on its website as, 'Centred around a
gala dinner, the "awards" themselves are both entertaining and raise awareness of a serious and growing prejudice.'[38] Previous winners and runners up
of the awards have included President George W. Bush, President Jacques
Chirac, Professor Colin Bundy, the Principal of the School of African and
Oriental Studies at the University of London, chat-show host Oprah Winfrey
and British *Guardian* newspaper columnist Polly Toynbee. These Islamist
organizations have also organized conferences and events to highlight the
Islamophobia issue. In 2004 the Muslim Association of Britain organized an
educational conference on Islamophobia in Scotland and in February 2006
the French Union des Organisations Islamiques de France issued a state-

ment expressing its concern about the 'rise of the Islamophobic tendency in France'.[39]

While it is true that Muslims have come increasingly under the spot-light in the post-9/11 era there appears to be a concerted effort by some of these organizations to stress to Muslim communities that there is a targeted campaign against them that stretches from the upper echelons of government to the police and the media. Indeed Islamophobia appears to have become a catch-all word and is cited as the reason even for socio-economic prob-lems that are generally associated with being from an immigrant community. Yasmin Alibhai-Brown has commented, 'By and large the lowest achieving communities in this country [Britain] are Muslim. When you talk to people about why this is happening, the one reason they give you, the only reason they give you, is Islamophobia. ... It is not Islamophobia that makes parents take 14-year-old bright girls out of school to marry illiterate men.'[40] This is not to suggest that there are not racist attacks against Muslims, that far-right groups have not upped the ante against Muslims or that anti-Muslim senti-ment and prejudice do not exist – far from it. It is also true that the war on terror, especially when it relates to issues such as stop and search, the arrests of Muslims or detention without trial, has made many within Muslim communities feel highly uncomfortable and as though they are a community under siege. These issues have undoubtedly fostered anger and frustration, potentially making individuals feel more alienated within European society.

However, by framing these issues and all the very real ills experienced by Muslim communities in the West in the simplistic terms of Islamophobia, community leaders are arguably exacerbating tensions and emphasizing differences. They are also contributing to the idea that Muslims represent one monolithic community for which they can act as a voice and on whose behalf they can fight against injustice. As commentator Kenan Malik argues, 'For Muslim leaders, inflating the threat of Islamophobia helps consolidate their power base, both within their own communities and wider society.'[41]

In addition, pushing the Islamophobia issue is another way of encourag-ing both Muslim communities and the host state to label Arabs and Asians as 'Muslims', almost foisting an Islamic identity upon them. We no longer talk about Moroccans, Egyptians or Pakistanis, for example, but immi-grants from all these nationalities are increasingly being lumped together and referred to as Muslims – something that mystifies and frustrates many non-practising Muslim immigrants, not least for the political overtones that such a label has increasingly come to acquire. Yet in pushing this issue, it makes it easier for the various Islamist organizations in Europe to appear to be speaking on behalf of Muslims across the board and to be given a far wider significance and remit than they in fact have. Indeed in many cases they have become the key interlocutors between Muslims and the state. As Amartya Sen has asked, 'Why should a British citizen who happens to be Muslim have to rely on clerics and other leaders of the religious community to communicate with the prime minister?'[42]

Yet it seems that the authorities of some European host countries have bought into this idea, not least the British who have hosted endless meetings with Islamist community leaders. One striking example can be found in the Topkapi Declaration that was drawn up after the UK's Foreign Office sponsored a large gathering of European Islamist organizations in Turkey in July 2006. One section of the declaration stated:

> The virtues of decency, goodness and ethical conduct in all aspects of life are espoused repeatedly in the Holy Qur'an. They are given primary importance and govern Muslim behaviour in all roles of life including that of active citizenship. Following the teachings of the Holy Qur'an and the high standard which it sets, Muslims can enrich Europe as exemplary members of society and role models of decency and goodness.[43]

This is an extraordinary statement that implies that all Muslims in Europe should abide by the Qu'ran. Indeed it could be construed as patronizing that the British government is so keen to advocate that Muslims should follow their lives according to the Qu'ran as interpreted by those politicized individuals who are invited to such events.

Even the multiculturalism debates that have raged in the aftermath of the attacks on European soil have been framed in a way that somehow seems to reduce Muslims to one single entity. Multiculturalism itself is a contested term that seems to mean different things to different people, making any discussion of the issues difficult at best. Yet while multiculturalism was originally conceived as a response to the influx of migrant communities and generally was used to mean the celebration of diversity of different cultures, the way it is being approached in the contemporary debate seems to lump Muslims together into one homogeneous unit that prioritizes Muslim identity over ethnic or other identities. It is no surprise therefore that many Islamist associations have prized the multiculturalist model, viewing it as a means of stressing Muslim identity and therefore enabling them to take the lead in determining what such an identity constitutes.

On the other hand, some of those on the right in Europe have seized upon multiculturalism as somehow being responsible for the radicalization of Muslims. These critics have condemned what they view as an overly liberal approach for encouraging segregation and ghettoizing society and for insisting that no culture is better than any other. Such criticisms were voiced very loudly in the UK in the aftermath of the London bombings. The think-tank Civitas, for example, produced a pamphlet called 'The Poverty of Multiculturalism', which stated, 'The fact that the London suicide bombers of July 7 and the would-be bombers of July 21 were born and bred in Britain – and encouraged by the state to be different – illustrates that hard multiculturalism has the capacity to be not only divisive but decidedly lethal.'[44] Even those on the left came to question the tolerant multiculturalist approach and there was much soul searching about how to blend liberal values with the kinds of conservative ideas being promoted by certain elements within Islamist communities over issues such as homosexuality, women's rights and the veil. As one commentator aptly framed the dilemma, 'Tolerance for intolerance is no tolerance at all.'[45]

Yet while the multicultural model might have created a situation whereby Muslim communities have been able to assert their own cultural values, multiculturalism itself cannot be held responsible for radicalization. Indeed integrating Muslims more into European society, providing better job opportunities and ironing out some of the very real socio-economic inequalities that these communities are facing is unlikely to result in support for such militant ideologies simply disappearing. The issue is much wider and more complex than this and the disaffection runs far deeper and is not simply related to socio-economic grievances. Moreover the different European countries, from France to Spain, to the UK and the Netherlands, despite their diverse approaches towards their migrant populations, have all experienced radicalism from both first- and second-generation communities. Therefore while all of the issues related to multiculturalism and integration are important in their own right, especially as they relate to how European countries come to terms with the make-up and identity of their own societies in the contemporary era, they are unlikely to explain why people adopt militant Islamist ideologies.

Moreover the assumption that by promoting moderate Islamist organizations one can somehow reduce extremism is also highly dubious. The more radical elements have a highly antagonistic attitude towards these moderates and Islamist organizations that they accuse of selling out. As one article posted on a fairly radical Islamist site noted, 'The British Home Office has become particularly skilful at hoodwinking Muslims. In the last two weeks they have managed to do it twice. Mind you it's not that difficult to pull the wool over Muslims' eyes when you have politically inept and naive Moderate (domesticated) Muslims for whom the chance of a cup of tea with Government officials is viewed as a sign of their influence.'[46] Similarly Mohammed Siddique Khan took time in his suicide video to lash out at community leaders, accusing them of having sold out:

Our so-called scholars today are content with their Toyotas and semi-detached houses. They seem to think that their responsibilities lie in pleasing the kufr instead of Allah. So they tell us ludicrous things, like you must obey the law of the land. Praise be God! How did we ever conquer lands in the past if we were to obey this law? ... By Allah these scholars will be brought to account, and if they fear the British government more than they fear Allah then they must desist in giving talks, lectures and passing fatwas, and they need to sit at home and leave the job to the real men, the true inheritors of the prophets.[47]

These comments reflect the fact that Islamist leaders have in many cases been put in a difficult position in the aftermath of 9/11. The war on terror has placed a new spotlight on Europe's Islamic communities and the differences between the 'moderates' and the 'radicals' have been forced out into the realm of public debate. Much of this has been driven by the policies of the host states that now expect those in the moderate camp to condemn terrorism and in some cases to work with the authorities to combat extremism. Islamist community leaders found themselves struggling to balance their response to the demands of the host authorities with those of their own communities, who in many cases themselves felt uncomfortable about such close cooperation with the state. Indeed some of the more politicized elements within the Muslim community in the UK, despite rejecting violence and terrorism, expressed their frustrations that Muslim associations such as the Muslim Council of Britain have sold out. One young British convert to Islam expressed his anger that these organizations had played along with the British state and as a result no one could be political in the mosques anymore.[48] He asserted that, as a result, some within the British Muslim community were moving away from the traditional mosques and finding other places where they could pray and express their real frustrations. Indeed some of those who feel uncomfortable about the perceived selling out by the moderates appear to be looking to more extreme groups who they feel can better represent their political views and demands. In fact the more these Islamist leaders issue condemnations of terrorist attacks in Europe, the more they are accused by those of a more militant bent of selling out to the establishment.

Therefore despite the fact that some of these Islamist organizations are keen to represent the interests of the Muslim community, they are often unable to really reach out beyond a very small circle. In addition, despite their keenness to promote the idea of a European Islam and a genuine desire to find a way to integrate and to retain their Muslim identity, some appear still not to feel that they are part of European society. Some Muslim leaders continue to frame their debates in terms of Muslims versus the West as if they are not themselves part of the Western world and as if Europe is an entirely different cultural identity. For example, Abu Laban himself spoke about the West as if, despite having lived in Denmark for many years, he still did not feel part of it. This is hardly surprising given that the majority of leaders of Islamic organizations in Europe are still run by first-generation immigrants who, although they may genuinely consider Europe as their home, are struggling to find their own place in the continent and still look at themselves as being part of the Islamic world.

In addition, being from the first generation brings its own anxieties about preserving cultural and traditional values and these organizations repeatedly stress the need to refrain from being contaminated by Western values. As a result these groups are keen to emphasize the need for separate Islamic education and for Muslim communities to be dealt with separately. In one mosque in Manchester the imam and Islamic community were pushing to be able to legislate for their own communities under *sharia* law. In a similar vein one moderate and very gentle Islamist leader in the UK explained how he was happy for his daughter to follow the UK's national curriculum but wanted her in a separate Muslim school so that she would not be contaminated by the influences of the Western girls around her.[49] Likewise an Islamist in Marseilles expressed his anxieties about the impact that mixing with French society would have on the next generation of Muslim children and was lobbying to get the funds to set up a private Islamic school in the city.[50] While this is understandable for the first generation who are still grappling to come to terms with being a minority community, it risks emphasizing and encouraging the differences between Muslims and non-Muslims and arguably makes life more challenging for the second and third generations.

Moreover, for the majority of Islamist leaders and practising Muslims in Europe, their references continue to come primarily from the Middle East or Islamic world. Despite the fact that many of these Islamists have been in Europe since the 1970s and 1980s, Europe has yet to produce its own Islamic scholar who can really have an influence or cut any ice outside his local environment. This is a painful issue that many Islamists in Europe are all too well aware of. Although French Islamists in the UOIF cite the Moroccan Tarek Oubru as one of their most important scholars, Oubru is little known outside of the French Islamist world. Even the European Council for Fatwa and Research, which was set up to provide religious rulings specifically for Muslims living as minority communities in Europe, is run by Sheikh Qaradawi who has never lived in Europe. His deputy in the council, the Lebanese Sheikh Yusuf Al-Moulawi, used to live in France but now resides in Egypt. In fact just over one-third of those on the council of this organization live in the Islamic world. Therefore as the cartoon affair showed, as much as they might wish it otherwise, the Arab world continues to be the main powerhouse for those Islamic organizations that have come to take up the middle ground of political Islam in Europe, and even issues that would appear to be concerned primarily with Europe have to be taken to the Islamic world to be granted any real legitimacy. Indeed, while the discourse of Islamist leaders in Europe has certainly become more sophisticated since the days of the Salman Rushdie crisis and displays a far better understanding of the political complexities of the debates they are engaging in, it would appear that some of these individuals still essentially feel themselves to be an extension of the Islamic world.

# CONCLUSION

One of the consequences of 9/11 was that it sparked unprecedented public interest in Islam and Muslims. However, this interest has been rather one dimensional and the richness and diversity of Islamic culture and its history have been lost among the debates that have raged about radicalism and radicalization. The Western media and countless commentators have taken to referring to Muslims as if they are one single block with the same aspirations and preoccupations, who can simply be conveniently divided into 'moderates' and 'extremists'. Talking about Muslims as if their national and local identities have been subsumed by an all-encompassing Islamic identity is clearly doing a disservice to those Muslim communities spread across Europe who are as diverse as any other group. Moreover to do so belies the persistent and very real differences that exist not only between different ethnic communities but also within them.

Furthermore the rather desperate attempts by some Western policy-makers to identify patterns and triggers of radicalization, as if this is some linear process that can be condensed into a simple equation, risks assuming that all radicals are the same and are driven by the same motivations and preoccupations. Likewise trying to boil Islam down to develop one accepted version of 'moderate' Islam – something that some European policymakers and analysts have suggested as a means of nipping extremism in the bud – is clearly absurd and belies the struggles that have been going on for generations in the Islamic world over what represents 'true' Islam. Moreover one of the problems of this approach is that what have been dubbed 'radical' and 'moderate' interpretations of Islam in the contemporary sense are essentially both expressions of politics.

Similarly assuming that militancy among Islamists in Europe is a problem that can be dealt with in isolation in the continent is probably an over-ambitious supposition and any policy aimed at tackling the problem in this way is likely to be doomed to failure, or at best would be like putting a sticking plaster on a gaping wound. It is true that being in Europe provides Islamists with a unique experience and that in some cases such experiences may have a bearing on radicalization. However, the developments that have occurred within Islamist communities in Europe are still primarily a reflection of what is occurring in the Islamic world more widely. Islamism has blossomed among Muslim communities in Europe in recent decades in line with the Islamic revivalism and increased religiosity that has developed in the Islamic world since the 1980s. Similarly the activists within Muslim communities in Europe in the 1950s and 1960s reflected the politics of the day in the Islamic world when nationalism and left-wing politics were strong. Just as the radical left-wing secularist tradition faded in the Islamic world, so too it withered away among Muslim communities in Europe and was replaced by the politics of Islam. Islamist activism of today is perhaps more noticeable than the nationalist or secular activism of the past. This is partly because Muslim communities across Europe are now much larger and more settled than they were in the 1950s and 1960s; partly because left-wing activists from Muslim communities often joined the socialist or anti-racism movements already present within the host countries; and partly because the symbols of the contemporary Islamist movement such as modes of dress are more visible as an outward display of difference. Indeed these issues and ideologies did not just spring up in Europe in isolation. As Islamist symbols and trends such as the *hijab* appeared in cities such as Cairo and Algiers, so they also appeared in the streets of Paris, Manchester and Brussels.

Therefore Muslim communities in Europe proved just as receptive to the Islamic revivalism that was spreading like wildfire across the Islamic world as those in the region itself. Islam was deemed to be as much of a solution for those in Europe as it was for those of the Islamic world and the type of Islam promoted in Europe was the same as that promoted in the region. This Islam, which has its roots in the revivalist movements of the nineteenth century, sought to promote a unified and 'pure' version of the faith that was stripped of its history and diversity. Islam was reduced to a set of essential permanent truths that could encompass every aspect of life. According to one Muslim scholar, these truths give out that Allah is one and is supreme; that Mohammed was his Prophet and the ultimate example of humanity; that the Qu'ran contains the last word in truth; and that the world can be divided into two camps, namely believers and non-believers.[1] As a result Islam was emptied of its rich and robust intellectual tradition and this boiled-down version of the faith became an ideology and a political tool that had a broad appeal among the masses. As such Islam came to offer a complete solution to every aspect of life for every Muslim wherever they happened to be.

This interpretation of Islam was encouraged by the propaganda efforts of the Gulf states and other interested parties, including some of the secular regimes, which viewed Muslim communities in Europe as an extension of the Islamic world and sought to spread their influence among them. These parties advised Muslims in Europe how they could weather the storm of living in a secular society where they risked 'temptation' and 'contamination' on a daily basis. The various Islamist movements based in the Middle East which undertook *dawa* in Europe also sought to 'bring Muslims back to the straight path' and to ensure that they did not lose the crucial cultural linkage to the Islamic world and to Islamic values. Despite being in Europe many Islamists took this advice to heart and a rejectionist mentality came to be a feature of Islamist discourse in the continent as much as it did in the Islamic world.

Similarly the politics and grievances of the Islamic world also continued to dominate the discourse of Islamist communities in Europe, again thanks partly to the propaganda efforts of the various Islamist states and organizations. As much as the Islamist movement in the region tapped into popular sentiment that held the West responsible for the ills of the Islamic world, so too did the Islamist activists in Europe. Indeed many Islamist activists and radicals in Europe focused their attentions on portraying the regimes of the Islamic world as mere puppets of their Western masters and anti-Western discourse also became a feature of the European Islamist scene.

It is true that some Islamist organizations have in recent years, and since 9/11 especially, been keen to promote a 'European Islam' that locates Muslims within the European context. This appears to be a genuine attempt to blend being Muslim with living in secular Western society, but as some Islamic leaders have themselves bemoaned, the centre is still located firmly in the Middle East, and figures such as Sheikh Yusuf Al-Qaradawi, the late Sheikh Abdulaziz Bin Baez or more radical elements such as Mohamed Al-Maqdisi hold a far greater sway and importance than any Islamist figure in Europe. This is hardly surprising given that Muslim communities are still a relatively recent phenomenon in the continent and most Islamist organizations are still largely the domain of the first generation. Moreover being part of the second or third generation does not necessarily mean that one does not share the same preoccupations and grievances or indeed in some cases the same antagonistic relationship towards the West as those from the first generation. In fact one could argue that the advancement of communications technology has made these communities even more strongly connected to their own cultural roots.

Living in Europe does not automatically change one's mindset or make people think in a different way, and traditions and cultural norms imported from the Islamic world are often still applied even within the second and third generations. Wearing Western clothes or living a Westernized lifestyle, just as many young people do in the Islamic world, does not necessarily mean one has fully embraced the values associated with the West. Reports of rapid conversions to militant Islam among seemingly secular young men in Europe often belie the cultural background and upbringing of those involved. Indeed those who embrace militant Islam, whether from the first, second or third generations, are brought up on the same ideological diet that has it roots, grievances and centre firmly anchored in the Islamic world. It is surely unsurprising, given the emergence in the Islamist world of a militant Islamist discourse, that those within Muslim communities in Europe where the same kinds of ideas are doing the rounds should also take these ideas and ideologies to extremes.

As such what is occurring within Islamist communities in Europe is still as much a reflection of what is occurring within the Islamic world as it is of local conditions. Therefore while local issues such as arrests of terror suspects, the banning of the *hijab* and anti-Muslim prejudice might serve to explain why some Muslims in Europe feel more alienated or angered by their situation, if one wants to get to the roots of radical Islam one still has to look at the ideology that is attracting young men from around the world and that has its roots in the stagnation and crisis that has characterized the Islamic world for decades. Rather than soul searching about the rights or wrongs of integration or multiculturalist policies, or working to try to construct a 'moderate' Islam, the West might be better to come to terms with understanding the conditions in the Islamic world that have resulted in the politics of despair and anti-Western discourse permeating the rhetoric of the region and beyond.

In addition Western policymakers should take a closer look at their own relationships to the regimes of the Islamic world. Supporting elites that suppress any form of genuine political expression, that have scant regard for human rights or the rule of law, that do not share the wealth of the country around with any sense of equity and that persist in denying their populations proper educational opportunities is unlikely to alter perceptions of the West in the region. As such the grievances that have fuelled the militant Islamist movement will persist, as will the perception that the West is responsible for all these ills. This can only have been compounded with the way in which the war on terror has been fought, with Western governments bolstering corrupt and authoritarian regimes in their bid to eliminate their Islamist opponents and supporting them in their bid to rush through even more draconian anti-terrorist legislation – something that only serves to perpetuate the ongoing stagnation in the region.

It was this sense of ongoing grievance and inability to effect change within the Islamic world that enabled Bin Ladin to strike such a symbolic victory on 9/11. It was also Bin Ladin's attacks, along with those in Palestine, that fostered a new culture of 'martyrdom' or suicide operation. The sense of vengeance and destruction that characterized the 9/11 attacks is what appears to have been carried through to the younger generation of militant Islamists including those in Europe. The new generation of jihad-ists appears to have descended into a nihilistic kind of violence, which is driven by revenge rather than by more tangible and political objectives such as those held by their predecessors who sought to overthrow corrupt regimes in individual Muslim countries. As the son of Abdullah Azzam bemoaned, 'We know jihad. It is something very precious and very honourable for a Muslim to do but not in the Al-Qaeda way. My father would have been completely against attacking civilian people living in their own countries like what happened in London, Spain and Amman. This is not jihad.'[2] Indeed this new way of fighting jihad is a far cry from the early days of Abu Musab Al-Suri and his jihadist band in London. To compare Abu Musab Al-Suri with London bomber Mohammed Siddique Khan reveals the vast differ-ence between them. Al-Suri had directly experienced the upheavals that had occurred in Syria and fought hard to bring down his own regime. He was a disciplined theologian as much as a fighter and had clear and precise aims and objectives. Khan meanwhile appears to have simply picked up an ideol-ogy that he did not know what to do with, and his attack on London was ultimately a useless act with no real purpose other than to express anger and distress. More than ever the new generation looks to be fighting un-winnable battles and their martyrdom operations, from the suicides in Madrid to the London bombings, look more to be acts of retribution and anger arising out of desperation.

The insistence on striking at the West as if it is the be all and end all and the only way to 'liberate Muslims' also smacks of a movement that is flail-ing around in the dark and no longer knows what it wants to achieve. Yet importantly it still serves as a vehicle for expressing the continuing distress and frustration felt throughout the Muslim world and which is reflected in Muslim communities in the West. Yet to interpret the expression of this distress as a globalized movement that has eroded national differences and priorities is probably to misrepresent those involved in militant Islamism. Indeed by globalizing everything and talking about militant Islamists as if they are one transnational movement the West is arguably only serving to bolster the militant camp, affording it a greater unity and sense of purpose than it probably has, not to mention giving it a far more amplified sense of menace. Similarly by framing everything in simplistic terms of assuming that young men blow themselves up as a direct response to foreign policy is also a means of playing into the hands of those doing the attacking. The reality is far more complex. As one former militant explained:

> I remember how we used to laugh in celebration whenever people on TV proclaimed that the sole cause for Islamic acts of terror like 9/11, the Madrid bombings and 7/7 was Western foreign policy. By blaming the government for our actions, those who pushed the 'Blair's bombs' line did our propaganda work for us. More important, they also helped to draw away any critical examination from the real engine of our violence.[3]

It does not take a war in Iraq or Afghanistan to provoke anger and radicalism or to turn someone against the society in which they are living. All the ingredients are already present and are tied up with the historical realities of the post-Cold War Islamic world. Yet of course it takes a certain type of individual to go down the path of radicalism, and determining what it is about that particular individual that makes him or her take that extra step will most likely remain a question we will be grappling with for the foreseeable future.

Finally one should not forget that not only the radicals but also the moderates are a minority within a minority, whose influence and importance should not be overplayed. Most Muslims living in Europe have no or limited interest in the politics of the Islamist movement and simply want to get on with life. The danger in overplaying the role of the Islamist camp is that it only serves to reiterate a discourse that talks about Islam versus the West or about a war on Islam which can only be to the detriment of the majority of Muslims living in Europe as well as to European societies themselves.

# NOTES

## Chapter 1. The First Wave of Radicals

1. 'Malaf abi Muasb al-Suri' (File on Abu Musab al-Suri), undated. Available in Arabic on the Al-Tawhed wa Jihad website. http://www.tawhed.ws/a?i=78&PH PSESSID=6e7cd3991ebce2b89175bbbacb81ca16.
2. 'Architect of New War on the West', *Washington Post*, 23 May 2006.
3. Available in Arabic on the Al-Tawhed wa Jihad website. http://www.tawhed. ws/a?i=78&PHPSESSID=6e7cd3991ebce2b89175bbbacb81ca16.
4. See Chapter 3.
5. Sheikh Abu Ithar, 'Sheikh Abu Talal Al-Qassem: Infatuated with the Pen and the Spear', undated. Available at http://www.cageprisoners.com/forums/ archive/index.php/t-243.html.
6. J. Nielsen, *Muslims in Western Europe*, 2nd ed. (Edinburgh: Edinburgh University Press, 1995), p 142.
7. Quoted in T. Ramadan, *Aux Sources du Renouveau Musulman* (Editions Tawhid, 2002), p 362.
8. N. Ayoubi, *Political Islam: Religion and Politics in the Arab World* (London: Routledge, 1991), p 90.
9. Sayid Qutb, *Milestones* (New Delhi: Islamic Book Service, 1998), p 139.
10. Ayoubi, *Political Islam*, p 138.
11. Ibn Taymiya's most famous *fatwa* was the Mardin *fatwa*. He applied this when he was asked to advise on the case of Mongols who were invading Syria and who were Muslim and with whom local Muslim leaders, including the Prince of Mardin, had allied themselves. Ibn Taymiya proclaimed that such people were infidels because, although nominally Muslim, they followed Turkic common law. Note: *kufar* means apostate (plural), *kafir* is apostate (singular) and *kufr* means apostasy.
12. Quoted in Ayoubi, *Political Islam*, p 144.

13.  http://www.abubaseer.bizland.com/books/read/b%2025.doc.

14.  *Ibid.*

15.  Dr Nashat Hamid Abdel Al-Majid, 'Asbab nashat al-Afghan al-Arab' (The reasons behind the creation of the Afghan Arabs), 7 October 2001. Available at http://www.islamonline.net.

16.  W. Laqueur, *No End to War* (New York: Continuum, 2003), p 52.

17.  Interview with members of the Parti Algérien pour la Démocratie et le Social-isme (PADS). Ellen Ray and Lenora Foerstal, 'Algeria: Theocracy by Terror?', October 1998. Available at http://www.covertaction.org/content/view/109/75.

18.  Interview by author with Libyan Afghan veteran, London, 2005.

19.  A. Pargeter, 'North African Immigrants in Europe and Political Violence', in *Studies in Conflict and Terrorism*, 29 (Taylor and Francis, 2006).

20.  'The legal ideologue of Al Qaeda leader, Mussa al Qarni, recalls the stages of the rise and fall of the Islamic state dream in Afghanistan', *Al-Hayat*, 13 March 2006.

21.  Interview by author with a member of the Libyan Brotherhood, UK, 2006.

22.  http://taarafu.islamonline.net/arabic/famous/2001/10/article2-a.shtml.

23.  Interview by author with former Afghan veteran, Amman, February 2006.

24.  As Fawaz Gerges has argued, 'Afghanistan had an overall radicalising impact on foreign combatants and served as a transformative experience on both hard-ened jihadis ... as well as on unseasoned ones.' F.A. Gerges, *The Far Enemy: Why Jihad Went Global* (Cambridge: Cambridge University Press, 2005), p 84.

25.  M. Al-Zayyat, *The Road to Al-Qaeda* (London: Pluto Press, 2004), p 55.

26.  Wissam Fouad, 'Al-Afghan al-Arab bayna wahdat al-manhaj al-tarbewi wa taditead al manarhij al-harakiya' (The Afghan Arabs: Between the Unity of the Educational Method and the Multiple Mobilising Methods), Future Centre for Studies and Research, undated. http://www.moragaat.com/moragaat/jun2000/go4.htm.

27.  'Rahilat al-Hilaq baine Kabul wa Kandahar' (The Journey of Death between Kabul and Kandahar), *Al-Sharq Al-Awsat*, 1 July 2001.

28.  *Ibid.*

29.  *Ibid.*

30.  Gerges, *The Far Enemy*, p 44.

## Chapter 2. Europe as Islamic Melting Pot

1.  'The Sweet Smell of Victory', *Crescent International*, 16–30 April 1982, in Kalim Siddiqui (ed), *Issues in the Islamic Movement 1981–82 (1401–1402)* (London:

Open Press, 1983), p 246.

2.  Interviews with members of the Muslim Brotherhood in various countries in Europe.

3.  K. Siddiqui, 'Impact of the Islamic Revolution on the Islamic Movement', in Siddiqui (ed), *Issues in the Islamic Movement*, p 363.

4.  M. Abedin, 'Libya, Radical Islam and the War on Terror: A Libyan Opposition-ist's View', 25 March 2005. http://www.jamestown.org/publications_details. php?volume_id=412&issue_id=3277&article_id=2369484.

5.  W. Abdelnasser, 'Islamic organizations in Egypt and the Iranian revolution of 1979: The experience of the first few years', *Arab Studies Quarterly*, Spring 1997. http://www.findarticles.com/p/articles/mi_m2501/is_n2_v19/ai_20046832.

6.  The Saudi regime had deliberately kept the eastern provinces where the Shi'ites lived starved of resources and infrastructure, so much so that in spite of the kingdom's riches, shanty towns were commonplace until the 1980s and the first modern hospital in the eastern province was only completed in 1987. See Graham E. Fuller and Rend Rahim Francke, *The Arab Shi'a: The Forgotten Muslims* (New York: St Martin's Press, 1999), p 181.

7.  Sadik J. Al-Azm, *Tha niyat al-Tahrim* (The Taboo Mentality) (Nicosia: The Centre for Social Studies and Research in the Arab World, 1994), p 196.

8.  'Who Speaks for the Ikhwan?', *Crescent International*, 1–15 January 1982, in Siddiqui (ed), *Issues in the Islamic Movement*, p 167.

9.  J. Bosch Vila, 'The Muslims of Portugal and Spain', *Journal of Muslim Minority Affairs*, vol. VII, no. 2 (January 1986).

10. *Thalathoun aman min al-amel al-Islami al-insani* (Thirty Years of Humanitarian Islamic Work) (The Islamic Call Society, n.d.).

11. F. Halliday, *Islam and the Myth of Confrontation* (London: I.B.Tauris, 1995), p 120.

12. G. Kepel, *Les Banlieues de l'Islam* (Editions du Seuil, 1991), p 229.

13. Trevor Stanley, 'Understanding the Origins of Wahhabism and Salafism', *Terrorism Monitor*, vol. 3, issue 14 (15 July 2005).

14. From http://www.bookrags.com/wiki/Wahhabism.

15. J.-Y. Camus, 'Islam in France', 10 May 2004. Available at http://www.ict.org. il/articles/articledet.cfm?articleid=514.

16. K. Siddiqui, 'Struggle for the Supremacy of Islam: Some Critical Dimensions', in Siddiqui (ed), *Issues in the Islamic Movement*, p 21.

17. J. Millard Burr and Robert O. Collins, *Alms for Jihad* (Cambridge: Cambridge University Press, 2006), p 29.

18. *Muslim World League Journal*, vol. 17, nos. 1 and 2 (September/October 1989).

19. *Muslim World League Journal*, vol. 19, no. 7 (January 1992).

20. *Ibid.*

21. Irfan Chishti, 'Comment on BBC Online. Sponsoring British Islam', 25 August 2005. http://newsrss.bbc.co.uk/1/hi/programmes/panorama/4172000.stm.

22. Siddiqui, 'Struggle for the Supremacy of Islam', pp 24–5.

23. Stanley, 'Understanding the Origins of Wahhabism and Salafism'.

24. 'Al-Mushid alam al Ikhwan al-muslimeen: nouayid tershia Mubarak wa atammana al-jillous mahahoo' (The Supreme Guide of the Muslim Brothers: I support the candidacy of Mubarak and I wish I could sit with him), *Akhbar Al-Youm*, 20 July 2005. http://www.akhbarelyom.org.eg/akhersaa/issues/3691/0501.html.

25. 'The Memoirs of Sheikh Yusuf Al-Qaradawi. No 3. *Ikhwan* outside Egypt'. Available in Arabic at http://www.islamonline.net/Arabic/Karadawy/part3/2003/11/article03.shtml.

26. 'Al-Tandeem al-Dawli lil ikhwan: al-wahd messira wal ma'al?' (The International Organization of the Ikhwan: The promise, the history and the outcome?), 20 September 2004. http://www.rezgar.com/debat/show.art.asp?aid=23729.

27. *Ibid.*

28. L. Vidino, 'The Muslim Brotherhood's Conquest of Europe', *Middle East Quarterly*, vol. XII, no. 1.

29. Muslim Association of Britain website. http://www.mabonline.info/english/modules.php?name=About.

30. UK Action Committee on Islamic Affairs, 'Letter from Dr Mughram Al-Ghamdi to Muslim Community, 28 October 1988', in Lisa Appignanesi and Sara Maitland (eds), *The Rushdie File* (London: Fourth Estate, 1989), p 59.

31. *Ibid.*

32. K. Malik, 'Born in Bradford', *Prospect*, October 2005.

33. Halliday, *Islam and the Myth of Confrontation*, p 71.

34. G. Kepel, *Allah in the West* (Cambridge: Polity Press, 1997), pp 139–40.

35. *Le Monde*, 28 February 1989.

36. Sadik J. Al-Azm: *Tha niyat al-Tahrim*, p 99.

37. See http://www.veronique-sanson.net/files/vero_18.html.

38. For a full description of the veil affair see Kepel, *Allah in the West*.

39. James Piscatori, 'Beyond East–West Relations: The Rushdie Affair and the Politics of Ambiguity', *International Affairs*, vol. 66, no. 4 (October 1990), pp 767–89.

40. *New Life*, 17 February 1989, quoted in Appignanesi and Maitland (eds), *The Rushdie File*, p 113.

41. *Ibid.*

42. *Death of a Princess* was a British docu-drama depicting the story of a young Saudi princess and her lover who had been publicly executed for adultery, based on the true story of Princess Misha'al. The Saudi establishment objected strongly to the programme and tried to censor it.

43. Tariq Modood, 'British Asian Muslims and the Rushdie Affair', *The Political Quarterly*, vol. 61, issue 2 (April 1990).

44. Appignanesi and Maitland (eds), *The Rushdie File*, p 58.

45. *Ibid.*, p 100.

46. Piscatori, 'Beyond East–West Relations'.

47. Dr Shabbir Akhtar, *Guardian*, 27 February 1989, quoted in Appignanesi and Maitland (eds), *The Rushdie File*, p 241.

48. Abdullah Kamal, 'Riyat al-sud Abdullah Azzam min al-jihad illa iktiyal' (The black banners: Abdullah Azzam from jihad to assassination), *Al-Sharq Al-Awsat*, 5 May 2002.

49. Aziz Al-Azmeh, *New Statesman and Society*, 20 January 1989, quoted in Appignanesi and Maitland (eds), *The Rushdie File*, p 73.

50. Piscatori, 'Beyond East–West Relations'.

51. *Muslim World League Journal*, vol. 17, nos. 1 and 2 (September/October 1989).

52. M. Haque, 'The Muslim Ummah in Crisis', *Muslim World League Journal*, vol. 22, no. 10 (March 1995).

53. K. Siddiqui, 'Generating "Power" without Politics', speech, 1990.

## Chapter 3. Recruitment for Jihad

1. 'Oh, what a lovely jihad', *Guardian*, 29 March 1997.

2. M. Taarnby, 'Recruitment of Islamist Terrorists in Europe', *Trends and Perspectives*, 14 January 2005. Available at http://www.jm.dk/image.asp?page=image& objno=73027.

3. P. Hodson, *Under a Sickle Moon: A Journey through Afghanistan* (London: Abacus, 1986), p 3.

4. Burr and Collins, *Alms for Jihad*, p 89.

5. 'Al-Guerbouzi: Al-Tahimu al-Mukhabarat al-Maghrebia bi wuquf wara ahda'ath 16 mai' (Al-Guerbouzi: I accuse the Moroccan intelligence service of being behind the events of 16 May), *Al-Jarida*, issue 44 (12–18 December 2005).

6. 'Al-Sirat Al-Mustaqeem' (The Straight Path). Interview with Sheikh Al-Muja-

hideen Abu Abdel Aziz, undated. Available at http://www.seprin.com/laden/barbaros.html.

7.   http://www.muslm.net/vb/showpost.php?p=690157&postcount=4.

8.   'Al-Sirat Al-Mustaqeem'. Interview with Sheikh Al-Mujahideen Abu Abdel Aziz, undated.

9.   B. Raman, 'Bosnia & Hyderabad', South Asia Analysis Group, Paper 306 (3 September 2001). Available at http://www.saag.org/papers4/paper306.html.

10.  'From under the Shade of Swords', Azzam Publications, 14 December 1995. Available at http://forums.islamicawakening.com/showthread.php?t=13.

11.  Interviews by author with North African immigrants in Italy, 2003.

12.  'Mujaheddin in Bosnia', Osservatorio sui Balcani, 1 March 2004. http://www.osservatoriobalcani.org/article/articleview/2846/1/42.

13.  Abu Hamza Al-Tunsi, 'Ana Naim Ala Tattoai Maa Maqatlin Almuslmeen' (I regret volunteering to fight with the Muslims), *Al-Sharq Al-Awsat*, issue 9208, 13 February 2004. http://www.asharqalawsat.com/details.asp?section=4&issue=9208&article=217651&search=???%20????%20???????&state=true.

14.  Sean O'Neill, 'The terrorist trained to fly bin Laden's plane', *Daily Telegraph*, 21 September 2001. http://www.telegraph.co.uk/news/main.jhtml?xml=/news/2001/09/21/wterr121.xml.

15.  *Ibid.*

16.  Hamid Al-Qatari, '55 Stikbalun muheeb wa haseen' (A great and sad reception, No. 55), undated. Available at http://www.saaid.net/Doat/hamad/1/55.htm.

17.  'Min Qassas al-Shuhadada al-Arab fil Bosna wal Herzeg' (Some of the Stories of the Arab Martyrs in Bosnia-Herzegovina), undated. Available in Arabic at http://www.saaid.net/Doat/hamad/16.htm.

18.  D. Pujades and A. Salam, *La Tentation du Jihad. L'Islam Radical en France* (J.C. Lattes, 1995), p 137.

19.  *Ibid.*

20.  'Biographies of Martyrs (Shaheed)', undated. Available at http://members.fortunecity.com/mist91/jihad/martyrs/martvarous.htm#.

21.  *Ibid.*

22.  *Ibid.*

23.  'Al-Isithan al-Akhir ...' (Final Permission ...), from 'Min Qassas al-Shuhadada al-Arab fil Bosna wal Herzeg' (Some of the Stories of the Arab Martyrs in Bosnia-Herzegovina), undated. Available in Arabic at http://www.saaid.net/Doat/hamad/16.htm.

24.  'Biographies of Martyrs (Shaheed)'.

25. Haque, 'The Muslim Ummah in Crisis'.

26. 'Arab states and Iran move closer to jihad in the Balkans', *The Times*, 2 September 1992.

27. A. Lebor, *A Heart Turned East* (Warner Books UK, 1997), p 56.

28. 'Arab states and Iran move closer to jihad in the Balkans'.

29. *Muslim World League Journal*, vol. 21, nos. 2–3 (August–September 1993).

30. Lebor, *A Heart Turned East*, p 46.

31. *Ibid.*

32. *Ibid.*, p 56.

33. *Ibid.*

34. 'Mujaheddin in Bosnia', Osservatorio sui Balcani, 1 March 2004. http://www.osservatoriobalcani.org/article/articleview/2846/1/42.

35. E. Kohlmann, *Al-Qaida's Jihad in Europe* (Oxford, 2004), p 30.

36. Burr and Collins, *Alms for Jihad*, p 137.

37. Reported in *British Muslims Monthly Survey* (BMMS), vol. 1, no. 5 (May 1993).

38. 'How Bosnia's Muslims Dodged Arms Embargo', *Washington Post*, 22 September 1996.

39. *Ibid.*

40. *Ibid.*

41. Burr and Collins, *Alms for Jihad*, p 136.

42. 'Al-Sirat Al-Mustaqeem' (The Straight Path). Interview with Comm. Abu Abdel Aziz Barbaros, August 1994.

43. J. Benthall and J. Bellion-Jourdan, *The Charitable Crescent: The Politics of Aid in the Muslim World* (London: I B.Tauris, 2003), p 77.

44. 'Hewar Maa Harz Ben Laden Al-Shakhzi' (An Interview with the Private Body-guard of Bin Ladin), *Al-Quds Al-Arabi*, 17 March 2005. Available in Arabic at http://hewar.khayma.com/showthread.php?t=46032.

45. 'Al-Sirat Al-Mustaqeem' (The Straight Path).

46. 'United States v. Enaam M. Arnaout'. Available at http://www.usdoj.gov/usao/iln/indict/2002/02cr892.pdf.

47. *Ibid.*

48. 'Al-Natq Besam al-maqatlin al-arab fi Bosna:Bin Laden arada Irsal al-mutween al-Arab ala Bosna' (The Spokesperson of the Arab fighters in Bosnia: Bin Laden objected to sending Arab volunteers to Bosnia), 31 May 2002. http://www.asharqalawsat.com/details.asp?section=4&issue=8585&article=106081&search=????%20?????%20???????&state=true.

49. Robert Fisk, 'Anti-Soviet Warrior Puts His Army on the Road to Peace', *Inde-*

*pendent*, 6 December 2003.

50. 'Hewar Maa Harz Ben Laden Al-Shakhzi' (An Interview with the Private Body-guard of Bin Ladin).

51. Quoted in Kohlmann, *Al-Qaida's Jihad in Europe*, p 22.

52. Yusuf Islam, 'Bosnia and the Issue of Music in Islam', 26 November 1997. Available at http://catstevens.com/articles/00029/index.html.

## Chapter 4. Islamist Opposition Groups and European Support Networks

1. *Al-Quds Al-Arabi*, 21 July 2001, quoted in Yotam Feldner, 'Radical Islamic Profile: Abu Hamza Al-Masri', 16 October 2001. Available at http://www.hrwf.net/html/world2001.html.

2. Interview by author with founding member of LIFG, London, 2006.

3. G. Kepel, *Jihad: The Trail of Political Islam* (London: I.B.Tauris, 2004), p 291.

4. Mohamed Abu Zayed, 'Min Kabul ila London. Ba'than An Al-Amaan am al-Dawa' (From Kabul to London. In search of safety or preaching), undated. http://www.balagh.com/islam/cy04d7li.htm.

5. 'The hunt for "Public Enemy No 2"', *Guardian*, 24 September 2001.

6. For a more detailed analysis of the GIA and the Algerian situation see Chapter 6.

7. '1995 Patterns of Global Terrorism,' US Department of State, Middle East Overview, April 1996.

8. Interview by author with Osama Rushdi, London, May 2006.

9. Interviewed in P. Denaud, *Le FIS: Sa Direction Parle* (Paris: L'Harmattan, 1997), p 163.

10. 'More than One Opinion. Arab Afghans Present and Past', Al-Jazeera, 3 June 2004. http://www.aljazeera.net/Channel/archive/archive?ArchiveId=89155.

11. 'The Islamic State in Egypt is Approaching. Interview with Sheikh Rifai Ahmed Taha', *Nidu'ul Islam*, issue 18 (April–May 1997).

12. *Ibid.*

13. Interview by author with Syrian immigrant, CGIL offices, Naples, June 2003.

14. Testimony of Steven Emerson with Jonathan Levin before the United States Senate Committee on Governmental Affairs. 'Terrorism Financing: Origination, Organization, and Prevention: Saudi Arabia, Terrorist Financing and the War on Terror', 31 July 2003.

15. Libya: News and Views website, 4 May 1997.

16. Al-Suri had a particular admiration for the LIFG because of their rigorous attitude towards military training.

17. Available in Arabic at Al-Tawheed wa Jihad website. http://www.almaqdese. net/r?i=1108&PHPSESSID=50a931aff534b807a0a5348f4a5635bd.

18. 'Min Tandeem al-Jihad al-Masri ila Tandeem al-Qa'ida' (From the Egyptian Al-jihad organization to Al-Qa'ida organization), 26 September 2004. Available at http://www.metransparent.com/texts/interrogation_minutes_najjar_to_qaida_ 1.htm.

19. *Al-Ansar*, no. 107 (27 July 1995).

20. *Al-Ansar*, no. 91 (6 April 1995).

21. Abu Musab Al-Suri, 'Mokhtasa shahadedti ala jihad fi djazair, 1988–1996' (The summary of my testimony on jihad in Algeria, 1988–1996), undated.

22. *Ibid.*

23. Lawrence Wright, 'The Man behind Bin Ladin', *The New Yorker*, 16 September 2002. Available at http://www.newyorker.com/fact/content/articles/020916fa_ fact2i.

24. *Sunday Times*, 29 December 1996.

25. *Ibid.*

26. Joseph Brewda, 'Mubarak Slams London for Harbouring Terrorist Groups', *The Executive Intelligence Review*, December 1997. http://members.tripod. com/~american_almanac/terror1.htm.

27. 'Brother Leader of the Revolution Moammar Ghadhafi presents an analysis about the actual crisis the world is passing through about terrorism', undated. Available at http://www.algathafi.org/terrorism/terrorism.htm.

28. Interview by author with Ahmed Nacer Yacine, Naples, June 2003.

29. 'Conflict, Drugs and Mafia Activities. Contribution to the Preparatory Work for the Hague Peace Conference, 11–16 May 1999', Available at http:// www.parl.gc.ca/37/1/parlbus/commbus/senate/com-e/ille-e/presentation-e/ labrousse2-e.htm.

30. *Ibid.*

31. 'L'Allemagne, terre d'asile du FIS et du GIA', *L'Humanité*, 3 January 1995.

32. B. Lia and A. Kjøk, 'Islamist Insurgencies, Diasporic Support Networks, and their Host States. The Case of the Algerian GIA in Europe 1993–2000', FFI/ Rapport-2001/03789.

33. Abdelkader Mostéfai, 'Mohamed Chalabi acquitté par la cour d'Alger', *Le Quotidien d'Oran*, 21 May 2002.

34. Lia and Kjøk, 'Islamist Insurgencies'.

35. Refugee Appeal No. 74540. Decision. Refugee Status Appeals Authority, New Zealand, 1 August 2003.

36. Reported in 'L'Allemagne, terre d'asile du FIS et du GIA', Le Web de l'Humanite, 3 January 1995. http://www.humanite.presse.fr/journal/1995-01-03/1995-01-03-715339.

37. 'Al-Makren amala mudariban fi Afghanistan wa muhariban li sila'a bil djazair' (Al-Makren worked as a trainer in Afghanistan and an arms smuggler in Algeria), Al-Sharq Al-Awsat, issue 9563, 2 February 2005. http://www.asharqalawsat.com/details.asp?section=4&article=280661&issue=9563.

38. Ibrahim Nafie, 'Choosing the Path to Stability', Al-Ahram Weekly, no. 438, 15–21 July 1999.

39. Kathy Evans, 'Radical time-bomb under British Islam', Guardian, 7 February 1994.

40. Interview with Algerian academic, London, 2000.

41. Interview with Libyan charity employee, Manchester, 2005.

42. Lia and Kjøk, 'Islamist Insurgencies'.

43. D. Pujadeas and A. Salam, La Tentation du Jihad. L'Islam Radical en France (Paris: J.C. Lattes, 1995), pp 168–9.

44. 'Terror links in Europe: MI5 knew for years of London mosque's role', Sunday Times, 25 November 2001. http://propagandamatrix.com/terror_links_in_europe_mi5.html.

45. Ibid.

46. Witnessed by author on numerous occasions during 2000/2001.

47. Pujadeas and Salam, La Tentation du Jihad. L'Islam Radical en France, p 171.

48. Guardian, 20 February 1996.

49. United States of America v Usama Bin Ladin. United States District Court. Southern District of New York.

50. Issa's story is told in Al-Hayat, 23 June 2005. The information about him provided here is taken from this article.

51. Conversation with illegal immigrant, Turin, 2003.

52. Interview with a friend of Zakariya who recounted his story, London, 2006.

## Chapter 5. Europe as Battleground

1. Interview with former member of Al-Jama'a Al-Islamiya, London, April 2006.

2. M. Allam, Bin Ladin in Italia: Viaggio nell'Islam Radicale (Milan: Mondadori, 2002), p 92.

3. Ibid.

4. Abu Musab Al-Suri, 'Mokhtasa shahadedti ala jihad fi djazair, 1988–1996' (The summary of my testimony on jihad in Algeria, 1988–1996), undated.

5.    *Ibid.*

6.    *Ibid.*

7.    Unpublished letter written by Abu Musab Al-Suri to Fouad Tallal Qassem, dated 17 June 1995. Unpublished material – copy given to author.

8.    *Al-Hayat*, no. 3 (17 September 2005). Much of this section about the LIFG is drawn from a series of articles that appeared in *Al-Hayat* in 2005 related to the group.

9.    Quoted in *Al-Hayat*, no. 3 (17 September 2005).

10.   *Al-Hayat*, no. 5 (19 September 2005).

11.   *Ibid.*

12.   Interview by author with Osama Rushdi, London, April 2006.

13.   *Ibid.*

14.   'Two Targets, One Enemy', *Al-Ahram Weekly Online*, issue 746 (9–15 June 2005). http://weekly.ahram.org.eg/2005/746/focus.htm.

15.   'Struggle within the ranks', *Al-Ahram Weekly*, no. 402 (5–11 November 1998).

16.   *Ibid.*

17.   *Ibid.*

## Chapter 6. Algerian Radicalism Targets France

1.    For an excellent explanation of this issue see Kepel, *Allah in the West*.

2.    Quoted in *ibid.*, p 159.

3.    *Ibid.*

4.    'Sheikh Abassi Madani fi Hiwarkhass ma'a al-Bayan: Hathihi khutati li waqf nazif al-dam fi Djazair' (Sheikh Abassi Madani in an exclusive interview with Al-Bayan: This is my plan to stop the bloodshed in Algeria), March–April 2004. http://www.albayan-magazine.com/bayan-198/aljeria/2.htm.

5.    Denaud, *Le FIS: Sa direction parle*, p 273.

6.    J. Cesari, 'Les Rapports France Algerie: L'effet Airbus', undated. Available in French at http://www.islam-fraternet.com/maj-0598/alger2.htm.

7.    Denaud, *Le FIS: Sa Direction Parle*, p 195.

8.    Between 1989 and 1993 the number of asylum requests from Algerians in France went from 101 to 1,099, although only 14 were granted refugee status in 1993 and ten in 1994. See Cesari, 'Les Rapports France Algérie: L'effet Airbus'.

9.    Denaud, *Le FIS: Sa Direction Parle*, p 160.

10.   Vitrine Légal, *L'Humanité*, 10 November 1993. Available at http://www.humanite.fr/journal/1993-11-10/1993-11-10-688038.

11. Denaud, *Le FIS: Sa Direction Parle*, p 209.

12. D. Pujadas and A. Salam, *La Tentation du Jihad. L'Islam Radical en France* (Paris: J.C. Lattes, 1995), p 65.

13. Reported in Human Rights Watch, 'Human Rights Developments Algeria', undated. http://www.hrw.org/reports/1994/WR94/Middle-01.htm.

14. *Ibid.*

15. 'Algeria Enters a New Djihad Era. Interview with Shaikh Abdelbaki Sahraoui', *Al-Munkidh*, July 1993. Available at http://www.library.cornell.edu/colldev/mideast/sahraui.htm.

16. *Ibid.*

17. *La Critère*, no. 5 (13 March 1992).

18. 'Les Ramifications du FIS en France', *Journal l'Humanité*, 29 October 1993.

19. Rachid Tlemçani, 'Islam in France: The French Have Themselves to Blame', *Middle East Quarterly*, vol. IV, no. 1 (March 1997).

20. Interview by author with Imam Abdulhadi, Marseilles, July 2006.

21. Pujadas and Salam, *La Tentation du Jihad. L'Islam Radical en France*, p 91.

22. *Ibid.*, p 100.

23. Quoted in M. Willis, *The Islamist Challenge in Algeria* (New York University Press, 1997), p 284.

24. *Ibid.*

25. See, for example, Cesari, 'Les Rapports France Algérie: L'effet Airbus'.

26. M. Stone, *The Agony of Algeria* (London: Hurst, 1997), p 196.

27. Willis, *The Islamist Challenge in Algeria*, p 275.

28. *Ibid.*, p 288.

29. Stone, *The Agony of Algeria*, p 195.

30. See, for example, Naima Bouteldja, 'Who really bombed Paris?', *Guardian*, 8 September 2005.

31. José Garçon, 'GIA, Bras de l'Armée', *Libération*, 4 November 2002.

32. Bouteldja, 'Who really bombed Paris?'.

33. 'Algerian "threat" lurks in Arsenal's shadow but the Islamic front is really here for the football', *Observer*, 15 December 1996.

34. See Pujadas and Salam, *La Tentation du Jihad. L'Islam Radical en France*, pp 175–86.

35. *Ibid.*, p 177.

36. *Ibid.*, p 179.

37. 'Moi, Khaled Kelkal', *Le Monde*, 7 October 1995.

38. 'Khaled Kelkal: Itinéraire d'un terroriste', *L'Express*, 26 September 1996.

39. 'Le "grand flic" qui a démantelé les GIA en 1995 a refusé d'éclaircir à la barre les mystères de l'enquête', *Le Monde*, 3 October 2002.

40. 'Islamists in court for Paris terror campaign: Militants accused of punishing France for supporting Algiers', *Guardian*, 2 June 1999.

41. 'Khaled Kelkal: Itinéraire d'un terroriste', *L'Express*, 26 September 1996.

42. 'Attentat de Saint-Michel: un témoin revient sur ses accusations', *Le Monde*, 14 October 2002.

43. 'GIA: Armed Islamist Groups Serving the Algerian Sécurité Militaire?', *Algeria-Watch*, March 2003.

44. 'Interview with the Former Leader of the Salafist Group for Call and Combat', *Al-Sharq Al-Awsat*, 17 October 2005. Available in English at http://www.asharq-e.com/news.asp?section=3&id=2212.

45. Special Immigration Appeals Tribunal. Appeal No. SC/1/2002, 29 October 2003. Available at http://www.hmcourts-service.gov.uk/legalprof/judgments/siac/outcomes/sc12002a.htm.

46. 'Hassan Hattab to Lil Hayat: Talakeina thamanat nin solta al-Djazairia' (Hassan Hattab to Al-Hayat: We received guarantees from the Algerian authorities), *Al-Hayat*, 7 November 2005.

47. Minbar Al-Tawhed wa Jihad, 'Hiwar Ma'a Rais al-ajna al-Ilimiya li Jama'a Salafiya Al-Dawa wa Kital' (Interview with the Head of the Media Committee of the GSPC), November 2004. Available at http://www.tawhed.ws.

48. Communiqué from the GSPC, 15 August 2005. Available at http://www.globalterroralert.com.

49. GSPC, 'A Call to the Muslims in France', GSPC communiqué, 15 August 2005. Available at http://www.globalterroralert.com.

50. Quoted in Dr Jean-Luc Marret, 'The GSPC/Al-Qaeda in Islamic Maghreb: A Mix of Low and High-Tech Capabilities', Working Paper, 25 April 2007.

51. 'Al-Qaeda "issues France threat"', BBC Online, 14 September 2006. Available at http://news.bbc.co.uk/1/hi/world/europe/5345202.stm.

## Chapter 7. The 9/11 Effect and 'Globalized' Islam

1. Simon Jenkins, 'We've globalised terror, but the solution is local', *Sunday Times*, 10 July 2005. http://www.timesonline.co.uk/article/0,,1059-1688040,00.html.

2. Tony Blair's speech to the World Affairs Council in Los Angeles. Available at http://news.bbc.co.uk/1/hi/uk/5236896.stm.

3. French analyst Olivier Roy, for example, who wrote a book called *Globalised Islam*, came up with the concept of 'Euro-Islam' which he describes as a transi-

tion from a faith that is imported from abroad to a 'universalist Islam' which is 'a transnational Islam divorced from its country of origin'. O. Roy, 'EuroIslam: The Jihad Within', *The National Interest*, Spring 2003.

4. Jon Ronson, 'No more playing the fool', *Guardian*, 15 August 2005. http://www.guardian.co.uk/comment/story/0,,1549448,00.html.

5. 'In Italia la Base dei Terroristi' (Terrorist bases in Italy), *Corriere della Sera*, 18 October 2000.

6. 'Terrorismo, arrestati a Milano sei fiancheggiatori di Al Qaeda', *La Repubblica*, 24 June 2003.

7. See the LIFG's website: http://www.almuqatila.com/index1.htm.

8. Z. Bangash, 'External enemies inside the House of Islam', *Muslimedia*, 16–31 July 1997. Available at http://www.muslimedia.com/archives/features98/external.htm.

9. 'Declaration of War against the Americans Occupying the Land of the Two Holy Places', published in *Al-Quds Al-Arabi*, August 1996.

10. 'Jihad against Jews and Crusaders'. World Islamic Front statement, 23 February 1998. Interestingly although this statement was issued in the name of the World Islamic Front, the collection of militants who actually joined with Bin Ladin and Al-Zawahiri at that time was not that extensive. The other signatories comprised only Sheikh Mir Hamzah of the Jamiat-ul-Ulema-e-Pakistan, Fazlur Rahman of the Jihad Movement in Bangladesh and Rifa'i Taher of Al-Jama'a Al-Islamiya. The latter had signed up to the declaration without the permission of the rest of his group and later withdrew (see Chapter 4). In fact Bin Ladin's appeal only appeared to have resonated at that point with his immediate entourage in Afghanistan and with the two south Asian groups. Other key jihadist movements had no real interest in Bin Ladin's Saudi-focused agenda at that time and were busy with their own preoccupations. The Algerian GIA had fallen out with Bin Ladin over money back in the early 1990s after they had demanded that he fund no other Algerian group apart from themselves – something the Saudi billionaire rejected. Likewise the LIFG had no interest in joining Bin Ladin, and as one former LIFG jihadist, Noman Bin Othman, explained, 'on the question of Al-Qa'ida, we never thought they had a realistic plan'. 'From Mujahid to Activist: An Interview with a Libyan Veteran of the Afghan Jihad', *Spotlight on Terror* (Jamestown Foundation), vol. 3, issue 2 (22 March 2005).

11. Interview: Osama Bin Ladin, PBS, May 1998. Available at http://www.pbs.org/wgbh/pages/frontline/shows/binladen/who/interview.html.

12. Tim Weiner, 'U.S. Case Against bin Laden in Embassy Blasts Seems to Rest on Ideas', *New York Times*, 13 April 1999.
13. 'From Mujahid to Activist: An Interview with a Libyan Veteran of the Afghan Jihad', *Spotlight on Terror* (Jamestown Foundation), vol. 3, issue 2 (22 March 2005).
14. Interview by author with Tunisian Islamist, London, July 2004.
15. 'Plot suspect "happy" after 9/11', BBC Online, 14 September 2006.
16. 'Celebrating 9/11 at the FBI', *Front Page*, 11 February 2004.
17. Sadik J. Al-Azm, 'Time Out of Joint. Western dominance, Islamist terror, and the Arab imagination', *Boston Review*, October/November 2004.
18. Analyst Faisal Devji, for example, stated, 'Like environmentalism, pacifism and other global movements, Al-Qa'ida's jihad is concerned with the world as a whole. In the same way that climatic warming or nuclear holocaust are not problems that can be dealt with regionally, the jihad's task of gaining justice for Muslims has meaning only at a global level.' F. Devji, 'Spectral brothers: Al-Qaida's World Wide Web', *Open Democracy*, 19 August 2005.
19. 'Kusat al-Afghan al-Arab min al-Duhoul ila Afghanistan hata al-Khourouj al-Ahir ma'a Taleban' (The Story of the Afghan Arabs: From Entering Afghanistan to the Final Exodus with the Taliban). Extract from a book written by an anonymous Al-Qa'ida ideologist and serialized in *Al-Sharq Al-Awsat*, issue 9522 (23 December 2004).
20. *Ibid.*
21. Gerges, *The Far Enemy*, pp 191–2.
22. Interviews conducted with second-generation Bangladeshis, Libyans, Algerians and Pakistanis in Europe.
23. Jocelyne Cesari, 'Muslim Minorities in the West: The Silent Revolution', in John Esposito and Francois Burgat (eds), *Modernizing Islam: Religion in the Public Sphere in the Middle East and in Europe* (Rutgers University Press, 2003), pp 251–69. Available at http://euro-islam.info/pages/pubs.html.
24. Interview with Algerian imam, Naples, June 2003.
25. 'Algeria and Terrorism: A Complex Web', *Strategic Comments* (International Institute of Strategic Studies), vol. 9, issue 6 (August 2003).
26. F. Khosrokhavar, *Suicide Bombers: Allah's New Martyrs* (London: Pluto Press, 2005), p 160.
27. 'Inside the Terror Network: Reporter's Notebook', PBS, undated. Available at http://www.pbs.org/wgbh/pages/frontline/shows/network/etc/notebook.html.
28. O. Roy, *Globalised Islam. The Search for a New Ummah* (London: Hurst and Co.,

2004), p 51.

29.   *Ibid.*, p 312.

30.   F. Ajami, 'Nowhere Man', *New York Times Magazine*, 7 October 2001.

31.   *Ibid.*

32.   'A Fanatic's Quiet Path to Terror', *Washington Post*, 22 September 2001.

33.   'Inside the Terror Network: Who were they?', PBS, undated. Available at
      http://www.pbs.org/wgbh/pages/frontline/shows/network/personal/whowere.
      html.

34.   'A Fanatic's Quiet Path to Terror', *Washington Post*, 22 September 2001.

35.   *Ibid.*

36.   'Suspected terrorist's will details final wishes', CNN, 2 October 2001.

37.   J. Corbin, *The Base* (London: Simon and Schuster UK Ltd, 2002), p 136.

38.   *Ibid.*

## Chapter 8. The Madrid Bombings

1.    Although in 1912 Morocco was formally made a French protectorate, Paris
      shared control of the country with Spain, but the latter retained 'protection'
      of some of the country's northern provinces as well as the Western Sahara,
      which it did not cede until 1975. To this day Spain still retains the two coastal
      enclaves of Ceuta and Melila in the north, prompting the indignation of
      many Moroccans who resent the continued hold that Madrid has on its terri-
      tory, despite the fact that it has become a convenient launch pad to get into
      Europe.

2.    Mohamed Darif, 'The Moroccan Combatant Group', *Análisis del Real Instituto*,
      no. 51 (2004). Available at http://www.realinstitutoelcano.org/analisis/465.
      asp.

3.    A. Pargeter, 'The Islamist Movement in Morocco', *Terrorism Monitor* (Jamestown
      Foundation), vol. 3, issue 10 (19 May 2005).

4.    Abdelsalam Razzak, 'Min el-Salafia el Watania ila Salfia Jihadia' (From nation-
      alist salafism to Jihadist Salafism), Al-Jazeera.net, 3 October 2004.

5.    K. Serraj, 'Dans le fief Islamist de Fizazi', *La Gazette du Maroc*, no. 329 (2003).

6.    'Jailed Moroccan Cleric Is Tied to Sept. 11 Pilots', *Los Angeles Times*, 6 July
      2005.

7.    *Ibid.*

8.    'La vraie histoire de Hassan Kettani', *Telquel*, 3 October 2003.

9.    *Ibid.*

10.   'Malaf al-harakat al-islamiya fil Maghreb' (A file on the Islamic Movements

in Morocco), *Nuctasa Kheina* (Hot Topic), 25 September 2003. Available in Arabic at http://www.aljazeera.net/NR/exeres/20589211-8460-40E7-9A5A-68BC9F2F002A.htm.

11.  Idris Wilt Al-Kabila, 'Mukahamat il irhab bil Maghreb al halaka thalith' (Terrorism on trial in Morocco. Article three), *Magazine of Palestinian Writers*, 19 April 2004. Available at http://www.falasteen.com.

12.  'Al Salafiya Jihadia al-Maghrebia takrouj min taht al-anqath' (The Moroccan Salafiyah Jihadia emerges from under the rubble), *Al-Ansar* magazine, 19 August 2003.

13.  S. Belaala, 'Morocco: Slums Breed Jihad', *Le Monde Diplomatique* (English edition), November 2004.

14.  Pargeter, 'The Islamist Movement in Morocco'.

15.  'Fikri défie la justice', *Maroc-Hebdo*, undated. Available at http://www.maroc-hebdo.press.ma/MHinternet/Archives_566/html_566/fikri.html.

16.  In Libya it is alleged that Libyan women working as prostitutes dress like Moroccan women to hide their nationality because of the shame of what they are doing.

17.  'The other side of Morocco. Sidi Moumen's shantytowns, home to human bombs', *Morocco Times*, 27 May 2005.

18.  *Ibid.*

19.  Ahmed R. Benchemsi, 'L'histoire extraordinaire d'un Marocain ordinaire. 30 Mai, prison centrale de Kénitra, midi quinze ...' (The extraordinary story of an ordinary Moroccan. Kenitra central prison, 30 May, quarter past twelve ...), *Telquel*, no. 228.

20.  *Ibid.*

21.  'The other side of Morocco'.

22.  *Ibid.*

23.  '16 Mai 2003. Le Bilan. 44 Morts dont 11 kamikazes' (16 May 2003. The Result. 44 Dead, of which 11 were kamikazes), *Telquel*, no. 176.

24.  Benchemsi, 'L'histoire extraordinaire d'un Marocain ordinaire'.

25.  'La double vie de Jamal Zougam', *Le Monde*, 19 April 2004.

26.  *Ibid.*

27.  *Ibid.*

28.  *Ibid.*

29.  'Jamal Zougam: Madrid bomb suspect', BBC Online, 18 March 2004.

30.  'Terrorism web emerges from Madrid bombing', *Christian Science Monitor*, 22 March 2004.

31. 'La double vie de Jamal Zougam', *Le Monde*, 19 April 2004.

32. Javier Jordan, 'Islamist Terrorist Rings in Spain. Current Situation and Future Outlook, *Análisis del Real Instituto*, no. 119 (13 October 2003).

33. Despite being Moroccan the role of two Syrians was also important in this network – these were two brothers Moutaz and Mohamed Dabas, the latter of whom lived in Spain, and who are both alleged to have had ties with Al-Qa'ida.

34. L. Wright, 'Terror at Large', *The New Yorker*, 2 August 2004.

35. L. Vidino, *Al Qaeda in Europe* (New York: Prometheus Books, 2006), p 304.

36. Ali Lmrabet, 'Aux racines de l'islamisme marocain: "Maman, je vais aller au paradis"', *Courrier International*, 13 May 2004.

37. 'Attentats de Madrid: "Ne pas vivre humilié sous le regard des infidèles"', Latinreporters.com, 16 February 2004.

38. Ali Lmrabet, 'Aux racines de l'islamisme marocain'.

39. James Graff, 'Morocco. The New Face of Terror?', *Time Magazine*, 21 March 2005.

40. Ali Lmrabet, 'Aux racines de l'islamisme marocain'.

41. Driss Bennani, 'Attentats de Madrid: Sur la piste des présumés coupables', *Telquel*, 120, undated. Available at http://www.telquel-online.com.

42. 'Morocco: Casablanca attacks ordered by Al Qaida', *World Tribune*, 5 July 2003.

43. ' "Nous ne sommes pas totalement à l'abri". Entretien avec Général Hamidou Laânigri', *Le Figaro*. Available at http://www.maroc-hebdo.press.ma/MHinter-net/Archives_605/html_605/nousne.html.

44. *Ibid.*

45. *Ibid.*

46. Youssef Sheli, 'Al-Salafiya al-jihadiya al-Maghrebia taqraju min that: al-Maghreb fi halat al-tawara' (The Moroccan Salafiyah Jihadia emerges from underneath: Morocco in an emergency state), *Al-Asr* magazine, 19 August 2003. http://www.alasr.ws/index.cfm?method=home.con&contentID=4436.

47. 'Al-Qaeda "claims Madrid bombings"', BBC Online, 14 March 2004.

48. Fred Halliday, 'Justice in Madrid: The "M-11" Verdict', *Open Democracy*, 5 November 2007. Available at http://www.opendemocracy.net/article/globalisa-tion/global_politics/11M.

49. Quoted in Emerson Vermaat, 'The Madrid Terrorism Trial Verdict: Some Critical Comments', *Militant Islam Monitor*, 18 November 2007.

50. Mohamed Al-Ashab, 'Maloumat Takshifuha Takikhat Al-Shourta fi Rabat'

(Police investigation in Rabat reveals information), *Al-Hayat*, 18 January 2006.

51. Declaración: Otman El Gnaoui. Enlaces Datadiar. Interrogatorio del Fiscal: Transcripción no. 87, 20 February 2007. Available at http://www.peones-negros.com/docs/juicio/transcripcionesvistaoral/I_Otman_El_Gnaoui.pdf.

52. 'Interrogatoria del M Fiscal a Otman El Gnaoui'. Datadiar.com, undated. Available at http://www.datadiar.tv/juicio11m/bd/intervencion.asp?idInterven cion=55&Idioma=es.

53. The videos of the questioning of each of the defendants are available at http://www.desiertoslejanos.com/wiki/index.php/Intervenciones_de_los_ acusados#Declaraci.C3.B3n_de_Abdelmajid_Bouchar.

54. Transcripción Derecho a la Ultima Palabra del Imputao Abdelilah El Fadoual El Akil. Sesion del Juicio 02/07/2007. Available at http://www.peones-negros. com/docs/Juicio/TranscripcionesVistaOral/UP_FadoualElAkil.pdf.

55. Mohamed Al-Ashab, 'Maloumat Takshifuha Takikhat Al-Shourta fi Rabat' (Police investigation in Rabat reveals information), *Al-Hayat*, 18 January 2006.

56. 'Al-Maghariba fil kharij bayna khataray al-Tashriq wal Tagreeb' (Moroccans abroad are in danger of being Easternized and Westernized), *Al-Ahdath Al-Maghrebia*, 14 January 2007.

57. Declaración de Hassan El Haski, 16 February 2007. Available at http://www. peones-negros.com/docs/juicio/transcripcionesvistaoral.

58. Javier Jordan, Fernando M. Mañas and Nicola Horsburgh, 'Strengths and Weaknesses of Grassroots Jihadist Networks: The Madrid Bombings', *Studies in Conflict and Terrorism* no. 31 (2008), pp 17–39.

59. *Ibid.*

60. 'Al-Maghariba fil kharij bayna khataray al-Tashriq wal Tagreeb' (Moroccans abroad are in danger of being Easternized and Westernized), *Al-Ahdath Al-Maghrebia*, 14 January 2007.

61. *Ibid.*

62. *Ibid.*

63. *Ibid.*

64. Mohamed Al-Ashab, 'Maloumat Takshifuha Takikhat Al-Shourta fi Rabat' (Police investigation in Rabat reveals information), *Al-Hayat*, 18 January 2006.

65. Declaración de Hassan El Haski, 16 February 2007. Available at http://www. peones-negros.com/docs/juicio/transcripcionesvistaoral.

66. Fred Halliday, 'Justice in Madrid'.

67. 'Madrid Attacks May Have Targeted Election', *Washington Post*, 17 October 2004.

68. 'Al-Qaida agent "introduced" top Madrid bomb suspects', *Irish Examiner*, 10 April 2004.

69. 'Madrid Attacks May Have Targeted Election', *Washington Post*, 17 October 2004.

70. 'Accuser les Marocains sert les intérêts des Espagnols', *La Gazette du Maroc*, 10 May 2004.

71. L. Wright, 'Terror at Large', *The New Yorker*, 2 August 2004.

72. Quoted in Andrew McGregor, '"Jihad and the Rifle Alone": Abdullah Azzam and the Islamic Revolution', *Journal of Conflict Studies*, vol. xxiii, no. 2 (Fall 2003).

73. Fizazi sermon. Video available at http://www.youtube.com/watch?v=MAF5v5x Ckcs&mode=related&search=.

## Chapter 9. The London Bombings

1. Chapter 10 deals specifically with the issue of converts to Islam including Germaine Lindsay. This chapter therefore focuses on the other three bombers.

2. Abdelrahman Al-Rashid, 'Al-Muslimoun hum awalu al-najeen' (The Muslims are the first survivors), *Al-Sharq Al-Awsat*, 12 August 2006.

3. Madeleine Bunting, 'Orphans of Islam', *Guardian*, 18 July 2005.

4. *Ibid.*

5. Ehsan Masood, 'A Muslim Journey', *Prospect*, August 2005.

6. Maruf Khwaja, 'Muslims in Britain: generations, experiences, futures', *Open Democracy*, 2 August 2005.

7. Kamran Nazeer, 'Beyond Grievance', *Prospect*, August 2005.

8. Masood, 'A Muslim Journey'.

9. 'Friends Describe Bomber's Political, Religious Evolution', *Washington Post*, 29 July 2005.

10. Khwaja, 'Muslims in Britain: generations, experiences, futures'.

11. Stephen McGinty, 'The English Islamic terrorist', *The Scotsman*, 16 July 2002.

12. 'The London Bombers', The Times Online, 15 July 2005.

13. Shiv Malik, 'My Brother the Bomber', *Prospect*, June 2007.

14. *Ibid.*

15. 'The London Bombers', The Times Online, 15 July 2005.

16. 'Making of a martyr. From pacifism to jihad', *Observer*, 4 May 2003.

17. 'What turned two happy teenagers into hate-driven suicide bombers?', *Daily Telegraph*, 2 May 2005.

18. Glenn Frankel, 'From Civic Activist to Alleged Terrorist', *Washington Post*, 28

November 2004.

19. Muslim Public Affairs Committee Website Forum, August 2006. Available at http://forum.mpacuk.org/showthread.php?p=174372#post174372.

20. Kenan Malik, 'Born in Bradford', *Prospect*, October 2005.

21. Dilwar Hussain, 'Bangladeshis in east London: from secular politics to Islam', *Open Democracy*, 7 July 2006.

22. Kamran Nazeer, 'Beyond Grievance', *Prospect*, August 2005.

23. *Ibid.*

24. Interviews by author with second-generation Muslims in the UK, 2005 and 2006.

25. 'One in four Muslims thinks the state was involved in 7/7 attacks', *This Is London*, 5 June 2007.

26. Kamran Nazeer, 'Pakistani Puzzles', *Prospect*, August 2006.

27. Khaled Ahmed, 'Not so good news about British Pakistanis', 21 September 2004. Available at http://www.hvk.org/articles/0904/57.html.

28. V.S. Naipaul, *Among the Believers. An Islamic Journey* (London: André Deutsch, 1981), p 85.

29. Abdelrahman Al-Rashid, 'Al-Muslimoun hum awalu al-najeen' (The Muslims are the first survivors), *Al-Sharq Al-Awsat*, 12 August 2006.

30. J. Stern, *Terror in the Name of God* (New York: HarperCollins, 2003), p 108.

31. Mohammad Shehzad, 'Jihad recruitment is on the rise', *The Friday Times*, 29 July 2003.

32. Quoted in *ibid.*

33. *Ibid.*

34. 'Suspects linked to hardline Islamic group', *Guardian*, 18 August 2006.

35. 'Suicide bombers flew to Pakistan together', *Daily Telegraph*, 19 July 2005.

36. Peter Bergen and Paul Cruickshank, 'London Broil: Kashmir on the Thames', New Republic Online, 4 September 2006.

37. 'Top al-Qaeda trainer "taught suspects to use explosive"', *The Times*, 12 August 2006.

38. 'For this college kid from UK, Mission Kashmir was suicide car bomb', *Indian Express*, 29 December 2000. Available at http://www.jammu-kashmir.com/archives/archives2000/kashmir20001229a.html.

39. 'British Muslims Join Holy War', BBC Online, 26 June 2000.

40. 'British Muslims take path to jihad', *Guardian*, 29 December 2000.

41. 'Profile: Omar Khyam', BBC Online, 30 April 2007. Available at http://news.bbc.co.uk/1/hi/uk/6149794.stm.

42. Sean O'Neill and Daniel McGrory, *The Suicide Factory* (London: Harper Perennial, 2006), p 80.

43. Khaled Ahmed, 'Not so good news about British Pakistanis', 21 September 2004.

44. 'Inside the breeding ground for fanatics', *Sunday Herald*, 17 July 2005.

45. *Ibid.*

46. 'A British Jihadist: Interview with Hassan Butt', *Prospect*, August 2005.

47. 'Sick Shrine to Killer', *Sun*, undated. http://www.thesun.co.uk/article/0,,2-2005520736,00.html.

48. 'London bomber video aired on TV', BBC Online, 2 September 2005.

49. Interviews with Muslims in the UK, Italy and France from 2003 onwards.

50. Naipaul, *Among the Believers*, p 111.

51. Lebor, *A Heart Turned East*, p 131.

52. 'Inside the breeding ground for fanatics', *Sunday Herald*, 17 July 2005.

53. Chatham House, 'Security, Terrorism and the UK', ISP/NSC Briefing Paper 05/01 (July 2005).

54. Shiv Malik, 'My Brother the Bomber, *Prospect*, June 2007.

55. *Ibid.*

56. 'My plea to fellow Muslims: you must renounce terror', *Observer*, 1 July 2007.

57. 'A new year's resolution for the chattering classes', *The Times*, 27 December 2006.

58. Michael Clarke, 'The contract with Muslims must not be torn up', *Guardian*, 26 August 2005.

59. Hizb ut Tahrir. Clarifying the meaning of Dar al-Kufr & Dar al-Islam, undated. Available at http://www.khilafah.com/kcom/islamic-thoughts/islamic-thoughts/clarifying-the-meaning-of-dar-al-kufr-&-dar-al-islam.html.

60. Quoted in Daniel Pipes, 'British Islamists Threatened Violence', 8 July 2005. Available at http://frontpagemagazine.com/Articles/Read.aspx?GUID=3761FD49-3138-4E51-85AA-A584D606597A.

61. David Cohen, 'Terror on the Dole', *Evening Standard*, 20 April 2004.

62. Newsnight, August 2006.

63. K. Baxter, 'Jihad and the Limits of Citizenship', undated. conference paper. Available at http://coombs.anu.edu.au/ASAA/conference/proceedings/Baxter-K-ASAA2004.pdf.

64. Peter Bergen and Paul Cruikshank, 'The Dangers of Tolerance', *The New Republic*, 8 August 2005.

65. Quoted in Daniel Pipes, 'London Terrorism: British "Covenant of Security"

with Islamists Ends', *Capitalism Magazine*, 8 July 2005.

66. 'A British Jihadist: Interview with Hassan Butt', *Prospect*, August 2005.

67. Paul Tumelty, 'Reassessing the July 21 London Bombings', *Terrorism Monitor* (Jamestown Foundation), vol. 3, issue 17 (8 September 2005).

68. 'Profile: Muktar Ibrahim', BBC Online, 11 July 2007. Available at http://news.bbc.co.uk/1/hi/email_news/6634901.stm.

69. *Ibid.*

70. 'Yassin Hassan Omar: Rebellious Foster Child Turned to Radicalism', *The Times*, 10 July 2007.

71. 'Defendants "Attracted to Islam"', BBC News, 17 January 2007. Available at http://news.bbc.co.uk/1/hi/uk/6272847.stm.

72. 'Ramzi Mohamed: Father of Two Who Left a Suicide Note', *The Times*, 10 July 2007.

73. *Ibid.*

74. 'Profile: Hussein Osman', BBC Online, 9 July 2007. Available at http://news.bbc.co.uk/1/hi/uk/6634923.stm.

75. Paul Tumelty, 'Reassessing the July 21 London Bombings'.

76. 'Profile: Adel Yahya', BBC Online, 13 November 2007. Available at http://news.bbc.co.uk/1/hi/uk/6634965.stm.

77. '"Terror camp plot" trial begins', BBC Online, 10 October 2007.

78. 'Profiles: Mohamed Hamid and His Followers', *Guardian*, 26 February 2008.

79. '"Osama bin London": Muslim Fanatic "trained 21/7 bombers"', *Evening Standard*, 11 October 2007. Available at http://www.thisislondon.co.uk/news/article-23416145-details/'Osama+bin+London'+Muslim+fanatic+'trained+217+bombers'/article.do.

80. 'The UK police terrorism arrest statistics (excluding Northern Ireland) from 11 September 2001 to 31 March 2007. Available at http://www.statewatch.org/news/2007/jul/05uk-terr-arrests.htm.

## Chapter 10. Radical Converts

1. Daniel Pipes, 'Converts to Terrorism', 6 December 2005. Available at http://www.danielpipes.org/article/3184.

2. S. Wheeler, 'Jihadists change terror stereotype; Iran and al-Qaeda have been recruiting and training brigades of blond, blue-eyed jihadists with Bosnian military experience to wage war against the West', *Insight on the News*, 10 December 2002.

3. 'Qaeda Position on Recruiting Europeans, Americans', *Al-Majalla* magazine, 3

August 2003. Available in English at http://www.religionnewsblog.com/12962.

4.  Rakan Bin Williams, 'Al-Qaeda Reveals its Latest Threat', *Al-Sharq Al-Awsat*, 8 November 2005.

5.  Memri TV Special Dispatch Series, no. 1112 (10 March 2006).

6.  'Messages by Al-Qaeda Operatives in Afghanistan to the Peoples of the West', Memri TV Monitor Project, clip no. 860, September 2005. Transcript available at http://www.memritv.org/Transcript.asp?P1=860.

7.  L. Vidino, *Al Qaeda in Europe* (Prometheus Books, 2006).

8.  Mohamed Al-Shafey, 'Muslim Converts: Why Do They Choose Extremism?', *Al-Sharq Al-Awsat*, 19 August 2006.

9.  'The Quintessential Englishman ... with Scottish Roots and an Eastern Religion: Richard Thompson Talks to Graeme Thomson', *Sunday Herald*, 31 July 2005.

10. 'Mustashar wazir al-Dahliya lishuoun ladian: irtinak al-Islam la yaklik al-dawla' (The Advisor to the Interior Minister for Religious Affairs: conversion to Islam doesn't worry the state), *Al-Hayat*, 9 March 2006. http://www.daral-hayat.com/special/features/03-2006/Item-20060308-db0e5a85-c0a8-10ed-00ad-9c6430fc5499/story.html.

11. From *In the Hearts of Green Birds* (Azzam Publications). Transcribed from cassette and available at http://www.militantislammonitor.org/article/id/258.

12. 'Rowe "bore al-Qaeda hallmarks"', BBC Online, 23 September 2005.

13. Interviews by author with converts to Islam in the UK, 2005–2006.

14. 'Tashia Janazat Fakeed al-Muslimeen yethulu kassisan al-Islam' (The Funeral Procession of the One who is Missed by Muslims Made a Priest Convert), *Al-Riyadh*, 19 August 2005.

15. Roy, *Globalised Islam*, p 317.

16. *Ibid.*

17. Interview by author with senior Hizb ut Tahrir member, London, 2005.

18. 'Lionel Dumont raconte sa guerre en Bosnie' (Lionel Dumont Tells of His War in Bosnia), Reuters, undated. Available in French at http://www.balkansecurity.com/news/index.php?l=fr&q=kriminal&enddate=2005-12-07&login=&passwd=.

19. 'L'intervention contre les fanatiques de Roubaix' (The Intervention against the Roubaix Fanatics), Recherche Assistance Intervention Dissuasion, undated. Available at http://raid.admin.free.fr/roubaix.htm.

20. Interviews with members of Hizb ut Tahrir, London, 2005.

21. Interview with member of Hizb ut Tahrir, London, 2005.

22. Abdur-Raheem Greene interviewed by *Islamic Voice*, vol. 11–11, no. 130 (November 1997). Available at http://www.themodernreligion.com/convert/convert_anthonygreen.htm.

23. 'Terror Suspect Left Brighton for Gun Training', *The Argus*, 31 March 2004.

24. Islam Online. Live Dialogue with Dr Jamal Badawi, 16 December 2004. Available at http://www.islamonline.net/livedialogue/english/Browse.asp?hGuestID=rQj546.

25. 'At School with the Shoe Bomber', *Guardian*, 28 February 2002.

26. *Ibid.*

27. 'From Tearaway to Terrorist: The Story of Richard Reid', *Daily Telegraph*, 30 December 2001.

28. Al-Muhajiroun, BBC Online, 29 April 2004. http://news.bbc.co.uk/1/hi/programmes/newsnight/3670007.stm.

29. 'Zaim harakat al-ghurraba al-usuliya al-jadid: Londistan in taht wal islam mioun sayakhterfoun taht al-arth' (The new leader of the fundamentalist group Al-Ghurraba: Londonistan is over and Islamist will go underground), *Al-Sharq Al-Awsat*, issue 1023 (8 May 2006). http://www.asharqalawsat.com/details.asp?section=11&issue=10023&article=362048&search=???????&state=true.

30. Quoted in 'Silence, race hatred and spiel', *Indian Express*, 18 August 2005. Available at http://iecolumnists.expressindia.com/full_column.php?content_id=76460.

31. New Muslims Study Circle, Regent's Park mosque. Attended by author, 2005.

32. Interview with convert, Slough, 2005.

33. 'Le Récit de Daoud. Air-Islam', undated. Available at https://impmail.kcl.ac.uk/horde-3.0.6/index.php?url=https%3A%2F%2Fimpmail.kcl.ac.uk%2Fhorde-3.0.6%2F.

34. David Cohen, 'The Rise of the Muslim Boys', *Evening Standard*, 7 February 2005.

35. 'Muslim Cleric Guilty of Soliciting Murder', *Guardian*, 24 February 2003.

36. 'Great Britain: Radical Preacher Incites Muslims to Rob Banks', *ADNKI*, 13 April 2005.

37. See http://www.blogistan.co.uk/blog/mt.php/2005/04/26/the_devils_deception_of_shaikh.

38. 'Bomber "influenced" by preacher', BBC Online, 11 May 2006. http://news.bbc.co.uk/1/hi/uk/4762123.stm.

39. 'Les Conversions à l'Islam Radical Inquiètent la Police Française', *Le Monde*, 13 July 2005.

40. *Ibid.*

41. 'Le Récit de Jamal. Air-Islam', undated. Available at http://www.air-islam.com/convertis/recits/recit-Jamal.html.

42. According to a French diplomatic source, at one point in 2002 there were around 50 young French Muslims studying in the universities of Mecca and Medina and one-third of those were converts. In a similar vein, it is striking to note that many of those converts who adopted militant interpretations of Islam or who became involved in terrorist-related activity spent time studying at these Saudi institutions. This includes Abdullah Faisal, Christian Ganczarski, who went to Saudi Arabia in 1991, and Pierre Antoine Robert and Djamel Herve Loiseau who reportedly both studied in Mecca.

43. Xavier Ternisien, 'L'essor des salafistes en banlieue inquiète policiers et musulmans', *Le Monde*, 24 January 2004.

44. *Ibid.*

45. Interviews conducted with Muslim converts and imams in south London, 2005.

46. 'Muslims Don't Bow', Mecca2Medina website. http://www.mecca2medina.com/audio/lyrics/muslimsdontbow.htm.

47. David Cohen, 'The Rise of the Muslim Boys', *Evening Standard*, 7 February 2005.

48. *Ibid.*

49. Interview by author with prisoner in Brixton prison, London, 2005.

50. *Ibid.*

51. Interview by author with imam of a Milan mosque, 2003.

52. Craig Smith, 'Islam in Jail: Europe's Neglect Breeds Angry Radicals', *New York Times*, 8 December 2004.

53. Interview by author with prisoner in a London prison, 2005.

54. *Ibid.*

55. Tracy Wilkinson, 'In a Prison's Halls, the Call to Islam', *Los Angeles Times*, 4 October 2005.

56. Roy, *Globalised Islam*, p 317.

## Chapter 11. The Danish Cartoon Row and the Dilemma of the Moderates

1. As explained in the introduction, by 'moderates' I am referring to those Islamists who are part of political organizations who advocate a non-violent reformist discourse. I am not referring to Muslim communities at large.

2. 'Muslims in Europe: Country Guide', BBC Online, 23 December 2005.

3.  Information available in Danish and English at http://www.wakf.com.

4.  Associated Press, 6 October 1995. Available at http://counterterror.typepad. com/the_counterterrorism_blog/2006/02/another_protest.html.

5.  Lorenzo Vidino, 'Creating Outrage', National Review Online, 6 February 2006.

6.  Helle Merete Brix and Lars Hedegaard, 'Islamic Extremists and Their Western Allies on the Offensive against Free Speech in Denmark', 1 March 2006. Available at http://www.sappho.dk/Den%20loebende/ekstremister_english.htm.

7.  Danish newspapers quoted on Ahmed Akkari, Wikipedia. http://en.wikipedia. org/wiki/Ahmed_Akkari#_note-7.

8.  'Timeline: How the crisis unfolded', Financial Times, 6 February 2006.

9.  Interview with German Ikhwan, December 2006.

10. 'Danish Muslims "Internationalise" Anti-Prophet Cartoons', IslamOnline.net, 18 November 2005.

11. Ibid.

12. See http://en.wikipedia.org/wiki/Image:Akkari-report-34.jpg.

13. 'What's Behind Muslim Cartoon Outrage', San Francisco Chronicle, 11 February 2006.

14. Sharq newspaper, 30 January 2006. http://www.al-sharq.com/site/topics/article. asp?cu_no=1&item_no=174902&version=1&template_id=92&parent_id=4.

15. 'How clerics spread hatred over cartoons', Daily Telegraph, 7 February 2006.

16. Imanen fra Århus Akkari har ansvaret for konflikten (In English). Hassan Fattah, 9 February 2006. Available at Islaminfo.dk.

17. 'Call for Jihad over prophet cartoon row goes online', Middle East Online, 3 February 2006.

18. Libya Focus, Menas Associates, February 2006. Subscription-only publication. Available at http://www.menas.co.uk.

19. Aatish Taseer, 'A Damascene Conversion', Prospect, March 2006.

20. 'Islamic Conference to Address Cartoon Controversy', Al-Sharq Al-Awsat, 7 March 2006.

21. 'Al-tandid walstinkar la yougnain an al-tabser wahwar' (Condemnation and rejection cannot replace thinking and dialogue), Al-Hayat, 25 March 2006. http://www.daralhayat.com/opinion/03-2006/Item-20060324-2db3b9b1-c0a8-10ed-0008-254db305126f/story.html.

22. 'Now Danes Respect Muslims', Al-Ahram Weekly, issue 787 (23–29 March 2006).

23. Ibid.

24. 'Islamic Conference to Address Cartoon Controversy', *Al-Sharq Al-Awsat*, 7 March 2006.

25. 'Qardawi vs Amr Khaled', *Al-Sharq Al-Awsat*, 9 March 2006.

26. 'Islamic Conference to Address Cartoon Controversy'.

27. 'Qardawi vs Amr Khaled', *Al-Sharq Al-Awsat*, 9 March 2006.

28. 'Qaradawi urges "peaceful" anger day', Islamonline, 18 September 2006.

29. 'What's behind Muslim Cartoon Outrage', *San Francisco Chronicle*, 11 February 2006.

30. 'Imam: Muhammedsagen var positiv', *Jyllands-Posten*, 20 May 2006. English translation available at http://sugiero.blogspot.com/2006/05/danish-imam-cartoon-controversy-good.html.

31. 'What's Behind Muslim Cartoon Outrage', *San Francisco Chronicle*, 11 February 2006.

32. *Ibid.*

33. 'More and More Moderate Muslims Speak Out in Denmark', *Brussels Journal*, 13 February 2006.

34. *Ibid.*

35. Anas Tikriti, 'This is not a cartoon war', *Guardian*, 10 February 2006.

36. MAB Press Release, 'Friday sermons to reflect on Islamophobia and to urge for peaceful protest', 9 February 2006.

37. 'Cartoons reflect Europe's Islamophobia', Al-Jazeera, 5 February 2006.

38. See http://www.ihrc.org.uk/islamophobia.

39. See http://www.uoif-online.com/modules.php?op=modload&name=News&file=article&sid=437.

40. Kenan Malik, 'Islamophobia Myth', *Prospect*, February 2005.

41. *Ibid.*

42. Amartya Sen, *Identity and Violence: The Illusion of Destiny* (W.W. Norton, 2006).

43. Topkapi Declaration, 2 July 2006. Available at http://www.muslimsofeurope.com/topkapi.php.

44. Quoted in 'Multiculturalism "Linked to London Bombings"', Press Association, 30 September 2005. Available at http://www.thetruthseeker.co.uk/article.asp?ID=3647.

45. Bruce Bawer, 'Tolerating Intolerance: The Challenge of Fundamentalist Islam in Western Europe', *Partisan Review*, vol. LXIX, no. 3 (2002).

46. 'How the Home Office Hoodwinks British Muslims', Article 1158, Islamicawakening.com.

47. 'The Making of a Terrorist', *Prospect*, June 2007.

48. Interview by author with British convert, Slough, 2005.
49. Interview with North African Islamist leader, Manchester, October 2004.
50. Interview with Tunisian Islamist leader, Marseilles, July 2006.

## Conclusion

1. Mohamed Argon, 'Aina houa al-fikra Islami al-muasser' (Where is the contemporary Islamic thinking?), Dar Al-Saqi, Beirut, 1993, p 163.
2. 'The son of the father of jihad', Irish Times, 27 June 2007.
3. Hassan Butt, 'My plea to fellow Muslims: you must renounce terror', Observer, 1 July 2007.

# INDEX